EUROPEAN CONSTITUTIONALISM
BEYOND THE STATE

The notion of a European constitution has, until recently, received un-favourable reactions within the European Union, with controversy surrounding its political and legal implications. Criticism has largely revolved around the threat of an emerging European federal state. Today, however, constitution-building has become a major point of debate among members of the European Community as the drafting of a European Constitution becomes more imminent. *European Constitutionalism Beyond the State* brings together some of the most innovative scholars in the field to highlight different facets of the new constitutional discussion. Provoking deep analysis of the different ideas of constitution and constitutionalism, the book delineates new ways of thinking about the future of Europe. In particular, it aims to challenge the idea of the European Union as an evolving federal polity. This book will appeal to anyone interested in the timely subject of constitutionalism, including students and practitioners of law, politics and philosophy.

J. H. H. WEILER is European Union Jean Monnet Professor at New York University School of Law, where he is the Director of the Jean Monnet Center for International and Regional Economic Law and Justice. His most recent publications include *The Constitution of Europe: Do the New Clothes have an Emperor?* (1999), *Kompetenzen und Grundrechte* (with Bruno Simma and Markus C. Zöckler, 1999), *The EU, the WTO, and the NAFTA: Towards a Common Law of International Trade?* (2000) and *The European Court of Justice* (edited, with Grainne de Burca, 2000).

MARLENE WIND is Associate Professor of European Integration in the Department of Political Science, University of Copenhagen. Her recent publications include 'Sovereignty, Anarchy and Law in Europe', in *International Relations Theory and the Politics of European Integration: Power, Security, Community* (edited by M. Williams and M. Kelstrup, 2000), 'Legal Globalisation and the New Human Rights Regime: Human Rights in a Post Sovereign World', in *The New Millennium: Challenges and Strategies for a Globalizing World* (edited by S. F. Krishna-Hensel, 2000), 'The Commission White Paper: Bridging the Gap Between the Governed and the Governing?', in *Symposium: Responses to the European Commission's White*

Paper on Governance (edited by C. Joerges, Y. Mény and J. H. H. Weiler, 2001), *Sovereignty and European Integration. Towards a Post-Hobbesian Order* (2001) and *Post-national Citizenship: The EU as a Rights Generator* (forthcoming).

Contributors include Philip Allott, Renaud Dehousse, Miguel Poiares Maduro, Francis Snyder, Neil Walker, J. H. H. Weiler, Antje Wiener and Marlene Wind.

EUROPEAN CONSTITUTIONALISM BEYOND THE STATE

Edited by

J. H. H. WEILER AND MARLENE WIND

CAMBRIDGE
UNIVERSITY PRESS

PUBLISHED BY THE PRESS SYNDICATE OF THE UNIVERSITY OF CAMBRIDGE
The Pitt Building, Trumpington Street, Cambridge CB2 1RP, United Kingdom

CAMBRIDGE UNIVERSITY PRESS
The Edinburgh Building, Cambridge, CB2 2RU, UK
40 West 20th Street, New York, NY 10011–4211, USA
477 Williamstown Road, Port Melbourne, VIC 3207, Australia
Ruiz de Alarcón 13, 28014 Madrid, Spain
Dock House, The Waterfront, Cape Town 8001, South Africa

http://www.cambridge.org

© Cambridge University Press 2003

This book is in copyright. Subject to statutory exception
and to the provisions of relevant collective licensing agreements,
no reproduction of any part may take place without
the written permission of Cambridge University Press.

First published 2003

Printed in the United Kingdom at the University Press, Cambridge

Typeface Adobe Minion 10.75/12.75 pt.   *System* LaTeX 2_ε [TB]

A catalogue record for this book is available from the British Library

ISBN 0 521 79225 8 hardback
ISBN 0 521 79671 7 paperback

The publisher has used its best endeavours to ensure that
URLs for external websites referred to in this book are
correct and active at the time of going to press. However,
the publisher has no responsibility for the websites and can
make no guarantee that a site will remain live or that the
content is or will remain appropriate.

CONTENTS

PART III

CONTRIBUTORS

PHILIP ALLOTT is Professor of International Public Law in the University of Cambridge and a Fellow of Trinity College, Cambridge. He was formerly a Legal Counsellor in the British Foreign and Commonwealth Office. He is the author of *Eunomia. New Order for a New World* (Oxford University Press, 1990/2001) and *The Health of Nations. Society and Law beyond the State* (Cambridge University Press, 2002).

RENAUD DEHOUSSE is Jean Monnet Professor of EU Law at the Institut d'Etudes politiques de Paris (*Sciences Po*) and Research Director at *Notre Europe*, a Paris-based think tank established and directed by Jacques Delors. He holds a PhD in Law from the European University Institute (Florence). He has held regular appointments at the European University Institute, Florence and at the University of Pisa. He had been adviser to various units of the European Commission and to the French Government on various issues. His recent work has focused in particular on the transformation of European governance, with specific reference to the growing importance of transnational bureaucratic structures (comitology, European agencies), as well as on the influence of the European Court of Justice on European policies. (For a list of publications, see http://www.portedeurope.org/centre europeen/whoiswho/dehousse.htm.)

MIGUEL POIARES MADURO is a Professor of European and International Law at the Universidade Nova de Lisboa. He is a Doctor of Laws by the European University Institute (Florence) where he was also a research assistant and Fellow. He is also an external Professor at the College of Europe (Natolin) Instituto Ortega y Gasset (Madrid) and the Institute of European Studies of Macao (China). He has taught at numerous other places including the European Masters on Human Rights and Democratisation and the Dubrovnik Summer Academy on Human Rights. He has been Fulbright Visiting Research Scholar at Harvard Law School. He is Co-Director of the Academy of International Trade Law (Macao). He co-edited with Joseph Weiler the Special Book Review Issue of the *European Law Journal* and is currently a member of the editorial board of the same journal. He is co-editor with Francis Snyder of the Hart Publishers Series Studies in European Law and Integration. He was the first winner of the Rowe and Maw Prize and winner of the Prize *Obiettivo Europa* (for the best PhD thesis at the EUI). He is the author of *We the Court – The European Court of Justice and the European Economic Constitution* (Oxford, Hart Publishing, 1997) and is currently preparing, with Damian Chalmers, a textbook on EU Law to be published by Cambridge University Press. He has published in several languages on issues regarding EU Law, European Constitutionalism, International Trade Law, Governance Issues and Human Rights.

FRANCIS SNYDER, Officier de l'Ordre des Palmes Académiques, is Professor of Public Law at the Université d'Aix-Marseille III, Centennial Visiting Professor at the London School of Economics and Professor of Law at the College of Europe (Bruges and Natolin). He serves as Co-Director of the Academy of International Trade Law (Macao, China). He is the Editor-in-Chief of the *European Law Journal*. His most recent books include *International Trade and Customs Law of the European Union* (Butterworths, 1998); *The Europeanisation of Law: The Legal Effects of European Integration* (editor) (Hart Publishing, Oxford, 2000); *Regional and Global Regulation of International Trade* (editor) (Hart Publishing, Oxford, 2001); and *La Sécurité alimentaire dans l'Union européenne* (co-editor) (Bruylant, Brussels, 2003).

NEIL WALKER has been Professor of European Law at the European University Institute, Fiesole since 2000, and before that he held posts in the Universities of Edinburgh and Aberdeen. He is the author of many articles and books on constitutional law in the UK and European context, and also on related matters of transnational police and justice co-operation. His most recent book is an edited collection on the development of sovereignty in the European Union (*Sovereignty in Transition*, Hart, 2003).

ANTJE WIENER is Professor of Political Science at Queen's University, Belfast. Her publications include *European Citizenship Practice – Building Institutions of a Non-State* (Westview, 1998); *European Integration After Amsterdam* (with K. Neunreither) (Oxford, 2001); *The Social Construction of Europe* (with Th. Christiansen and K. E. Joergensen) (SAGE) and *Evolving Norms of Constitutionalism* (with J. Shaw) (Blackwell). She is currently completing a manuscript on 'The Invisible Constitution' of politics.

Introduction
European constitutionalism beyond the state

J. H. H. WEILER AND MARLENE WIND

The pace of change in European public discourse has been dizzying. At the beginning of the last decade, in the heady days before Maastricht, the Socialists and the Christian Democrats in the European Parliament were poised to divide the reporting spoils – such as they were then – between themselves. The two big prizes were the report to be presented as Parliament's input into the Maastricht process and the grand project, dating back to Spinelli's Draft Treaty, of writing a constitution for Europe. The Socialists held the majority and had the right of first choice. They chose Maastricht and they chose wisely. Readers are more likely to remember the Martin Report than the eventual Draft Constitution that was presented to plenary, provisionally approved and instantly forgotten. The C word (Constitution) was just as bad as the F word (Federalism) – both were considered as useless toys of the almost lunatic federalist fringe. But that was last century, of course.

How things have changed in the first few years of the new century. The floodgates were opened with that latter-day Joshua, alias Joschka (Fischer), and Jacob, alias Jacques (Chirac), and a lot of fellow travellers eager to take us into a new Promised Land in which Europe (or at least the bit of Europe that, in their opinion, counts) will have a constitution. Even *The Economist* jumped into the fray with its Draft Constitution. And now we have the Convention whose President has not shied away from naming the European Philadelphia and which in all likelihood will produce a document in the title of which the word 'constitution' will surely figure.

What is interesting and, indeed, admirable is the speed by which constitutional rhetoric has been normalized and mainstreamed and how quickly

The writing of this book was completed in October 2002.

the debate has moved from 'Does Europe need a constitution?'[1] to 'What should be in the new European Constitution? A list of competences? A Constitutional Court? A reconfigured Council with a president? An elected president? et cetera et cetera.' The debate and reflection, such as they have been, have also been fuelled, in a very typical European fashion, by a political agenda (enlargement) and timetable (the Inter-governmental Conference (IGC) 2004). This is not to plead for an ivory tower conception of academia which is detached from the so-called 'real world'. But it is to point out that this 'real world' can at times be inimical to the quiet, long-term and profound virtues of La Vita Contemplativa.

The sudden popularity of a 'Constitution for Europe' is rooted in many factors. Here are just a few. In part 'constitution' simply became a fashion-able code word, like 'governance', for the need to engage in more profound institutional reform in view of enlargement. In part it seemed a ready-made model for solving some of the legitimacy problems of an enlarging community and even a subterfuge for *not* dealing with deep-seated prob-lems of democracy. In the Union of 2003 the democracy deficit seems to have been resolved by arguing that it does not exist – 'and we will have a constitution to prove it'. Clearly, if the Constitution of Europe is to repli-cate more or less the existing structures and processes adapted to deal with twenty-five members it will do no more than entrench, constitutionally, the existing democratic deficit.

At the political level the discussion of a Constitution for Europe re-sembles the discussion of democracy. Most people are not theorists of democracy. The democracy they have in mind when they examine and discuss Europe is the national model to which they are accustomed. That experience defines the democratic benchmark for most. Likewise, most people are not constitutionalists. And many constitutionalists are not con-stitutional theorists. Thus, their discussion of a Constitution for Europe is largely conditioned by their experience and understanding of constitu-tionalism in some national setting.

A common characteristic of this debate was, and is, a sometimes facile assumption that one could transfer and adapt constitutional frameworks which have been associated, inextricably, with the state to the European level. One can of course transfer the vocabulary, even the institutions such as a Constitutional Court and various constitutional doctrines. Even some of the more thoughtful contributions to the 'do we need a constitution?' side of the discussion are implicitly operating within a statal notion of

---

[1] D. Grimm, *Braucht Europa eine Verfassung?* (Munich: Werner von Siemens Stiftung, 1994).

constitutionalism. One can transfer and adapt statal constitutional frameworks to Europe (just as we transfer and adapt state institutions such as a parliament) and one can theorize on the need for a European constitution with a statal model in mind – that may be the very normative purpose of both exercises.

The underlying rationale of this volume is that there is a difference between constitution and constitutionalism. Constitutionalism, for example, embodies the values, often non-stated, which underlie the material and institutional provisions in a specific constitution. At this level, separating constitution from constitutionalism would allow us to claim, rightly or wrongly, for example, that the Italian and German Constitutions, whilst very different in their material and institutional provisions, share a similar constitutionalism, vindicating certain neo-Kantian humanistic values, combined with some notion of the *Rechtstaat*.

At an even deeper level constitutionalism is a self-referential concept – not a reflection of something that contains or embodies something else (like values) but the reflection of the very thing itself. This is abstract, we know. But rather than engage in further abstract clarification, we invite you to read the chapter by Miguel Poiares Maduro or Neil Walker in this volume – it will become a lot clearer. Falling in love provides a lesson in love that is rarely bettered by academic discourse.

It is the focus on constitutionalism on the one hand, and the very banal affirmation that it is not, decidedly not, a European state that we are after on the other hand, that underlies our project and this volume. For what is under investigation is a series of questions which may be termed of a 'pure' constitutional nature. We are not primarily interested in the various options concerning the Council or Commission, or the precise mechanisms for protecting the jurisdictional lines between Union and Member States. We are instead interested in, for example, the extent to which constitutions are inherently concepts associated with statehood and peoplehood. We are interested in the possibilities of constitutional 'translation' from Member State to Union without losing the distinct differences between State and Union. We are not totally in the rarified climates of abstract theory. But to the extent that we look expressly at democratic structures or processes, or at some other central features of, yes, Union governance such as comitology or enhanced cooperation, we examine these under an optic of a transformed constitutionalism. Ours then is not a contribution as to how to do it, but as to how to think about it.

Like many such volumes, this book began in a conference held, as is often the case, some time ago. Time has been on our side. What once seemed like an intellectual indulgence has suddenly become a central strand in political and academic discourse. We have purged some of the older papers, amended some others and added a few freshly baked, hot out of the oven.

Please do not be disappointed by, and do not accuse us of, a certain measure of 'incoherence'. We think it is inevitable. There is as yet no developed field of comparative constitutionalism, especially if our interest is in non-statal constitutionalism. Ours in not a project driven by a systematic plan. Think of it the way you would of a Festschrift – a collection of papers animated by central preoccupation and sensibility but not constrained by a schema; an invitation for 'think pieces'. Could there be more pieces included? Of course. Could the pieces be tied together more effectively than we have done? Maybe. But we firmly believe that no single person could achieve the richness of thought and reflection which these pieces achieve when placed side by side, even if there is a price to pay in eclecticism for that richness.

We have made a gesture towards organization through a certain clustering. We open with a chapter in which J. H. H. Weiler, in a rearguard and losing battle, returns to his defence of the status quo – his understanding of the extant European constitutionalism expressed in the notion of constitutional tolerance, and his fear that this may be lost by the adoption of a formal European constitution.

This is followed by Neil Walker, theorizing about constitutional translation, and then by Francis Snyder and Miguel Poiares Maduro actually doing some translation of their own – imagining a European constitutional order which is not a simple transfer from the national to the supranational.

After this Marlene Wind, Renaud Dehousse, and Antje Wiener examine certain features of the process and/or structure in the Union or certain fundamental doctrines and give them, in a variety of ways, a new intellectual twist.

We conclude the book with an Epilogue by Philip Allott which defies categorization but which we publish with no hesitation.

PART I

1

In defence of the status quo: Europe's constitutional *Sonderweg*

J. H. H. WEILER

Introduction: Europe's fateful choice

To judge by the renewed popularity of the idea of a Constitution for Europe one might get the impression that right now Europe is in some kind of constitutional desert. And now we have a European Philadelphia busy preparing yet another document in which the word 'constitution' is almost certain to figure. If a formal constitution is to be the European Promised Land, I think I will join Moses and stick to the desert. In this chapter I will explain this preference.

The idea of a constitution is presented as indispensably part and parcel of a legitimating reform package of an enlarged Europe. It is not, of course, an original idea and can be traced back at least to Spinelli's Draft Treaty for European Union. Whether one can have a Europe which would respect the current constitutional *acquis* and embed it in a formal constitution adopted through a *European constituent power* and, at the same time, not become a federal state in all but name is very doubtful.[1] I think it is a chimera. But the very idea of a formalized constitution requires some serious critical reflection. What appears to be progressive may in fact be regressive. This new fad of a new constitution for Europe may, in fact, be leading us away from the Promised Land into a familiar and boring desert.

Let us step back a minute to review our well-known history.

As a result of a combination of express Treaty provisions, such as those stipulating that certain types of Community legislation would be directly applicable;[2] of foundational principles of international law, such as

---

[1] If a 'constitution' by anything other than a European constituent power, it will be a treaty masquerading as a constitution.

[2] Originally Article 189 EEC (Treaty of Rome).

the general principle of supremacy of treaties over conflicting domestic law, even domestic constitutional law;[3] and of the interpretations of the European Court of Justice,[4] a set of constitutional norms regulating the relationship between the Union and its Member States, or the Member States and their Union, has emerged which is very much like similar sets of norms in most federal states. There is an allocation of powers, which (as has been the experience in most federal states) has often not been respected; there is the principle of the law of the land, in the EU called Direct Effect; and there is the grand principle of supremacy every bit as egregious as that which is found in the American federal constitution itself.

Put differently, the constitutional discipline which Europe demands of its constitutional actors – the Union itself, the Member States and state organs, European citizens and others – is in most respects indistinguishable from that which you would find in advanced federal states.

But there remains one huge difference: Europe's constitutional principles, even if materially similar, are rooted in a framework which is altogether different. In federations, whether American or Australian, German or Canadian, the institutions of a federal state are situated in a constitutional framework which presupposes the existence of a 'constitutional demos', a single *pouvoir constituant* made up of the citizens of the federation in whose sovereignty, as a constituent power, and by whose supreme authority the specific constitutional arrangement is rooted. Thus, although the federal constitution seeks to guarantee state rights and although both constitutional doctrine and historical reality will instruct us that the federation may have been a creature of the constituent units and their respective peoples, the formal sovereignty and authority of the people coming together as a constituent power is greater than any other expression of sovereignty within the polity, and hence the supreme authority, of the Constitution – including its federal principles.

---

[3] The general rule of international law does not allow, except in the narrowest of circumstances, for a state to use its own domestic law, including its own domestic constitutional law, as an excuse for non-performance of a treaty. That is part of the ABC of international law and is reflected in the Vienna Convention on the Law of Treaties, Article 27. *Oppenheim's International Law* is clear: 'It is firmly established that a state when charged with a breach of its international obligations cannot in international law validly plead as a defence that it was unable to fulfil them because its internal law ... contained rules in conflict with international law; this applies equally to a state's assertion of its inability to secure the necessary changes in its law by virtue of some legal or constitutional requirement', *Vol. I: Peace*, 84–5 (Sir Robert Jennings and Sir Arthur Watts eds., 9th edn (Harlow, Essex: Longmans, 1992)).

[4] See generally J. H. H. Weiler, 'The Transformation of Europe', in *The Constitution of Europe* (Cambridge and New York: Cambridge University Press, 1999).

Of course, one of the great fallacies in the art of 'federation build-ing', as in nation building, is to confuse the juridical presupposition of a constitutional demos with political and social reality. In many instances, constitutional doctrine presupposes the existence of that which it creates: the demos which is called upon to accept the constitution is constituted, legally, by that very constitution, and often that act of acceptance is among the first steps towards a thicker social and political notion of constitutional demos. Thus, the empirical legitimacy of the constitution may lag behind its formal authority – and it may take generations and civil wars to be fully internalized – as the history of the USA testifies. Likewise, the juridical presupposition of one demos may be contradicted by a persistent social reality of multiple ethnoi or demoi who do not share, or grow to share, the sense of mutual belongingness transcending political differences and fac-tions and constituting a political community essential to a constitutional compact of the classical mould. The result will be an unstable compact, as the history of Canada and modern Spain will testify. But, as a matter of empirical observation, I am unaware of any federal state, old or new, which does not presuppose the supreme authority and sovereignty of its federal demos.

In Europe, that presupposition does not exist. Simply put, Europe's constitutional architecture has never been validated by a process of con-stitutional adoption by a European constitutional demos and, hence, as a matter of both normative political principles and empirical social ob-servation the European constitutional discipline does not enjoy the same kind of authority as may be found in federal states where federalism is rooted in a classic constitutional order. It is a constitution without some of the classic conditions of constitutionalism. There is a hierarchy of norms: Community norms trump conflicting Member State norms. But this hierarchy is not rooted in a hierarchy of normative authority or in a hierarchy of real power. Indeed, European federalism is constructed with a top-to-bottom hierarchy of norms, but with a bottom-to-top hierarchy of authority and real power.

You would think that this would result in perennial instability. As we shall see, one of the virtues of the European construct is that it produces not only a surprisingly salutary normative effect but also a surprisingly stable political polity. Member States of the European Union accept their constitutional discipline with far more equanimity than, say, Quebec. There are, surely, many reasons for this, but one of them is the peculiar constitutional arrangement of Europe.

This distinct constitutional arrangement is not accidental. Originally, in a fateful and altogether welcome decision, Europe rejected the federal state model. In the most fundamental statement of its political aspiration, indeed of its very telos, articulated in the first line of the Preamble of the Treaty of Rome, the gathering nations of Europe 'Determined to lay the foundations of an ever closer union among the peoples of Europe'. Thus, even in the eventual Promised Land of European integration, the distinct peoplehood of its components was to remain intact – in contrast with the theory of most, and the praxis of all, federal states which predicate the existence of one people. Likewise, with all the vicissitudes from Rome to Amsterdam, the Treaties have not departed from their original blueprint as found, for example, in Article 2 EC of the Treaty in force, of aspiring to achieve 'economic and social cohesion and solidarity among Member States'. Not one people, then, nor one state, federal or otherwise.

Europe was relaunched twice in recent times. In the mid-1980s the Single European Act introduced, almost by stealth, the most dramatic development in the institutional evolution of the Community achieved by a Treaty amendment: majority voting in most domains of the Single Market. Maastricht, in the 1990s, introduced the most important material development: Economic and Monetary Union. Architecturally, the combination of a 'confederal' institutional arrangement and a 'federal' legal arrangement seemed for a time to mark Europe's *Sonderweg* – its special way and identity. It appeared to enable Europe to square a particularly vicious circle: achieving a veritably high level of material integration comparable only to that found in fully fledged federations, while maintaining at the same time – and in contrast with the experience of all such federations – powerful, some would argue strengthened,[5] Member States.

At the turn of the new century, fuelled, primarily, by the Enlargement project, there is a renewed debate concerning the basic architecture of the Union. Very few dare call the child by its name and only a few stray voices are willing to suggest a fully fledged institutional overhaul and the reconstruction of a federal-type government enjoying direct legitimacy from an all-European electorate.[6] Instead, and evidently politically more

---

[5] See three classics: A. S. Milward *et al.*, *The European Rescue of the Nation State* (Berkeley: University of California Press, 1992); Stanley Hoffmann, 'Reflections on the Nation-State in Western Europe Today', in Loukas Tsoukalis (ed.), *The European Community – Past, Present and Future* (Oxford: Basil Blackwell, 1983); A. Moravcsik, *The Choice for Europe* (Ithaca, NY: Cornell University Press, 1998).

[6] See e.g. Giscard d'Estaing and Helmut Schmidt, *International Herald Tribune*, 11 April 2000. For a more honest discussion, admitting the statal implications of the new construct, see, for example, G. Federico Mancini, 'Europe: The Case for Statehood', 4 *European Law Journal* (1998), 29, and Harvard Jean Monnet Working Paper 6/98, and see, of course, Jürgen Habermas's suggestions in 'The European Nation-State and the Pressures of Globalization',

correct, there has been a swell of political and academic voices[7] calling for a new constitutional settlement which would root the existing discipline in a 'veritable' European constitution to be adopted by a classical constitutional process and resulting in a classical constitutional document. The Charter of Human Rights is considered an important step in that direction. What is special about this discourse is that it is not confined to the federalist fringe of European activists, but has become respectable Euro-speak in both academic and political circles.

Four factors seem to drive the renewed interest in a formal constitution rather than the existing 'constitutional arrangement' based on the Treaties. The first factor is political. It is widely assumed, correctly it would seem, that the current institutional arrangements would become dysfunctional in an enlarged Union of, say, twenty-five. A major overhaul seems to be called for. In the same vein, some believe, incorrectly in my view, that the current constitutional arrangements would not work. In particular, the absence of a formal constitution leaves all important constitutional precepts of the Union at the mercy of this or that Member State, threatening both the principle of uniformity of, and of equality before, the law as well as an orderly functionality of the polity. One is forever worried: 'What will the German/Italian/Spanish, or whatever, constitutional court say about this or that?' A formal constitution enjoying the legitimacy of an all-European *pouvoir constituant* would, once and for all, settle that issue.

The second factor is 'procedural' or 'processual'.[8] The process of adopting a constitution – the debate it would generate, the alliances it would form, the opposition it would create – would, it is said, be healthy for the democratic and civic ethos and praxis of the polity.

The third factor is material. In one of its most celebrated cases in the early 1960s, the European Court of Justice described the Community as

New Left Review no. 235 (May 1999), 46, and *Die Einbeziehung des Anderen* (Frankfurt: Suhrkamp, 1996), ch. 3 'Hat der Nationalstaat eine Zukunft?', 128–91. There is an interesting political–legal paradox here. A 'flexible' Europe with a 'core' at its centre will actually enable that core to retain the present governance system dominated by the Council – the executive branch of the Member States – at the expense of national parliamentary democracy. Constitutionally, the statal structure would in fact enhance even further the democracy deficit.

[7] In the political sphere see, for example, the over-discussed Berlin speeches of Joschka Fischer and Jacques Chirac. For text and comments on these interventions, see the special symposium on the Harvard Jean Monnet site: www.JeanMonnetProgram.org.

[8] I am grateful to Professor Günther Frankenberg, University of Frankfurt, for sharing his idea.

a 'new legal order for the benefit of which the States have limited their sovereign rights, albeit in limited fields'. There is a widespread anxiety that these fields are limited no more. Indeed, not long ago a prominent European scholar and judge wrote that there 'simply is no nucleus of sovereignty that the Member States can invoke, as such, against the Community'.[9] A constitution is thought an appropriate means to place limits on the growth of Community competences.

Of greatest interest to me is the final normative and conceptual drive behind the discussion. Normatively, the disturbing absence of formal constitutional legitimization for a polity that makes heavy constitutional demands on its constituent Members is, it may be thought, problematic. If, as is the case, current European constitutional discipline demands constitutional obedience by and within all Member States, their organs and their peoples, even when these conflict with constitutional norms of the Member State, this, it is argued, should be legitimized by a constitution which has the explicit consent of its subjects instead of the current pastiche which, like Topsy, just 'growed'.

Conceptually, the disquiet with the current European constitutional arrangement must be understood against a European constitutional discourse, which for years has been dominated by a strange combination of Kelsen[10] and Schmitt.[11] It is Kelsenian in its attempts, under many guises, to describe, define and understand the European *Grundnorm* – the source whence the authority of European constitutional disciplines derives. The search for this Kelsenian holy grail, whether or not acknowledged explicitly, underscores the great bulk of the academic literature theorizing European constitutionalism. And this holy grail is, typically, understood in Schmittian terms: the search is for the ultimate source of authority, the one that counts in the case of extremity, of conflict.[12] That is the true criterion of the real *Grundnorm*.

---

[9] Koen Lenaerts, 'Constitutionalism and the Many Faces of Federalism', 38 *American Journal of Comparative Law* (1990), 205 at 220. The Court, too, has modified its rhetoric: in its more recent Opinion 1/91 it refers to the Member States as having limited their sovereign rights 'in ever wider fields': [1991] ECR 6079, Recital 21.

[10] Hans Kelsen, 'On the Pure Theory of Law', 1 *Israel Law Review* (1966), 3.

[11] See C. Schmitt, *The Concept of the Political* (Chicago: University of Chicago Press, 1996), at, for example, 35, 43ff.

[12] Whether the *Grundnorm* is internal to the legal order or outside it is a contested matter. For insight see Pavlos Eleftheriadis, 'Begging the Constitutional Question', 36 *Journal of Common Market Studies* (1998), 255; and 'Aspects of European Constitutionalism', 21 *European Law Review* (1996), 32.

Early 'Europeanists' liked to argue that the *Grundnorm*, typically expressed in, say, the principle of supremacy of European law over national law in case of conflict, had shifted to the 'central' or 'general' power: that is, to Europe. That view is less in fashion today and is contested by those who point out that, both in fact and in law, ultimate authority still rests in national constitutional orders which sanction supremacy, define its parameters, and typically place limitations on it.

According to this latter view, the statal *Grundnorm* would shift. Only if one were to take the existing constitutional precepts and enshrine them in a formal constitution adopted by a European 'constitutional demos' – the peoples of Europe acting on that occasion as one people – would constitutional authority in fact and in law shift to Europe. For the most part, both for friends and for foes of European constitutionalism the debate is conducted on this Kelseno-Schmittian turf.

I am far from certain whether the constitutional discussion will actually result in the adoption of a formal constitution and I am even more doubtful whether we will see in the near future a European state even of a most limited core. My interest in this debate is, thus, that of neither the international relations expert nor the social scientist trying to explain or predict the course that European integration has taken or will take. I am, instead, mostly interested in the normative values of which the constitutional and political discourse is an expression.

I want to explain why the unique brand of European constitutional federalism – the status quo – represents not only its most original political asset but also its deepest set of values. I also do not think that a formal constitution is a useful response to other concerns such as the issue of competences.

Authority, submission and emancipation: a parable

Before offering a normative reading of the European constitutional architecture, I want to tweak some of the assumptions on which the constitutional debate is typically premised. The following parable is offered with this purpose in mind.

There is an inevitable and scary moment in the growing up of an observant Jew and in the raising of religiously observant children. In a religion the constitutive and defining feature of which is Nomos – the Law – and which has no theology, there is no easy answer to the inevitable question: why observe this law? The Pauline antinomian revolution derives from a failure to find a convincing justification for submission to Nomos. To the sceptical reader one may point out that a similar question may be asked regarding submission and loyalty to a constitution.

The simplest, and deepest, answer is rooted in covenant and in the authority – and the Author – whence Nomos derives. But submission and obedience to God surely do not exhaust the significance of a Nomos-based life. One intriguing reply, given by the polymath philosopher Isaiah Leibowitz,[13] is relevant to our current discussions of European constitutionalism.

Take the core set of ritualistic observances: kosher laws, Sabbath laws and the laws of purity in sexual relations. They are the core set because they affect the three central features of our mundane existence: eating, working, loving. Living by Nomos means a submission to a set of constraints in all these areas. The constraints are designed in such a way that they cannot be explained in rational utilitarian terms. Kosher rules actually exclude some of the healthiest foods; the Sabbath rules have a niggardly quality to them that militates, in some respects, against a vision of rest and spirituality; and the ritualistic laws of purity, involving the messy subject of menstruation and sexual abstention, have arbitrary elements galore. It is, indeed, as if they were designed to force the observer into pure and mindless obedience and submission. One observes for no other reason than having been commanded. No wonder Paul[14] shrugged off this yoke.

There is, however, an interesting paradox in this submission which orthodox Judaism as well as several strands of Islam share. Total obedience and submission are to a transcendent authority which is not of this world. In that very act of submission is encapsulated an emancipation and liberation from any authority of this world. By enslaving oneself to an authority outside of this world, one declares an independence of, and refusal to submit – in the ultimate sense – to, any authority of this world. By abstaining from eating everything that one fancies, one liberates oneself from that powerful part of our physical existence. By arranging life so as not to work on the Sabbath, one subjugates the even more powerful call of career and the workplace. And by refraining from sexual abandon, even if loving, even if within wedlock, one asserts a measure of independence

---

[13] Y. Leibowitz, *Judaism, Human Values and the Jewish State* (Cambridge, MA: Harvard University Press, 1992), *passim.*

[14] St Paul needs no citation. But for a somewhat troubling latter-day reincarnation of this aspect of Pauline dogma, see R. M. Unger, *What Should Legal Analysis Become?* (London and New York: Verso, 1996), at 186ff.

even over that exquisite part of our lives too. Isaiah Berlin, a town mate, friend, and admirer of Isaiah Leibowitz, gives the secular equivalent to this insight in his discussion of rational liberty.

There are three relevant lessons for the constitutional and European discourse in this parable.

The first: an act of submission can often be simultaneously an act of emancipation and liberation.

The second: as Aristotle teaches us, virtue is a habit of the soul and habits are instilled by practice.

The third: the purpose of obeying the law is not co-terminous with the consequences of obeying the law. One may obey to submit to the author of the Command. A consequence, not a purpose, may be emancipation.

Let us see now how these play out in the normative understanding of European constitutionalism.

Neither Kelsen nor Schmitt: the principle of European constitutional tolerance – concept and praxis

The reason the question of ultimate authority and constitutional *Grundnorm* seems so important is that we consider the integrity of our national constitutional orders as a matter not simply of legal obedience and political power but of moral commitment and identity. Our national constitutions are perceived by us as doing more than simply structuring the respective powers of government and the relationships between public authority and individuals or between the state and other agents. Our constitutions are said to encapsulate fundamental values of the polity and this, in turn, is said to be a reflection of our collective identity as a people, as a nation, as a state, as a Community, as a Union. When we are proud and attached to our constitutions we are so for these very reasons. They are about restricting power, not enlarging it; they protect fundamental rights of the individual; and they define a collective identity which does not make us feel queasy the way some forms of ethnic identity might. Thus, in the endless and tiresome debates about the European Union constitutional order, national courts have become, in the last decade, far more aggressive in their constitutional self-understanding. The case law is well known. National courts are no longer at the vanguard of the 'new European legal order', bringing the rule of law to transnational relations and empowering, through EC law, individuals vis-à-vis Member State authority.

Instead they stand at the gate and defend national constitutions against illicit encroachment from Brussels. They have received a sympathetic hearing, since they are perceived as protecting fundamental human rights as well as protecting national identity. To protect national sovereignty is passé; to protect national identity by insisting on constitutional specificity is à la mode.

Thus, on this new reading, to submit to the constitutional disciplines of Europe without a proper Kelsenian constitution, which formally vests in Europe Schmittian ultimate authority, is something that not only contradicts an orderly understanding of legal hierarchy but also compromises deep values enshrined in the national constitution as well as a collective identity which is tied up with these values. Indeed, it is to challenge the idea of constitution itself.

Miguel Poiares Maduro, one of the most brilliant of the new generation of European constitutional thinkers, gives eloquent expression to this concern:

> European integration not only challenges national constitutions . . . it challenges constitutional law itself. It assumes a constitution without a traditional political community defined and proposed by that constitution . . . European integration also challenges the legal monopoly of States and the hierarchical organisation of the law (in which constitutional law is still conceived of as the 'higher law').[15]

Is this challenge so threatening?

In part it is. Modern liberal constitutions are, indeed, about limiting the power of government vis-à-vis the individual; they do, too, articulate fundamental human rights in the best neo-Kantian tradition; and they reflect a notion of collective identity as a community of values which is far less threatening than more organic definitions of collective identity. They are a reflection of our better part.

But, like the moon, like much which is good in life, there is here a dark side too.

---

[15] M. P. Maduro, *We, the Court, the European Court of Justice and the European Economic Constitution* (Oxford: Hart Publishing, 1998), at 175. Maduro himself does not advocate a European constitution. I cite him simply for his striking diagnosis of the issue. It is superior to my own clumsy attempt to formulate the dilemma as a 'constitution without constitutionalism', as 'doing before hearkening'. J. Weiler, ' "We Will Do, and Hearken" – Reflections on a Common Constitutional Law for the European Union', in Roland Bieber and Pierre Widmer (eds.), *The European Constitutional Area* (Zurich: Schulthess, 1995).

It is, first, worth listening carefully to the rhetoric of the constitutional discourse. Even when voiced by the greatest humanists, the military overtones are present. We have been invited to develop a patriotism around our modern, liberal, constitutions. The constitutional patriot is invited to defend the constitution. In some states we have agencies designed to protect the constitution whose very name is similar to our border defences. In other countries, we are invited to swear allegiance to the constitution. In a constitutional democracy we have a doctrine of a fighting democracy, whereby democratic hospitality is not extended to those who would destroy constitutional democracy itself. To be a good constitutional liberal, it would seem from this idiom, is to be a constitutional nationalist and, it turns out, the constitutional stakes are not only about values and limitations of power but also about its opposite: the power which lurks beneath such values.

Very few constitutionalists and practically no modern constitutional court will make an overt appeal to natural law. Thus, unlike the 'constitution' in the parable, the formal normative authority of the constitutions around which our patriotism must form and which we must defend is, from a legal point of view, mostly positivist. This means that it is as deep or as shallow as the last constitutional amendment: in some countries, like Switzerland or Germany, not a particularly onerous political process. Consequently, vesting so much in the constitutional integrity of the Member State is an astonishing feat of self-celebration and self-aggrandizement, of bestowing on ourselves, in our capacity of constituent power, a breathtaking normative authority. Just think of the near sacred nature we give today to the constitutions adopted by the morally corrupted societies of the Second World War generation in, say, Italy and Germany and elsewhere.

A similar doubt should dampen somewhat any enthusiasm towards the new constitutional posture of national courts, which hold themselves out as defending the core constitutional values of their polity, indeed its very identity. The limitation of power imposed on the political branches of government is, as has been widely noticed, accompanied by a huge dose of judicial self-empowerment and no small measure of sanctimonious moralizing. Human rights often provoke the most strident rhetoric. Yet constitutional texts in our different polities, especially when it comes to human rights, are remarkably similar. Defending the constitutional identity of the state and its core values turns out in many cases to be a defence of some hermeneutic foible adopted by five judges voting against four. The banana saga, which has taxed the European Court of Justice, the German Constitutional Court, the Appellate Body of the World Trade Organization, and endless lawyers and academics, is the perfect symbol of this farce.

Finally, there is also an exquisite irony in a constitutional ethos which, while appropriately suspicious of older notions of organic and ethnic identity, at the very same time implicitly celebrates a supposed unique moral identity, wisdom and, yes, superiority, of the authors of the constitution, the people, the constitutional demos, when it wears the hat of constituent power and, naturally, of those who interpret it.

It was Samuel Johnson who suggested that patriotism was the last refuge of a scoundrel. Dr Johnson was, of course, only partly right. Patriotism can also be noble. But it is an aphorism worth remembering when we celebrate constitutional patriotism, national or transnational, and rush to its defence from any challenges to it. How, then, do we both respect and uphold all that is good in our constitutional tradition and yet, at the same time, keep it and ourselves under sceptical check?

The advocacy for a European constitution is not what it purports to be. It is not a call for 'a' constitution. It is a call for a different form of European constitution from the constitutional architecture we already have. And yet the current constitutional architecture, which of course can be improved in many of its specifics, encapsulates one of Europe's most important constitutional innovations, the Principle of Constitutional Tolerance.

The Principle of Constitutional Tolerance, which is the normative hallmark of European federalism, must be examined both as a concept and as a praxis. First, then, the concept. European integration has been, historically, one of the principal means by which to consolidate democracy within and among several of the Member States, both old and new, with less than perfect historical democratic credentials. For many, thus, democracy is the objective, the end, of the European construct. This is fallacious. Democracy is not the end. Democracy, too, is a means, even if an indispensable means. The end is to try, and try again, to live a life of decency, to honour our creation in the image of God, or the secular equivalent. A democracy, when all is said and done, is as good or bad as the people who belong to it. The problem of Haider's Austria is not an absence of democracy. The problem is that Austria is a democracy, that Haider was elected democratically, and that even the people who did not vote for him are content to see him and his party share in government. A democracy of vile persons will be vile.

Europe was built on the ashes of the Second World War, which witnessed the most horrific alienation of those thought of as aliens, an alienation which became annihilation. What we should be thinking about is not simply the prevention of another such carnage: that is the easy part and it is unlikely ever to happen again in Western Europe, though events in the Balkans remind us that those demons are still within the continent. More difficult is dealing at a deeper level with the source of these attitudes. In the realm of the social, in the public square, the relationship to the alien is at the core of such decency. It is difficult to imagine something normatively more important to the human condition and to our multicultural societies.

There are, it seems to me, two basic human strategies for dealing with the alien and these two strategies have played a decisive role in Western civilization. One strategy is to remove the boundaries. It is the spirit of 'come, be one of us'. It is noble since it involves, of course, elimination of prejudice, of the notion that there are boundaries that cannot be eradicated. But the 'be one of us', however well intentioned, is often an invitation to the alien to be one of us, by being us. Vis-à-vis the alien, it risks robbing him of his identity. Vis-à-vis oneself, it may be a subtle manifestation of both arrogance and belief in my superiority as well as intolerance. If I cannot tolerate the alien, one way of resolving the dilemma is to make him like me, no longer an alien. This is, of course, infinitely better than the opposite: exclusion, repression, and worse. But it is still a form of dangerous internal and external intolerance.

The alternative strategy of dealing with the alien is to acknowledge the validity of certain forms of non-ethnic bounded identity but simultaneously to reach across boundaries. We acknowledge and respect difference, and what is special and unique about ourselves as individuals and groups; and yet we reach across differences in recognition of our essential humanity. What is significant in this are the two elements I have mentioned. On the one hand, the identity of the alien, as such, is maintained. One is not invited to go out and, say, 'save him' by inviting him to be one of us. One is not invited to recast the boundary. On the other hand, despite the boundaries which are maintained, and constitute the I and the Alien, one is commanded to reach over the boundary and accept him, in his alienship, as oneself. The alien is accorded human dignity. The soul of the I is tended to not by eliminating the temptation to oppress but by learning humility and overcoming it.

The European current constitutional architecture represents this alternative, civilizing strategy of dealing with the 'other'. Constitutional Tolerance is encapsulated in that most basic articulation of its meta-political objective in the preamble to the EC Treaty mentioned earlier in this chapter: 'Determined to lay the foundations of an ever closer union among the peoples of Europe.' No matter how close the Union, it is to remain a union among distinct peoples, distinct political identities, distinct political communities. An ever closer union could be achieved by an amalgam of distinct peoples into one which is both the ideal and/or the de facto experience of most federal and non-federal states. The rejection by Europe of that One Nation ideal or destiny is, as indicated above, usually understood as intended to preserve the rich diversity, cultural and other, of the distinct European peoples as well as to respect their political self-determination. But the European choice has an even deeper spiritual meaning.

An ever closer union is altogether more easy if differences between the components are eliminated, if they come to resemble each other, if they aspire to become one. The more identical the 'Other's' identity is to my own, the easier it is for me to identify with him and accept him. It demands less of me to accept another if he is very much like me. It is altogether more difficult to attain an ever closer Union if the components of that Union preserve their distinct identities, if they retain their 'otherness' vis-à-vis each other, if they do not become one flesh, politically speaking. Herein resides the Principle of Tolerance. Inevitably I define my distinct identity by a boundary which differentiates me from those who are unlike me. My continued existence as a distinct identity depends, ontologically, on that boundary and, psychologically and sociologically, on preserving that sentiment of otherness. The call to bond with those very others in an ever closer union demands an internalization – individual and societal – of a very high degree of tolerance. Living the Kantian categorical imperative is most meaningful when it is extended to those who are unlike me.

In political terms, this Principle of Tolerance finds a remarkable expression in the political organization of the Community, which defies the normal premise of constitutionalism. Normally in a democracy, we demand democratic discipline, that is, accepting the authority of the majority over the minority only within a polity which understands itself as being constituted of one people, however defined. A majority demanding obedience from a minority, which does not regard itself as belonging to the same people, is usually regarded as subjugation. This is even more so in relation to constitutional discipline. And yet, in the Community, we subject the European peoples to constitutional discipline even though the European polity is composed of distinct peoples. It is a remarkable instance of civic tolerance to accept being bound by precepts articulated not by 'my people' but by a community composed of distinct political communities: a people, if you wish, of others. I compromise my self-determination in this fashion as an expression of this kind of internal – towards myself – and external – towards others – tolerance.

Constitutionally, the Principle of Tolerance finds its expression in the very arrangement which has now come under discussion: a federal constitutional discipline which, however, is not rooted in a statist-type constitution.

This is where the first and third lessons of the parable come into play. Constitutional actors in the Member State accept the European constitutional discipline not because, as a matter of legal doctrine, as is the case in the federal state, they are subordinate to a higher sovereignty and authority attaching to norms validated by the federal people, the constitutional demos. They accept it as an autonomous voluntary act, endlessly renewed on each occasion, of subordination, in the discrete areas governed by Europe, to a norm which is the aggregate expression of other wills, other political identities, other political communities. Of course, to do so creates in itself a different type of political community, one unique feature of which is that very willingness to accept a binding discipline which is rooted in and derives from a community of others. The Quebecois are told: in the name of the people of Canada, you are obliged to obey. The French or the Italians or the Germans are told: in the name of the peoples of Europe, you are invited to obey. In both, constitutional obedience is demanded. When acceptance and subordination are voluntary, and repeatedly so, they constitute an act of true liberty and emancipation from collective self-arrogance and constitutional fetishism: a high expression of Constitutional Tolerance.

The Principle of Constitutional Tolerance is not a one-way concept: it applies to constitutional actors and constitutional transactions at the Member State level, at the Union level and among the Member States too. This dimension may be clarified by moving from concept to praxis, to an examination of Constitutional Tolerance as a political and social reality.

It is, in my view, most present in the sphere of public administration, in the habits and practices it instils in the purveyors of public power in European polities, from the most mundane to the most august. At the most mundane administrative level, imagine immigration officials overturning practices of decades and centuries and learning to examine the passport of Community nationals in the same form, the same line, with the same scrutiny of their own nationals. And a similar discipline will be practised by customs officials, housing officers, educational officials and many more subject to the disciplines of the European constitutional order.

Likewise, a similar discipline will become routine in policy-setting forums. In myriad areas – whether a local council or a parliament itself – every norm will be subject to an unofficial European impact study. So many policies in the public realm can no longer be adopted without examining their consonance with the interest of others, the interest of Europe.

Think, too, of the judicial function, ranging from the neighbourhood *giudice conciliatore* to the highest jurisdictions: willy-nilly, European law, the interest of others, is part of the judicial normative matrix.

I have deliberately chosen examples which both occur daily and are commonplace but which also overturn what until recently would have been considered important constitutional distinctions. This process operates also at Community level. Think of the European judge or the European public official who must understand that, in the peculiar constitutional compact of Europe, his decision will take effect only if obeyed by national courts, if executed faithfully by a national public official with whom he belongs to a national administration which claims from them a particularly strong form of loyalty and habit. This, too, will instil a measure of caution and tolerance.

It is at this level of praxis that the second and third lessons of the parable come into play. What defines the European constitutional architecture is not the exception, the extreme case which definitively will situate the *Grundnorm* here or there. It is the quotidian, the daily practices, even if done unthinkingly, even if executed because the new staff regulations require that it be done in such a new way. This praxis habituates its myriad practitioners at all levels of public administration to their concealed virtues.

What, then, of the non-Europeans? What of the inevitable boundary created by those within and those without? Does not Constitutional Tolerance implode as an ethos of public mores if it is restricted only to those chosen people with EU passports? Let us return to the examples mentioned above, such as the new immigration procedures which group all Community nationals together. What characterizes this situation is that, though national and Community citizens will be grouped together, they will still have distinct passports, with independent national identities, and still speak in their distinct tongues, or in that peculiar Eurospeak that sometimes passes itself off as English. This is critical, because in the daily practices which I am extolling, the public official is invited and habituated to deal with a very distinct 'other', but to treat him or her as if he/she was his own. One should not be starry-eyed or overly naïve; but the hope and expectation is that there will be a spillover effect: a gradual habituation to various forms of tolerance and with it a gradual change in the ethos of public administration which can be extended to Europeans and non-Europeans alike. The boundary between European and 'non-European' is inevitable, dictated if by nothing else by the discipline of numbers. In too large a polity the specific gravity of the individual is so diminished that democracy, except in its most formal sense, becomes impossible. But just as at the level of high politics the Community experience has conditioned a different ethos of intergovernmental interaction, so it can condition a different ethos of public interaction with all aliens.

To extol the extant constitutional arrangement of Europe is not to suggest that many of its specifics cannot be vastly improved. The Treaty can be pared down considerably, competences can be better protected[16] and vast changes can be introduced into its institutional arrangements. But when it is objected that there is nothing to prevent a European constitution from being drafted in a way which would fully recognize the very concepts and principles I have articulated, my answer is simple: Europe has now such a constitution. Europe has charted its own brand of constitutional federalism. It works. Why fix it?

[16] The issue of competences is particularly acute since there has been a considerable weakening of constitutional guarantees to the limits of Community competences, undermining Constitutional Tolerance itself. See B. Simma, J. H. H. Weiler and M. Zöckler, *Kompetenzen und Grundrechte – Beschränkungen der Tabakwerbung aus der Sicht des Europarechts* (Berlin: Duncker & Humblot, 1999). History teaches that formal constitutions tend to strengthen the centre, whatever the good intentions of their authors. Any formulation designed to restore constitutional discipline on this issue can be part of a Treaty revision and would not require a constitution for it. For pragmatic proposals on this issue see J. H. H. Weiler *et al.*, 'Certain Rectangular Problems of European Integration' (http://www.iue.it/AEL/EP/index.html) (1996).

PART II

2

Postnational constitutionalism and the problem of translation

NEIL WALKER

A few years ago Joseph Weiler spoke of the deep-seated 'problems of translation'[1] of the core normative concepts of constitutionalism from the state to the European Union setting, and by inference to other settings beyond the state. As we shall see in due course, the problems of translation are profound indeed, but before we can begin to address them we must pose a prior question. Is it at all legitimate even to attempt to translate the language and normative concerns of constitutionalism from the state to the non-state domain? If it is not, there is no problem that merits, still less requires, our attention. Let us begin, then, with that prior question before proceeding to a substantive examination of issues of constitutional translation. Throughout the discussion the main focus is on the European Union as the most developed site of postnational constitutionalism, but it will hopefully become apparent that the arguments brought forward also apply to non-state sites of 'constitutional' discourse more generally.[2]

Why translation is a problem worth addressing

Talking about constitutional talk

In the diplomatic world of national or transnational ethnic conflict res-olution, we have become increasingly familiar with the vocabulary of 'talks about talks'. In South Africa, in the former Yugoslavia, in Israel, in Northern Ireland and in many other places, the development of terms of

---

[1] J. H. H. Weiler, *The Constitution of Europe* (Cambridge: Cambridge University Press, 1999), 270.

[2] Elsewhere, I have begun to try to develop arguments about the relevance of postnational constitutionalism to the WTO. See N. Walker, 'The EU and the WTO: Constitutionalism in a New Key', in G. de Burca and J. Scott (eds.), *The EU and the WTO: Legal and Constitutional Issues* (Oxford: Hart Publishing, 2001), 31.

reference on which polarized parties can agree to engage in substantive talks is increasingly identified – even institutionalized – as a necessary initial stage[3] in addressing the resolution of conflict. In the domain of postnational constitutionalism, on the other hand, and most evidently in the context of the European Union, we see a strange inversion of this logic. As we shall see, there is much explicit constitutional debate in the European Union context, and now in the post-Laeken Convention on the Future of Europe an institutional framework which facilitates and legit-imates that debate.[4] However, beneath the surface of the constitutional debate, as part of its often unacknowledged or under-articulated political and intellectual substratum, lies continuing uncertainty and disagreement as to whether and on what terms we should be having the debate at all. In turn, this 'second order'[5] debate may be framed in terms of the general problem of translation.

Those who see constitutionalism as a state-centred idea in terms of its historical elaboration, preconditions of settled political community and symbolic associations (i.e. where there is a constitution, there should also be a state) would reject the transposition of constitutionalism to non-state contexts as illegitimate, and perhaps impossible. Such a belief, with its deep roots in the modern Westphalian scheme which sees states as the major or perhaps only co-ordinates on the global political map, has a

---

[3] One which, moreover, is always protracted and sometimes insurmountable. See e.g. C. Bell, *Peace Agreements and Human Rights* (Oxford: Oxford University Press, 2000).

[4] The possibility of a Convention was anticipated in the Treaty of Nice, Annex, Declaration on the Future of the European Union. The Convention was set up by the Laeken Decla-ration on the Future of the European Union, Annex to the Conclusions of the Laeken European Council, 14–15 December 2001, SN 300/101 REV 1. It is made up of a Chair and two Vice-Chairs, one representative of the government of each Member (fifteen) and Candidate (thirteen) State, two representatives of the national Parliaments of each Member and Candidate State, sixteen members of the European Parliament and two members of the Commission. In addition, a number of other agencies may attend as observers, and a separate (Civic) Forum may receive information from the Convention and contribute to its debates. Although under Valéry Giscard d'Estaing's forceful leadership the Convention seized the constitutional baton from the outset, it is worth recalling that its specifically constitutional mandate is slim, restricted to asking whether the tasks of simplification and reorganization with which it was charged 'might not lead in the long run to the adoption of a Constitutional text in the Union'. It remains to be seen what the Intergovernmental Conference to be convened in 2004 will make of its conclusions, as the IGC's role will be decisive in the authorization of any constitutional document that the Convention might propose.

[5] See N. Walker, 'European Constitutionalism and the Finalité of Integration', forthcoming in B. de Witte (ed.), *An Emerging Constitution for Europe?* (Oxford: Oxford University Press, 2003).

resilient political and ideological currency, and it is also inscribed in and supported by the traditional division of labour within the study of law. In some parts of the academy, one continues to find an obdurately 'defensive internationalism'.[6] This tendency, which seeks to grasp and contain all the transformations of authoritative structures and processes beyond the state within the traditional paradigm of international law,[7] is premised on the continuing integrity of state sovereignty, and is the external complement and counterpart to internal state constitutionalism. As regards the debate about the proper legal character of the EU, for example, there is a school of thought which emphasizes the continuing role of the states as 'masters of the treaties' and which, on that basis, continues to depict the new legal order in terms of a very old international law pedigree.[8]

For their part, some of those who see constitutionalism as a mobile set of ideas, equally at home in non-state settings as state settings, believe implicitly – and less commonly explicitly – that there is *no problem* of translation. This assumption manifests itself in both critical and constructive perspectives. In critical vein, as Shaw and Wiener report, the 'often invisible touch of stateness'[9] is apt to compromise understanding of non-state or post-state entities or processes. There is an enduring tendency, as they have observed, to measure many of the supposed normative shortcomings of post-state entities such as 'deficits of democracy, legitimacy, accountability, equality and security'[10] in terms of a statist template and against the benchmark of a (real or imagined) statist standard. In constructive

---

[6] N. Walker, 'The Idea of Constitutional Pluralism', 65 *Modern Law Review* (2002), 317 at 322.

[7] Although by no means all international lawyers work within this paradigm and reject the idea of terming some of the forms of postnational regulation which may encroach upon the traditional domain of international law as 'constitutional', any more than all constitutional lawyers work within their traditional paradigm of state constitutional law and refuse the label 'constitutional' to these same forms of postnational regulation because they may stray beyond the state domain.

[8] See e.g. A. Pellet, 'Les Fondements Juridiques Internationaux du Droit Communautaire', *Collected Courses of the Academy of European Law*, vol. V (Dordrecht: Kluwer, 1994), Book 2, 211. See also T. Schilling, 'The Autonomy of the Community Legal Order: An Analysis of Possible Foundations', 17 *Harvard International Law Journal* (1996), 389, together with his 'Rejoinder: The Autonomy of the Community Legal Order', (1996) Harvard Jean Monnet Working Paper 96/10, responding to Joseph Weiler's reply to Schilling's earlier article; Weiler, *Constitution of Europe*, ch. 9. This argument is developed in Walker, 'Constitutional Pluralism'.

[9] J. Shaw and A. Wiener, 'The Paradox of the European Polity', in M. Green Cowles and M. Smith (eds.), *State of the European Union 5: Risks, Reform, Resistance and Revival* (Oxford: Oxford University Press, 2000).

[10] *Ibid.*

vein, too, as the present post-Laeken 'Constitutional' Convention on the Future of Europe demonstrates, many of the background assumptions of constitution-building in non-state contexts are drawn from the state tradition. This is as true of the very 'Philadelphian' form of the debate – that it takes place in a Convention, and that the preferred option of that Convention is to write a documentary Constitution[11] – as it is of its *content* – from Charters of Rights to Madisonian conceptions of the horizontal division and vertical separation of powers. All of this is unsurprising. After all, the vocabulary with which we seek to make normative sense of political entities, including all the key values listed above, even if it does not originate with the modern state, has nonetheless undergone centuries of development and refinement within the context of the state. Unsurprising, but, for reasons developed below, just as unsatisfactory as the attitude that refuses even to contemplate the possibility of translation.

Paradoxically, these opposite attitudes can be mutually reinforcing. The attitude which sees constitutional translation to non-state contexts as illegitimate is in some measure in reaction or response to the claims of those who believe that the form, content and, perhaps, status associated with state constitutionalism can be translated literally and without remainder to the non-state setting. If the state constitutional template is suggested or, more frequently, simply assumed as the only available template for postnational settings by those who advocate the constitutionalization of post-state entities, then this may present itself either as a genuine danger or as a convenient dystopia to those who continue to see constitutionalism as an exclusive affair of states. We may also observe a more subtle causal connection running in the opposite direction, between the suspicious disengagement of many sceptics of postnational constitutionalism on the one hand and the insouciant assumptions of those who assume the viability and legitimacy of direct transcription on the other. If, as has been the case in the European debate at least until recently when the momentum behind the constitutional approach has begun to force a strategic rethink on the part of some state constitutionalists,[12] the sceptics simply fail to

---

[11] In line with his consistent preference from the outset of the Convention's deliberations to take the constitutional route, Valéry Giscard d'Estaing announced on 6 October 2002 that an outline Constitution would be presented to the plenary Convention on 28 October, so seeking to lock any subsequent discussion into an explicitly constitutional frame. As it transpired, this skeletal draft did indeed provide a template for all subsequent debate within the Convention.

[12] The sceptics have begun to come on board with a view to using the European Constitution as a way of *limiting* power at the European level. This was the theme of *The Economist* magazine (4 November 2000) and also of many of the 'Eurosceptics' present in the Laeken Convention. However, two points should be noted. (1) The attitude of the sceptics

participate in the postnational constitutional debate for fear of so dig-
nifying that debate as to legitimate the postnational constitutional process, then the perspective of uncritical transcription may flourish more
easily than it would if subject to the detailed interrogation of a critical
perspective.

What the mutually reinforcing positions of the postnational constitutional 'refuseniks' and the literal translators have in common is a failure
fully to *engage* with problems of translation. EU constitutional 'talk' may
now be *de rigueur* in and around the post-Laeken Convention and, indeed, increasingly in other public, institutional and academic fora,[13] but
the absence of a sufficiently reflective preliminary phase of 'talk about
constitutional talk' entails that the legitimacy and coherence of official
constitutional discourse rests on insecure foundations.

The resilient value of the constitutional frame

Of course to point to the limitations of exclusive state constitutionalism,
or of literal translation, or to the dialogue-chilling consequences of the

remains highly ambivalent, vacillating between general antipathy to a Constitution and
acknowledgement that one, and only one, particular type of Constitution may be acceptable. (2) A number of distancing tactics are used, often with the consequence of minimizing
active engagement in the debate over the full implications of a constitutional settlement. So,
for example, the attitude of the British Government, *inter alios*, has been one of symbolic
trivialization, marked by the frequent interventions of the Foreign Secretary Jack Straw to
the effect that since may entities, including golf clubs, have Constitutions, there is nothing
of general political significance in the European Union adopting one (see, for example,
The Economist, 12 October 2002). This attitude fails to acknowledge that the European
Union, unlike any golf club with which I am acquainted, is an active geo-political player,
implicated like all such active players in the competition for scarce symbolic resources.

[13] This is not the place to attempt a detailed history of the development of a specifically
European constitutional discourse in the ECJ, the European Parliament and other public
and institutional settings, or indeed in the academy. It suffices to say that while many would
agree that the secular tendency of the European Union to develop ever more intensive and
extensive authoritative claims, powers and institutional structures without developing an
adequate normative language to keep pace with these developments meant that, in Weiler's
words, by the late 1990s the EU had become 'a constitutional order the constitutional theory
of which has not been worked out' (*Constitution of Europe*, 8), many would also conclude
that the development of a political project of constitutionalization in the post-Laeken
Convention has at last allowed the constitutional theory to 'catch up'. Yet the failure to
resolve background questions about the translatability of constitutional thinking to the
postnational setting suggests that the constitutional fanfare may be premature. As Maduro
says, '[T]he claim by Europe to independent political authority... has never been fully
legitimised. Instead we have moved directly into discussing how to legitimate the processes
and institutional system through which the power derived from that claim is exercised':
'Where to Look for Legitimacy?' in E. O. Eriksen, J. E. Fossum and A. J. Menendez (eds.),
Constitution Making and Democratic Legitimacy, ARENA Report No. 5/2002, 81; see also
Walker 'European Constitutionalism'.

opposition of these two approaches, does not prove that, even if it is possible, anything of value can be achieved by developing a more general conception of constitutional translation from the state to the post-state context. Many may talk of wanting it, but what, if anything, is the point of translation? A positive answer to this question requires us to demonstrate that there is something of value in our statist constitutional heritage that is worth preserving and applying to the non-state context of political organization. We must show that there is something which flows from the ethic of responsible self-government which lies at the heart of all publicly defensible constitutional discourse which, if transferred to the non-state setting, is helpful in solving problems of responsible self-government in these settings too and, indeed, in legitimating the solutions it provides. In so doing, we must overcome two objections. One is to the effect that constitutionalism is not just about the history of legitimate self-government, but also about the history of *illegitimate* domination – of cloaking illegitimate regimes and the illegitimate acts of sometimes legitimate regimes with the inauthentic robes and mystifying aura of legitimate authority – and that if a positive constitutional legacy is to be retained we have to be able to differentiate between the virtuous promise of constitutionalism and much of what it has delivered. A second objection is to the effect that, as developed below, even if we assume that at least some constitutional discourse consists of good-faith attempts to solve problems of responsible self-government, the particular solutions offered are so disparate and so much in mutual tension that it is difficult to find any common heritage on which we might usefully draw.

Patently, these are strong objections. If they are not to be insurmountable objections, our claims for the value of constitutional translation have to be suitably modest. We must concede that constitutionalism translated cannot provide us with the definitive answers to puzzles and conflicts of political organization in the post-state setting any more than constitutionalism untranslated can provide us with definitive answers to puzzles and conflicts of political organization in the state setting. Nevertheless, the constitutional frame of reference may be worth retaining for at least[14]

---

[14] In my view, there is a third sense in which constitutionalism provides an important frame for postnational regulation, namely as an *authoritative* frame. This is a complex and controversial claim that cannot easily be defended in a few paragraphs. Moreover, it is not necessary to defend this claim for the purposes of the present argument, as the case for translation can rest adequately enough on the twin pillars of constitutionalism as a *symbolic* and as a *normative* frame. Accordingly, I make no attempt here to defend this third argument in detail. Synoptically, the case for viewing constitutionalism as an indispensable

two related reasons – reasons that in acknowledging these very limitations of constitutionalism also discern its strengths.

In the first place, we must consider the significance of constitutionalism as a symbolic frame of reference. Viewed as a general discursive register rather than a specific set of state-puzzle-solutions, constitutionalism is linked in a powerful and resilient chain of signification to a whole series of *substantive* institutional values – such as democracy, accountability, equality, the separation of powers, the rule of law and fundamental rights, with their strong association to the freedom and well-being of the individual within a framework of collective action and protection, as well as, at the *procedural* level, to the idea that the institutional specification, interpretation and balanced application of these values as an exercise in practical reasoning is a matter of contestation and should accordingly be resolved through forms of deliberation and decision (constitutional

authoritative frame in the postnational context depends upon two propositions. In the first place, it depends upon the proposition that we miss something of significance if we try to trace all forms of postnational regulation to state authority sources. Secondly, in so far as state authority sources are not sufficient to ground the various forms of postnational regulation, they are instead grounded in other authoritative sites beyond the state. In the European context at least, this argument can be defended empirically, as it tracks the claims to supremacy actually made by the European Court of Justice; on this see G. de Burca, 'Sovereignty and the Supremacy Doctrine of the European Court of Justice', in N. Walker (ed.), *Sovereignty in Transition* (Oxford: Hart Publishing, forthcoming). More fundamentally, the argument can also be defended as a necessary feature of the ordering power of law in general. Legal norms may claim legitimacy on various grounds, but these invariably include a claim based on the internal authority of a particular legal order, whose initial claim to authority itself is presented as self-authorizing and so independent of any other authoritative claim. In so far as constitutionalism is concerned with the presentation and representation of the fundamental norms of the legal order, it provides a necessary register in which this claim of self-authorization, rather than simply being assumed, can be articulated, justified and refined. That is to say, for all that many constitutional norms are claimed to be universal (for example, in the area of fundamental rights), and for all that this claim is important for us to make sense of the idea of constitutional translation, part of constitutional discourse is also concerned with the representation of the *particular* authority and ordering power of a distinctive polity or authoritative site. However much we recognize and encourage an outward-looking constitutionalism in which different legal orders seek mutual coherence and recognition and claim an authority or influence for some of the constitutional norms which they validate that transcends their particular legal order, we can only begin to make sense of this process if we recognize, as a fundamental feature of legal epistemology, the existence and reflexive development of identifiable legal *orders*. Or, in Hartian language, legal norms must always have a pedigree in a particular legal order with its particular complex of secondary rules of recognition, adjudication and change, the adequate articulation of which secondary rules requires a constitutional discourse. See e.g. H. Lindahl, 'Sovereignty and Representation in the European Union' and N. Walker, 'Late Sovereignty in the European Union', both in Walker, *Sovereignty in Transition*. See also Walker, 'Constitutional Pluralism'.

Conventions, referenda, constitutional courts, etc.) which satisfy those involved or otherwise affected of their legitimacy.[15] In this regard, we may think of constitutionalism as a 'condensing symbol',[16] a general category of thought and effect through which the concerns and commitments of the community with regard to the establishment and operation of just political institutions for that community are traditionally and commonly made sense of and expressed. It follows that those who wish, from whatever motive or combination of motives, to make a plausible claim for their version of constitutionalism, must at least *be seen to* take these substantive values seriously – so addressing the problem of good faith – and also to be taking the procedural imperative of the deliberative negotiation or resolution of difference seriously – so addressing the problem of the marked disparity of substantive preferences. As Jon Elster points out, 'hypocrisy can have civilizing effects',[17] and the invocation of constitutionalism, just because of the expectations thus aroused and the constituencies and arguments thus mobilized, tends to structure the ensuing debate between those who would claim, challenge or counterclaim its associated symbolic power – and in turn, tends to inform the institutional consequences of that debate – in ways which escape the original intentions of the protagonists.[18]

It is the very potency of constitutionalism as a condensing symbol for the problems and aspirations associated with the institutional specification of a viable and legitimate framework for political community, moreover, which accounts for its abstraction from its statist domicile and its increasingly insistent invocation at the postnational level. Earlier we pointed to the current momentum behind constitutional talk at the EU level, and indeed it is the very dangers associated with the premature escalation of such talk against a background of continuing fundamental disagreement over the second order question of whether and to what extent

---

[15] For a development of a sociologically sensitive model of the procedural side of constitutional legitimacy within a context of agonistic discursive democracy, see e.g. J. Tully, 'The Unfreedom of the Moderns in Comparison to Their Ideals of Constitutional Democracy' 65 *Modern Law Review* (2002), 203.

[16] V. Turner, *Dramas, Fields and Metaphors: Symbolic Action in Human Society* (Ithaca: Cornell University Press, 1974).

[17] J. Elster, 'Introduction', in Elster (ed.), *Deliberative Democracy* (Cambridge: Cambridge University Press, 1998), 14.

[18] The 'civilizing effect' can operate in both a weak and a strong sense. Weakly, it imposes an external discipline upon those who would use the language of constitutionalism for purely strategic motives. More strongly, the requirement to use constitutional discourse and the acquired habit of engagement of debate in a constitutional register may transform the original motives of the strategic protagonist and lead to the internalization of a substantive and procedural constitutional ethic. See, for example, Tully, 'Unfreedom of the Moderns'.

constitutionalism is an appropriate discourse at all at this level which lends such urgency to the present inquiry. Yet the heavy mobilization of constitutional language within the EU context remains an undeniable and telling sociological phenomenon.

But our caution about the spread of constitutional language indicates that it is not enough merely to say that constitutionalism can provide a public and so constraining context of debate in which a number of very general substantive and procedural values are loosely coupled. Alongside the sociological constraints associated with constitutionalism as such a public and consequential exercise in practical reasoning within and concerning the polity, constitutionalism must also provide some epistemological dividend. It must do so both as a way of imposing some kind of tangible discipline on the substantive 'good faith' and procedural 'reasonable engagement' values and as a way of ensuring that even those prepared to act in good faith and reasonably to engage *inter se* in the sketchily mapped world of post-state governance are able so to do. That is to say, constitutionalism should also provide a normative frame of reference to build on its symbolic power, an ideational framework to justify and civilize its ideological power. It must have some value as a form of knowledge production at the postnational level just as it must have some value as a form of knowledge production at the national level, even if the constraint of modesty in such a contested domain entails that this cannot take the form of providing definitive answers and must instead be limited to the framing of the right questions. This, then, brings us back full circle to the problem of translation. The task of translation of constitutionalism into the postnational context is, in acknowledging the strength of constitutionalism as a powerful and mobile symbolic frame, to vindicate the promise of constitutionalism as a normative frame. The test, then, of the adequacy of any attempt at general translation lies precisely in whether or not it succeeds in elucidating the questions which must inform and animate constitutionalism in its search for a viable and legitimate regulatory framework for political community in postnational settings.

Addressing the problem of translation

The terms of translation

Even for those who are prepared to engage in this task, who do not – willingly or otherwise – submit to fatalism about the prospects of constitutionalism beyond the state, nor follow the treacherously easy path of

literal translation, the acknowledgement that translation is a problemat-
ical yet feasible and vital task does not readily yield insights which will
actively advance the task of translation. To be sure, within constitutional
thinking there are many, often ingenious, efforts in specific translation;
that is to say, translations of particular concepts – in particular those
of democracy[19] and federalism[20] – to one particular level of non-state
governance (EU, WTO, UN, etc.). But there has been less progress in developing a general methodological framework in this area. The reasons
for this clearly have much to do with particular intellectual priorities and
perspectives, but in an echo of the more profound scepticism of those
who believe constitutionalism to be inextricably tied to the state, may
also have to do with a perception that any such general project is doomed
to failure.

Perhaps translation of constitutional concepts between different levels
and sites of governance *can* only be specific. My sense, however, is that this
need not be so, and, indeed, that to the extent that analysis is limited to
the particular translation, it will be of limited explanatory and normative
value, and will do little to assuage the doubts and fears of the postnational
sceptics. In its original sense of *linguistic* translation – or indeed in the
rather closer sense of the translatability of legal concepts between different
state jurisdictions in comparative law,[21] the very idea of good translation
involves three things. First, it involves a 'thick' conception of what is to be

---

[19] For a recent example, see P. Schmitter, *How to Democratise the European Union . . . and Why Bother?* (Lanham: Rowman & Littlefield, 2000).

[20] For a recent example, see K. Nicolaidis and R. Howse (eds.), *The Federal Vision: Legitimacy and Levels of Governance in the United States and the European Union* (Oxford: Oxford University Press, 2001).

[21] Many of the problems of translation of constitutional discourse between state and non-state sites find parallels in the traditional discipline of comparative law between state sites to the extent that this too is approached as an exercise in practical reasoning – as the identification of common problems across sites and the translation of optimal solutions. The work of Pierre Legrand is especially noteworthy in this regard in that it contains a powerful critique of the tendency within some comparative work to see translation as unproblematical, but does so from a position which in stark contrast sees translation between differently socially embedded legal *mentalités* as quite impossible. The similarity to the polar opposition in attitudes to translation within the European constitutional debate is striking. See, for example, P. Legrand, *Fragments on Law-as-Culture* (Deventer: Willink, 1999). For an exchange of views in the particular context of comparative public law, see P. Legrand, 'Public Law, Europeanization and Convergence: Can Comparatists Contribute?' and N. Walker, 'Culture, Democracy and the Convergence of Public Law: Some Scepticisms about Scepticism', both in P. Beaumont, C. Lyons and N. Walker (eds.), *Convergence and Divergence in European Public Law* (Oxford: Hart Publishing, 2002) at 225 and 257 respectively.

translated, in the sense of a detailed hermeneutic understanding both of the context in which it was originally embedded and of the new context for which it is destined. Secondly, it involves some non-linguistic or meta-linguistic way of comparing these 'thick' contexts – of working out what is commonly or equivalently signified by these different local signifiers.[22] Thirdly, the translation must be plausible to those who are competent in both languages. That is to say, those who can claim membership of both linguistic communities must agree that the method and product of the

---

[22] As a number of commentators on the first draft of this chapter pointed out, here we run up against the limitations of the translation metaphor. Much of twentieth-century philosophy was concerned with the critique of what Rorty terms 'representationalism' – the combination of (1) the Kantian idea that knowledge must be understood in terms of some relation between what the world offers up to the thinker on the one hand, and the cognitive structures through which the thinker processes these offerings on the other, and (2) the Platonic idea that there must be some form of description of these things that the world offers up which through its privileged ability to discern and map these things counts as a true or accurate or otherwise valid description (see R. Rorty, *Philosophy and the Mirror of Nature* (Princeton: Princeton University Press, 1979), ch. 4). We can see a strong critique of one or both of these foundationalist premises in various diverse strands and schools of modern philosophy – for example, in Wittgenstein, in Quine, in Davidson, in Rorty himself – and, indeed, the anti-foundationalist conclusions of such a critique are included within the settled premises of much other influential contemporary philosophy. One manifestation of this critique is Quine's well-known thesis concerning the indeterminacy of translation. If there is no privileged access to the object world but only different theory-dependent and language-dependent forms of access, the accuracy of any particular translation from one language to another can never be warranted, and we can end up with radically different and mutually inconsistent but equally plausible (or implausible) translations (see e.g. W. V. Quine, *Pursuit of Truth* (Cambridge, MA: Harvard University Press, 1990)).

But, of course, we are not here concerned with language *tout court*, but with a particular discourse associated with a specific form of practical reasoning. 'Translation' here concerns not whether a speech act which is embedded in the totality of ways a community has of speaking about the world can be rendered meaningful in a speech act which is embedded in the totality of ways another and quite distinct community has of speaking about the world, to which no determinate 'yes' can be provided in any particular instance in the absence of a correspondence theory of truth – one relying on an objective world which exists independently of perception which can be accessed and described independently of the source and destination language. Rather, 'translation' in this specialist context concerns whether a particular type of applied normative reasoning which does not exhaust the linguistic resources of the user, but which is instead concerned with the circumscribed task of articulating a viable and legitimate regulatory framework of political community at the level of the state, can be applied to forms and levels of political community other than the state. 'Translation' in this context does not depend for its determinacy upon an implausible correspondence theory of truth, but rather on the coherence of the discourse, and in particular on the generality and transferability of its theoretical objects, whose articulation can draw on second-order linguistic resources distinct from the first-order 'user' language of constitutionalism. See further below.

translation is adequate to capture and convey a similar meaning in the two languages.

So what, then, do our conditions of adequate translation require when applied to the specialist normative domain of constitutionalism? They entail, first, that we cannot regard particular concepts in isolation, but must look at the overall constitutional scheme and indeed the deeper context of political opportunity, constraint and motivation in which it is embedded. So, for example, we cannot understand the meaning of democracy within a particular state context unless and until we see how it is elaborated and articulated with other constitutional values – fundamental rights, separation of powers, dispersal of powers, etc. – in an overall constitutional scheme within that local context, and unless and until we understand how that scheme is in turn informed by underlying social and political forces. Similarly, we cannot begin to conceive of a normatively adequate translation of a particular constitutional value to a postnational setting unless we have an equally rich understanding of its situation within the existing or envisaged overall constitutional scheme and relative to underlying political forces within that destination setting. Secondly, and crucially, our translation manual is deficient unless and until we have a conception of the *constitutionally signified* which is independent of but commonly referred to by or implied by our familiar *constitutional signifiers*. Finally, the common set of general references for the various site-specific constitutional discourses which this provides must be one which is capable of commanding broad agreement as a basis on which we may ask pertinent questions as to the appropriate deployment of constitutional reasoning and the appropriate articulation of constitutional design across sites.

Some candidate solutions

It seems, therefore, that the process of translation cannot get off the ground unless we have some broadly agreed sense of what constitutionalism *is about* which transcends particular contexts and which thus acts as a benchmark for translations between these particular contexts. Immediately, the criteria of meaningful translation confront us with a number of related problems that rule out various candidate solutions.

In the first place, as we have already noted, definitions of constitutionalism are often more or less ideologically loaded. In public discourse constitutionalism, as such a potent condensing symbol, is often seen as code for legitimate government. And just because there is so much at stake symbolically in the acceptance of a position or an argument as constitutional or otherwise, constitutional actors both in the political domain and, if more subtly, in the academic domain invest much, and often without much scruple or at least without full awareness or acknowledgement of the commitments already built into their first premises, in the effort to win such acceptance or deny it to others. The power of legitimate naming, in other words, counts for much within constitutional discourse.[23] So we should not be surprised to find constitutionalism invoked not just in connection with, but even as synonymous with, preferred normative ends or mechanisms of government, whether this be the general idea of limited government, the idea of fundamental rights-based constraints upon or 'trumps' over the policy values of a particular regime, the idea of deliberative democracy, etc.[24] Regardless of the internal coherence or external attractiveness of these various schemes of though – in which, incidentally, the concept of constitutionalism if used in such a selective fashion often does little work and performs no function other than as a crowning label – their partial quality and their mutual irreconcilability do not mark them out as candidates capable of commanding broad agreement.

A second problem concerns the difficulty of escaping constitutional discourse – the 'constitutional signifier' – in developing a framework for translation. For, as noted, we cannot find principles for discovering what is in common between two discourses in either of the discourses themselves. On reflection, this problem divides into two more specific difficulties. The first concerns the dominance of the host or source language of *state* constitutionalism. The 'touch of stateness' which Shaw and Wiener refer to takes us to the heart of the problem, and reminds us of the dangers of literal translation. Just because state constitutionalism

---

[23] As already intimated, this is true not only of 'regime legitimacy', that is the legitimacy of particular systems of government, but also of 'polity legitimacy', that is whether a particular system of political organization counts as a polity at all – the accepted and familiar use of constitutional discourse in relation to the polity being an important element in the affirmation of such a status. On the distinction, and overlap, between 'polity legitimacy' and 'regime legitimacy', see N. Walker, 'The White Paper in Constitutional Context', in C. Joerges, Y. Mény and J. H. H. Weiler (eds.), *Mountain or Molehill? A Critical Appraisal of the Commission White Paper on Governance* (2001), Harvard/NYU Jean Monnet Programme.

[24] See, for example, the criticism made by Carlos Closa of Christian Joerges's work as identifying constitutionalism in general with a particular variant of constitutionalism based upon deliberative democracy: C. Closa, 'The Implicit Model of Constitution in the EU Constitutional Project', in Eriksen, Fossum and Menendez, *Constitution Making*, 53 at 55, n. 5; see also in the same volume, C. Joerges, 'The Law in the Process of Constitutionalizing Europe', 13.

is the dominant or defining template, and just because the 'destination language' of non-state constitutionalism is underdeveloped, there is a danger that, in Schmitter's words, 'both scholars and actors in the integration process presume an isomorphism between the EU [or, by extension, any other post-state site of political capacity] and their respective national polities'.[25] But the problem of the 'constitutional signifier' is not just a problem of state-centredness. Imagine, if such a thing is possible, that non-state sites had developed their own constitutional discourse significantly and had done so in ways which owed little to the statist heritage, or in ways which had been as much influential of as influenced by the state heritage.[26] Imagine, in other words, a greater autonomy of non-state constitutionalism or a more equal mutual interdependence of state and non-state constitutionalism. Even then, one could not find a basis for translation between the discourses in any of the discourses themselves or arising out of them, for one would still lack the independent mechanism necessary for comparative interpretation and evaluation.

An example may help to make these points. Many constitutional theorists who do not associate constitutionalism with any one particular *Eigenwert* instead see the true arena or centrepiece of constitutional debate and development as involving the reconcilation of two values or clusters of constitutional values, those associated with the collective capacity of democratic institutions on the one hand and those associated with the fundamental rights of individuals and, perhaps, other 'non-public' legal personalities on the other.[27] Might this balancing of the scales between these two supposedly fundamental imperatives be seen as the basis for translation between sites? If, on the one hand, the reference point remains that of the state, then the problem of state-centredness persists,

---

[25] P. Schmitter 'What is there to Legitimize in the European Union . . . And How Might This Be Accomplished?', in Joerges, Mény and Weiler, *Mountain or Molehill?*, 79, 81–2.

[26] Of course, some non-state sites do have a tradition of constitutional discourse, some a very recent tradition, as in the case of the WTO (see n. 2 above), and some a more longstanding one, as in the case of the United Nations: see e.g. B. Fassbender, 'The United Nations Charter as the Constitution of the International Community', 36 *Columbia Journal of International Law* (1997), 529. Yet, unsurprisingly, in all such cases, as in the European Union itself, the statist legacy is strong, in that the point of departure is the discovery of an analogy between institutions and principles at the non-state level and those long embedded in state constitutional discourse, or even, in more active mode, is an argument that particular state-level constitutional institutions or principles should be transplanted to the particular non-state site in question. There is no question, in other words, that the state site remains the dominant site and basepoint of reference in the process of translation.

[27] The centrality of this point of departure within constitutional theory is discussed at length in Tully, 'Unfreedom of the Moderns'.

and no translation is possible. If, on the other hand, the reference point is not any particular site of authority, then the difficulty lies in locating a meaningful basis of comparative interpretation and evaluation. If that basis is said to be the relationship between rights and democracy in constitutional settings *in general*, then we cannot work out what this might mean by looking at any particular site of constitutional authority, for that takes us back to the problem of site-specific bias, and in effect to the problem of state-centredness. Thus, we cannot escape the conclusion that we have to look beyond constitutional discourse itself to find a basis for meaningful translation of constitutional concerns from one site to another, even where we may have a constitutional *problématique* – the reconciliation of rights and democracy – which involves a less partial prioritization of values and which thus might otherwise appear to provide a more promising candidate to command general agreement as a common feature of constitutionalism across sites.[28]

Yet even if we are sensitive to the problems of selectivity of values, of state-centredness and of the need to move beyond 'constitutional signifiers' to find a basis for translation, if we look more closely at our conditions of adequate translation there remain considerable difficulties in discovering such a basis. The identification of that which is commonly 'constitutionally signified' must involve a balance between the requirement of *relevance* which demands that the translation is sensitive to a

---

[28] Of course, ideas of 'rights' and 'democracy' register not only in constitutional discourse, but in the deeper discourse of political theory, and the balance between the two at this deeper level might seem an obvious candidate basis for translation of concerns at the more institutional level of constitutional theory. However, as Jeremy Waldron has pointed out, particularly in respect to the language of rights, there is much slippage between the levels of constitutionalism and political theory in debate (as much by political theorists as constitutional lawyers!) – and often an apparent lack of appreciation that we *are* dealing with quite different registers of debate. So, for instance, when we talk about rights as deep entitlements flowing from a theory of human nature or human society on the one hand and rights as justiciable claims against government (and less frequently, private actors) within an institutional framework of law on the other, then we are not talking about the same thing, but the suspicion remains that the semantic identity of the objects of analysis leads many to use these terms interchangeably. As Waldron shows, moreover, there is, on closer inquiry, no obvious relationship, but only complex and contestable ones, between the same terms within the different registers, and certainly no guarantee, to take the instant case, that the underlying meaning, if any such general meaning exists, of the *constitutional* relationship between rights and democracy is revealed by an examination of their relationship at the level of political theory, and thus little prospect that the latter might in fact provide an agreed basis for translation of the core concerns of constitutionalism between sites. See J. Waldron, *Law and Disagreement* (Oxford: Clarendon Press, 1999); see also Walker, 'Culture, Democracy'.

sufficiently 'thick' understanding of each local context, the requirement of *generality* which demands that translation is indeed possible between all constitutional sites and so must have some interpretive or explanatory purchase in all constitutional contexts, and the requirement of *normative salience* which recalls that constitutionalism is an exercise in practical reasoning whose value as such depends upon its supplying a lens through which it can draw upon and evaluate a legacy of comparative constitutional thought and experience to propose solutions to the question of providing a viable and legitimate regulatory framework for political community.

The 'constitutionally signified', therefore, must not be so general and so abstract, its relationship to the concerns of particular constitutional contexts so attenuated and so varied, that it lacks any meaningful and normatively significant common purchase on these concerns. To take an extreme example, to say that all constitutional sites are concerned with the promotion and stabilization of the 'good society' would meet with few, if any, objections, yet the common denominator – the 'good society' – is pitched at such a level of abstraction that it provides us with no explanatory or normative basis on which to conduct an evaluative comparison of particular constitutional doctrines and mechanisms operating in particular contexts.

Conversely, in ensuring that its relevance to and relationship to particular constitutional schemes is legible and capable of generating meaningful scheme-specific questions and propositions, the 'constitutionally signified' should not sacrifice on the altar of contextual appropriateness the generality of explanation or the capacity to provide a deep normative underpinning which a legitimate site-transferable constitutionalism implies and requires. That is to say, the value of the 'constitutionally signified' which provides the basis for translation is reduced to the extent that, for the sake of contextual 'fit', it is not of universal explanatory relevance across constitutional sites and does not speak to the deepest justificatory roots of consitutionalism's normative orientation.

Again an example may help to illustrate these points. An instructive instance of the difficulties in finding a 'constitutionally signified' that, while being well honed to the requirements of contextual 'fit', is also of sufficient generality and normative power, can be found in a recent study by Christian Joerges of the Nazi heritage in European legal thought. Though interested in comparisons over time rather than space, and in translation between different postnational contexts rather than between state and postnational, Joerges's methodological concerns mirror those that animate the present inquiry. He is concerned to provide a framework which shows the continuities and discontinuities between the pre-war German legal tradition and other times and places, and – of particular concern for present purposes – with discovering the lessons for the profoundly different type of supranationalism at the centre of the contemporary European constitutional configuration that may be learned from reflecting upon the *Grossraum* – the German imperialist dystopia suggested by the Nazi apologist Carl Schmitt.[29] Joerges makes the telling point that for all the pathologies of the Third Reich and its schemes for extinguishing other national sovereignties in accordance with the *Führung* principle, 'the problems of the order of the economy, of the exposure of society to technological problems and necessities, and of the difficulty of ensuring the political and social accountability of the administration did not resolve themselves with the disappearance of National Socialism'.[30] That is to say, underlying both transnational models although responded to very differently in each, we can identify the same puzzles of governance: first, as regards the economy, how to ensure the *relative* insulation of an increasingly complex transnational economy from protectionist or otherwise market-jeopardizing interventionist political forces; secondly, as regards technology, how to ensure that the increasing range of questions of modern governance which require technical knowledge in areas as varied as environmental impact, product safety standards, public health and internal and external security are treated with the requisite expertise while preserving the scope for open political contestation over those associated normative choices which are not reducible to merely technical considerations; thirdly, as regards administration, how to ensure fairness, consistency and calculability of administration in an era of increasingly 'big government' without succumbing to the pathologies of bureaucracy's 'iron cage'[31] – where legality descends into mere legalism[32] and public administration becomes insensitive to differing social needs and

---

[29] For Joerges's essay and my commentary, see 'Europe: A Grossraum?', EUI Law Department Working Paper 2002/2, incorporating Joerges, 'Europe: A Grossraum? Rupture, Continuity and Re-Configuration in the Legal Conceptualization of the Integration Project' and Walker 'Putting the European House in Order: From Grossraum to Condominium – A Comment'. Both also forthcoming in C. Joerges (ed.), *The Darker Legacy of European Law* (Oxford: Hart Publishing).

[30] Joerges, 'Europe: A Grossraum?', 20.

[31] In Weber's famous metaphor. See M. Weber, *The Theory of Social and Economic Organization* (Glencoe: Free Press, 1947).

[32] For a recent discussion of this distinction, see Z. Bankowski, *Living Lawfully: Love in Law and Law in Love* (Dordrecht: Kluwer, 2001), esp. ch. 3.

unsusceptible to supervision, guidance or transformation in accordance with a legitimate normative vision.

Importantly, these problems are of course staples of *all* modern advanced societies, including states, and are not peculiar to systems of multi-level governance. Yet in its recognition that the complexities and potential of transnational economic circuits and the boundary-transgressing ramifications of new technological processes may be usefully addressed through political mechanisms other than the state, multi-level governance can be seen both as a particular response, or at least as a reaction to the problems in question, and also as a setting in which these problems, through being merely reconfigured rather than transcended, are as likely to be exacerbated as resolved. The general explanation for such a perverse possibility, which is explored in more depth below, is not hard to seek, for the various problems outlined by Joerges speak to the significance and delicate balance of a plurality of values which remain in tension with one another regardless of how many levels of government are involved in their treatment and in what combination, and where often the prioritization of one value may be to the unhealthy detriment of others. So the relentless Nazi emphasis on the primacy of the political beyond the German state and throughout the occupied *Grossraum*, and Schmitt's apologia for this strategy,[33] seeks to exorcise the demons of soulless technocracy and rudderless bureaucracy, but does so at the expense not only of the virtues of independent expertise and unbiased and non-arbitrary administration but also of any conception of the political itself as democratically pluralist and so 'weak' (in National Socialist terms) rather than authoritarian and ideologically 'strong'. In the context of the European Union, both ordo-liberalism and functionalism, two of its deepest founding roots, stand in stark contrast to fascist doctrine in terms both of the moral defensibility of their intentions and of their explicit *defence* of economic and technical rationality patterns in an economic constitution protected from the vicissitudes of politics, whether quotidian or millenarian. Nevertheless, as Joerges indicates,[34] these approaches may err too much in the other direction and create an opposite imbalance, even if profoundly less dangerous in consequence. For, as the European Union, through an increasingly deep-rooted and wide-ranging process of positive integration, is transformed 'into a political community of open and undetermined political

---

[33] Even though, as Joerges points out ('Europe: A Grossraum', 16), there was much in Schmitt's pre-Grossraum writings that could have mitigated this emphasis.

[34] And see, more expansively, his ' "Good Governance" in the European Internal Market: An Essay in Honour of Claus-Dieter Ehlermann', EUI Working Papers, RSC No. 2001/29.

goals',[35] the relationship between the economic, the technocratic and the political logics which inform decision-making and regulation within the Union defy any simple demarcation into different compartments, while the traditional indirect, state-centred democratic legitimation of the expanding Union mandate looks ever more threadbare.

Yet, however insightful Joerges's work and however appropriate to the particular historical comparison in which he is engaged, for the purposes of providing a general framework of constitutional translation the balance between contextual appropriateness, generality of explanatory scope and depth of normative foundations required to provide a sound basis for such translation has to be further adjusted to allow normative questions to be abstracted from issues of governance and to be granted a separate and more prominent status. By concentrating on problems of governance and the diverse and sometimes contending values associated with these, Joerges indeed develops a non-constitutional language for a comparative evaluative framework that succeeds in indicating many of the constitutional dilemmas of modern advanced societies in both state and non-state sites. But although the questions of administration, expertise and economics which he highlights do underpin and inform constitutional choices, we have to dig deeper in search of a fundamental and generalizable set of normative concerns which in turn inform these problems of governance in the various site-specific settings. That is to say, beneath the governance puzzles which Joerges identifies and places in mutual tension may lie other even more fundamental political values and an even more basic set of objective tensions concerning the reconciliation of these values. If constitutionalism as a form of practical reasoning is to begin to meet its aspiration of finding a context-transcending way of approaching the legitimate regulation of political community these more fundamental values must be drawn out and rendered explicit within the conceptual framework.

A modest proposal

Recent work by the social theorist Ralf Dahrendorf may be helpful in identifying this configuration of fundamental values.[36] For him, *the* great problem of modern political thought lies in the reconciliation of the three

---

[35] Maduro, 'Where to Look for Legitimacy?', 81.
[36] R. Dahrendorf, 'A Precarious Balance: Economic Opportunity, Civil Society and Political Liberty', 5(3) *The Responsive Community* (1995), 13.

virtues of economic or material well-being, social cohesion and effective freedom (both the political 'liberty of the ancients' and the personal 'liberty of the moderns', the latter being both intrinsically valuable and a necessary underpinning of full political freedom).[37] Affluence, community and (personal and political) liberty, in other words, are the often inarticulate major premises on which we base our political visions, frame our governance dilemmas and, finally, make our constitutional choices. Here, at last, then, we may be on more promising ground to develop a mechanism to aid a general translation of the constitutional *problématique* between sites.

It was argued earlier that the proof of the value of any system of constitutional translation is to be found in the questions it allows us to ask across constitutional sites embedded in very different social and political contexts as to the significance of the various institutional choices available in the construction of particular constitutional schemes. How, if at all, might Dahrendorf's approach be developed to meet this challenge? In addressing this question, let us again look at the European context – not as a way of avoiding the requirement of generality, but simply as a method of illustrating with some concreteness the issues which might arise in a particular context of translation in light of the general principles of translation.

Weiler himself provides a useful general orientation towards the key issues of translation between state and European Union. He argues[38] that two of the main founding imperatives, even ideals, of the European Union were 'peace' and 'prosperity'. Lasting peace was to be achieved through the binding of the states and peoples of Europe (with Western Europe as a starting point rather than a terminus) into 'an ever closer Union' of economic interdependence and, increasingly, social interaction and 'interculturality'.[39] Lasting prosperity was to be achieved by the pooling of the factors of production at the level of the continent and ensuring the free circulation of goods, services, capital and – if with less conviction – people across the old state borders. A third ideal, which Weiler argues exists only in emergent form, is that of 'supranationality' itself, here defined as

---

[37] On this distinction, see famously B. Constant, 'The Liberty of the Ancients Compared with That of the Moderns', in B. Fontana (trans. and ed.), *Constant: Political Writings* (Cambridge: Cambridge University Press, 1988).

[38] Weiler, *Constitution of Europe*, ch. 9.

[39] To use Tully's nice expression depicting the permeability of all cultural boundaries. See *Strange Multiplicity: Constitutionalism in an Age of Diversity* (Cambridge: Cambridge University Press, 1995), 11.

a way of introducing a scheme of interdependent national and European citizenships in which each curbs the excesses or supplies the deficiencies of the other. Supranational citizenship tames nationalism – its tendency to internal discrimination and external aggression, to cultural insularity and imperialism – 'with a new discipline',[40] – the self-binding of the states of Europe in a framework which involves 'transnational affinities to shared values which transcend the ethno-national diversity'.[41] Likewise, national identities guard against the alienating tendencies of the broader and more cosmopolitan European identity, preserving the best of the creative and solidary impulses of national identity which may be in shorter supply at the European level.

With the help of some 'stylized facts'[42] about the 'thick' context of national and postnational political communities, the framework of mobilizing factors supplied by Weiler allows us to indicate how concern for the treatment of the fundamental political values identified by Dahrendorf helps both to explain the opening up of a European constitutional space and to make sense of the problems arising and concerns articulated within that new space as belonging to a general category of constitutional problems and concerns. Following some liberal nationalist thinkers,[43] we may think of national identity as the 'battery'[44] which helps modern nation states, and even 'pluri-national states'[45] run. Briefly, we may identify three types of 'constitutive public goods'[46] as key interrelated components of the 'battery'. These goods are aptly described as 'constitutive' because not only do they produce results that are public goods in themselves but they also help to *constitute* or reinforce the very collectivity or public which is the subject of such goods. One is the good of political dialogue – the basic sense of a political community as a community of communication and mutual understanding. The second is the good of solidarity – the creation

---

[40] Weiler, *Constitution of Europe*, 251.   [41] *Ibid.*, 346.

[42] To borrow a term of J. Cohen and C. F. Sabel in 'Sovereignty and Solidarity: EU and US', in J. Zeitlin and D. Trubek (eds.), *Governing Work and Welfare in a New Economy* (Cambridge: Cambridge University Press, 2002), ch. 13.

[43] See e.g. Y. Tamir, *Liberal Nationalism* (Princeton: Princeton University Press, 1993); M. Canovan, *Nationhood and Political Theory* (Cheltenham: Edward Elgar, 1996); D. Miller, *On Nationality* (Oxford: Oxford University Press, 1995); N. MacCormick, *Questioning Sovereignty* (Oxford: Oxford University Press, 1999); W. Kymlicka, *Politics in the Vernacular* (Oxford: Oxford University Press, 2001), esp. ch. 2.

[44] Canovan, *Nationhood and Political Theory*, 80.

[45] M. Keating, *Plurinational Democracy: Stateless Nations in a Post-Sovereign Europe* (Oxford: Oxford University Press, 2001).

[46] See further Walker, 'European Constitutionalism'.

48 NEIL WALKER

of a sense of common concern, a preparedness to think of the collectivity or other parts of the collectivity as part of the same community of attachment whose welfare and interests have to be considered when engaging in political decisions. The third constitutive good, which both derives from and reinforces the first two, is the creation of a societal infrastructure – the production of the minimum means of social co-ordination necessary to produce certain other primary goods such as security, media, education and mobility, which are in turn necessary to produce second-order public goods and private benefits (e.g. cultural goods, material wealth) which may themselves reinforce the sense of community.

This basic set of constitutive public goods – or elements of a 'societal culture'[47] – exists in a paradoxical relationship with supranational polity developments and the broader globalization of political, economic and cultural circuits of which these developments are part. On the one hand, the limitations of the 'battery' help to stimulate supranational polity-building. Both its stuttering (but still not inconsiderable) capacity to drive these functions to which it is suited – its decreasing purchase on the establishment and maintenance of the 'constitutive public goods' of communication, solidarity and infrastructural development in the face of new circuits of power – *and* its intrinsic pathologies and limitations – its tendency to cultural insularity and external aggression, the limitations of production scale, competition and choice its favouring of nationally framed markets and production processes imposes, its incapacity to deal with market 'externalities' which transcend national boundaries – encouraged the call for supranational political development in the name of peace and prosperity. In Dahrendorf's terms, what we see, then, is a series of tensions within and between the core values: (1) a secular decline in the capacity of the nation state as a host of political community and social cohesion, particularly in plurinational societies, together with (2) certain associated declines in its capacity to produce and distribute affluence and risks, which is at the heart of material well-being, and, finally, (3) the perennial vulnerability of the nation state to its social cohesion project being prosecuted at the cost of an intolerance to personal freedom within the state and reasonable communication across states, together with an effective decline in the potential of individual and group political freedom and participation 'to make a difference' in consequence of the declining overall political capacity of the state.

On the other hand, these supranational developments at EU level (and beyond) exacerbate some dimensions of the very problems of the state they

[47] Kymlicka, *Politics.*

are intended to alleviate or resolve. In particular, they threaten to acceler-
ate the secular decline of the socially constitutive and broader economic
regulatory capacity of the state, with the various linked consequences in
terms of social cohesion, material well-being and effective freedom. At the
same time, the EU's capacity to supply those omissions and counterbal-
ance those excesses of the state which are both cause and consequence of
its very assumption of supranational political capacity, and so its capacity
to address its historical agenda in the best or 'idealized' sense identified
by Weiler, is both limited and deeply contested.

Again, in Dahrendorf's terms, just as we can at the state level, we can
make sense of these limitations and contestations at the supranational
level in terms of a series of tensions within and between the core values, underscored by the elusiveness of the conditions for the flourishing
of these values. To start with the value of social cohesion, it is far from
clear or uncontested to what extent the constitutive attributes of dialogue,
solidarity and common societal infrastructure are relevant at the supranational level. If public goods associated with these attributes of community are already generated at the national level, even if to a declining degree,
any assessment of the potential and warrant for the development of the
attributes of community at supranational level is bound to be complex.
It must take account of the ways in which the existence of prior national
community encourages or inhibits the development of a new and broader
sense of community. It must also take account of the nature and extent of
the justification for 'added value' in terms of the generation of additional
public goods or, indeed, of those existing constitutive and other public
goods which the state finds increasingly difficult to deliver.

These questions, then, which are central to Scharpf's analysis of the
'joint decision trap'[48] – the gap created by the declining political capacity of the state coupled with the absence of the legitimating conditions
for the European Union to assume the displaced political capacity thus
displaced – are both empirical and normative, and closely engage the
two other core values, namely freedom and material well-being. They depend upon an analysis of the social forces at the national level that would
deter the transfer of political capacity, as well as of the forces available
at EU level to nurture such a capacity. That nurturing capacity in turn
depends upon the extent to which the EU, like other postnational sites,

[48] F. Scharpf, *Governing in Europe: Effective and Democratic?* (Oxford: Oxford University
Press, 1999) esp. ch. 2; see also his 'The Joint Decision Trap: Lessons from German Fed-
eralism and European Integration', 66 *Public Administration* (1988), 239. For critique, see
O. Gerstenberg, 'The New Europe: Part of the Problem or Part of the Solution to the
Problem?', *Oxford Journal of Legal Studies* (forthcoming).

can help provide new answers to collective action problems by generating new bonds of association which, either alternatively or in combination, (1) are parasitic upon the statist political configuration (i.e. simply endorsing the existing social and political infrastructure as 'the intergovernmental' or, more generally, 'inter-existing solidary units', framework of decision-making),[49] or (2) recreate some features of the statist configuration at the supranational level,[50] or (3) encourage new, less centralized decision-making sites organized around discrete transnational communities of interest and practice,[51] or perhaps around existing or emerging non-nation-state-based communities of attachment.[52] In turn, these questions demand an understanding and articulation of the conditions in which effective voice and participation – political freedom – may be optimized in a postnational context.

Crucially, the answers to the questions concerning the value of social cohesion at the supranational level also depend upon preferences concerning the level of solidarity-presupposing political initiatives – in particular initiatives which directly or indirectly redistribute wealth and risks and so speak to the value of material well-being, a redistributive task made harder by the increasingly modest reach of existing forms of pooled resources in an eastward-enlarging Union – which are appropriate at the supranational level, and indeed appropriate *tout court*. In turn this raises complex questions about the relationship between these three solidarity-presupposing activities – risk redistribution, wealth redistribution and the involvement of the collectivity in the public-revenue-based support of the creation of private wealth[53] – about whether, and to what extent, these forms of intervention are divisible, and about whether, and to what extent, they each have different solidarity 'tariffs' or preconditions.

Finally, we must bring these dimensions of personal freedom which are less closely linked to political freedom and participation into the complex equation. As we have seen, social cohesion has traditionally been viewed

---

[49] What Cohen and Sabel call the 'association of associations' approach: 'Sovereignty and Solidarity'.

[50] What Cohen and Sabel (*ibid.*) call the 'Eurodemocracy approach', which they associate with Habermas. See e.g. J. Habermas, 'Why Europe Needs a Constitution', *New Left Review* no. 11 (September–October 2001).

[51] See Cohen and Sabel's own vision of 'experimental democracy': 'Sovereignty and Solidarity'.

[52] Tully's analysis of agonistic democracy is relevant here. See Tully, 'Unfreedom of the Moderns'.

[53] See, in particular, G. Majone's work. For example, 'The Credibility Crisis of Community Regulation', 38 *Journal of Common Market Studies* (2000), 273.

as a particularly strongly sustained core value at the nation state level, yet examination reveals that this is both a fragile strength and a strength that is indivisible from certain weaknesses. Similarly, at the postnational level, personal freedom has tended to be seen as the least threatened and most comfortably embedded core value, but again close analysis reveals a more complex and troubling picture. To begin with, the traditional distance of postnational political sites from the 'state-defining' questions of internal and external security has narrowed as the European Union has gradually assumed a capacity in both Foreign and Security Policy and Justice and Home Affairs, the two outer 'pillars' of the post-Maastricht Three Pillar Treaty structure. Once these capacities gained a jurisdictional foothold, the questions of personal freedom from public interference associated with them – questions of the limits of police and military power to interfere with freedom and privacy and of general administrative and regulatory power to control freedom of movement and entry – were bound to become less abstract and to lie more at the mercy of broader political developments. Witness, in particular, the controversial acceleration of supranational initiatives in the field of anti-terrorism, common policing and public order capacity and common immigration and asylum policies encouraged by Brussels after 11 September.[54] Moreover, if, as Weiler suggests, we should also think of the supranational level's stewardship of personal freedom in more positive terms – as a potential moderator of internally and externally directed national-level intolerance – it is not clear how effectively it is capable of pursuing this more ambitious role beyond the EU's more general (if by no means insignificant) promotion of a more mobile and interpenetrating European cultural space helping to foster an attitude more tolerant of the diversity of forms of expression of human dignity and lifestyle preference. As a vast literature attests, questions concerning the relationship between universalism and localism in human rights protection are deeply complex and controversial.[55] What is clear is that there is no obvious 'positive sum' relationship between the two levels of protection. We cannot assume that the protection afforded

---

[54] These developments, including the proposal of a common arrest warrant, the development of a common definition of terrorism and the creation of a European Corps of Border Guards, are moving at such a pace that it is pointless to cite specific references charting their progress. Probably the best ongoing commentary is that supplied by the bimonthly *Statewatch* Bulletin (http://www.statewatch.org).

[55] For an interesting recent overview, see, for example, W. Sadurski, 'It all Depends. The Universal and the Contingent in Human Rights', EUI Law Department Working Paper No. 2002/7.

at supranational level, now consolidated in the newly minted Charter of
Fundamental Rights for the European Union which was given declaratory status at Nice in 2000, even to the limited extent that it bears upon
state-level practices will necessarily *augment* protection of freedom already provided at the state level. Different aspects of personal freedom –
privacy, expression, life, bodily integrity, etc. – are often in tension with
one another and indeed with other values – including those such as security and social welfare intimately associated with the promotion of social
cohesion and material well-being – and so European-level protection,
although perhaps of value in reinforcing existing national standards, to
the extent that it differs from and 'goes beyond' these national standards
will produce results more complex and troubling for the ensemble of core
political values than some simple and cost-free 'freedom dividend'.

Conclusion

Hopefully, the use of the basic co-ordinates of social cohesion, material
well-being and personal freedom provides at least a rudimentary framework through which we might be able to translate constitutional concerns
from the state level to the supranational level. When we ask questions of
the value and function of the various constitutional institutions and principles at the EU level or in other postnational settings we should do so
from a starting point which never assumes that a superficial institutional
or doctrinal similarity with the state level – say between national Parliaments and the European Parliament, or between national administrations
and the European Commission, or between national Supreme Courts and
the ECJ, or between 'states rights' within national federations and 'subsidiarity', or between state Bills of Rights and the European Charter – is
the basis for translation and modelling, but rather from a starting point
which moves from the general framework of core values through their
particular configuration at particular levels of political community and
only then and against that deep background to what is required in order
to develop a viable and legitimate regulatory framework at the level of
political community in question. That does not, of course, imply institutional innovation for its own sake, or that we can never learn from the
experience of state constitutional institutions and principles and adapt
them to the postnational context, but for such learning and adaptation
to be meaningful it must proceed through an examination of the common core values and of how they inform and condition the normative
frame of constitutionalism in any particular context. The results then, as

forewarned, are modest, a mere framing of some of the common questions which should inform and validate constitutional analysis across all sites of authority rather than a set of definitive solutions, but this modesty is hopefully not just a failure of imagination or analytical rigour, but at least in some part also due to the particular character of constitutionalism as a deeply contested but indispensable symbolic and normative frame for thinking about the problems of viable and legitimate regulation of the complexly overlapping political communities of a post-Westphalian world. Two closing remarks may help to reinforce the value of the approach taken.

In the first place, an appreciation of the inextricability of the three core values may encourage us to resist the temptation to focus too closely on one or more core values, and on the institutional implications of the pursuit of these values, to the neglect of others. Even the best work on the legal and political theory of European Union has a tendency to bracket some of the core values at the expense of others, whether the emphasis is on political freedom and the democratic deficit,[56] or on the meaning and mutual articulation of national and supranational identity in citizenship discourse,[57] or on the regulatory structure necessary to achieve an effective internal market without neglecting the importance of retaining a problem-solving capacity which can fairly and effectively distribute the risks and resources associated with an affluent economy.[58] Yet however understandable this selective framing, the complex political puzzle which lies at the core of the European Union, as of any multi-level polity, means that in the final analysis *all* the relevant values must be held equally in focus.

Secondly, it is worth noting that there is an inherently reflexive element involved in the process of translation. It is a trite truth of multi-level political organization that particular polities and political communities, still less the specific institutions of these polities and political communities, cannot be regarded in isolation. Where there is no one 'centre' of political life, ideally each institution which exercises political authority should address from a particular simple or compound constituency perspective – regional, national, Union, functional group, expert – and in a particular simple or compound governance modality – legislative, executive, administrative, judicial, executive – the particular constitutional puzzle with which it is concerned *in the light of* the same complex master-puzzle

---

[56] See e.g. Schmitter, *How to Democratise.*   [57] See e.g. Weiler, *Constitution of Europe.*
[58] See e.g. Scharpf, *Governing in Europe.*

involving the optimal articulation and balance of core values, and always bearing in mind the need to complement the contribution of each of the other differently constituted and tasked institutions towards that same master-puzzle. In terms of constitutional discourse, this development points to the increasing significance of the relational dimension generally within the post-Westphalian configuration. In this plural configuration, unlike the one-dimensional Westphalian configuration, the 'units' are no longer isolated, constitutionally self-sufficient monads. They do not purport to be comprehensive and exclusive polities, exhausting the political identities and allegiances and personal and group aspirations of their members or associates. Indeed, it is artificial even to conceive of such sites as having separate internal and external dimensions, since their very identity and *raison d'être* as polities or putative polities rests at least in some measure on their orientation towards other sites. The overlap of jurisdictions and governance projects is emerging as the norm rather than the exception, the constitutional processes developed to address these becoming 'central at the margins'.

Accordingly, constitutional translation should be conceived of as an active and dynamic process, one where the lessons of translation must be internalized in each constitutional site, including the source state sites. Institutional design, even in the most venerable and venerated constitutional settlements, must always be viewed as a derivative and contingent exercise, always at the service of the core values and the changing detail of material and cultural conditions and of diversely located solutions which influence the articulation and optimal balance of these core values. The lessons of historical experience and of political theory are that there is no timeless key to good constitutional design and practice. Rather, this depends first and foremost upon a critical reflexivity – upon a healthy awareness within constitutional discourse of the contingent and provisional quality of its multifaceted and intricately interdependent solutions to the remorseless puzzle of the balance of the core values of political organization.

3

The unfinished constitution of the European Union: principles, processes and culture

FRANCIS SNYDER

Introduction

How can we best conceive of the European Union (EU) constitution?[1] In my view it is essential to try to elaborate a conception of the EU constitution which engages with the concerns, not only of the elite, but also of ordinary citizens. I suggest that an adequate conception of the EU constitution requires systematic attention to its social, economic, political and cultural contexts. Consequently, this chapter seeks to sketch a model of the EU constitution that takes account of the various contexts that produce EU law and shape its operation in practice. To facilitate this task, it is useful first to circumscribe the object of inquiry, to define the term 'constitution', and to identify some ways in which the EU constitution has so far been conceived.

Most work so far has either focused solely on the EC or, though concerned with the EU, lamented the fact that, in contrast to its predecessor, it could no longer be understood in constitutional terms. In contrast, partly in view of the past history of European integration, but even more because of its future, I suggest that we should be concerned with the EU, not only the EC, for two reasons. On the one hand, nowadays it is difficult, if not impossible, to understand EC law from the technical legal standpoint except in the broader legal context of the EU. On the other hand, only the more inclusive view takes account of the different political tendencies, and thus different interpretations and practices regarding the law, which have always been inherent in the European Community, were recognized

---

[1] This chapter is based on my 'General Course on Constitutional Law of the European Union', *Collected Courses of the Academy of European Law*, vol. VI (Dordrecht: Kluwer, 1998), book 1, 41–155, which gives further references. I wish to acknowledge the help of Vassil Breskovski, Katarzyna Gromek Broc, Candido Garcia Molyneux, John Stanton Ife, Wolf Sauter, Song Ying and Anne-Lise Strahtmann. The usual disclaimer applies.

in the Single European Act and the Maastricht and Amsterdam Treaties, and now constitute the dynamic element of the system. In other words, taking the EC alone as the unit of analysis risks neglect of crucial elements of structure and process.

What do we mean by 'constitution'? For present purposes it is useful to distinguish four possible meanings. One meaning refers to a constitution in the empirical sense, the way in which the polity, such as the state, is organized in fact. A second meaning connotes the constitution in a *sens matériel* or material sense, namely the totality of fundamental legal norms which make up the legal order of the polity. A third meaning concerns the constitution in an instrumental sense, the written document or fundamental legal act which sets forth at least the principal constitutional legal norms. A fourth meaning refers to the constitution simultaneously in a material, instrumental and subjective sense, that is, a written document or fundamental legal act which has been deliberated by the people, either directly or through representatives.

The EU has a constitution in the first, empirical sense. It also has a constitution in the second, or material, sense. In addition, it may be said to have a constitution in the third, formal sense. It should also be noted that there is a wide gap between the EU constitution in the formal sense (i.e. the Treaties) and the EU constitution in the substantive sense (including its interpretation by the European Court of Justice (ECJ)). The EU does not, however, have a constitution in the last sense, that is, also in the subjective sense.

To analyse the EU constitution, I suggest that we need to refocus our constitutional lens. Let us concentrate on the meaning of a constitution in the subjective sense. This expression is sometimes limited to a constitution that has been approved by a constitutional convention. In the EU context, however, it may be misleading to focus on this specific form of expression of popular consent. We can use the expression 'constitution in the subjective sense' to refer, not to deliberation by the people, but rather to people's subjective orientation: that is, to use Weber's terms, whether people are subjectively oriented to the constitution in a substantive sense as if it were their fundamental legal act. It is this particular combination of meanings, constitution in a material sense and constitution in a subjective sense, which I wish to emphasize here.

The EU constitution does not necessarily have to be enshrined in one document or even in writing. Nor do all its rules need to be rigid. We must however deal with three sets of difficult questions. One set concerns the relationship between the constitution and the 'living society': is the EU constitution a form of social contract, an organic expression of a society as a whole, or both? Another set of questions asks: what is the substance of the constituent power? A final set of questions refers to 'acceptance conditions', or legitimacy: who accepts the EU constitution, why and within what limits?

These sets of questions are part of our theoretical problem. How does a 'constitution in the material sense' become also a 'constitution in the subjective sense'? I have stated this problem in terms of the discourse of constitutional law. However, it could also be expressed in terms of popular acceptance, democratic consensus and political legitimacy.

The principal models that have been used to conceptualize the EC/EU so far can be grouped into three categories.[2] The first category comprises models of structure. Structural models are designed to identify essential features of governmental structure. The most frequently used structural models are: (1) international organization, (2) special-purpose association, (3) federation, (4) confederation, and (5) regime. The second category refers to models of ideals underlying European integration in general and the EC (or more rarely EU) in particular, such as unification, communitarianism, or participation in shared activities such as sport. A third category of model includes jurisprudential (or legal theoretical) models. Designed to elucidate the contribution which different schools of legal theory can make to our understanding of European integration, these models focus mainly on types of analytical strategy.

How can we create a model of the EU constitution? A challenging alternative to existing models is the technique of constitutional analysis proposed by Laurence Tribe.[3] Tribe organizes constitutional principles, rules and theories according to seven basic models that 'have represented the major alternatives for constitutional argument and decision in American constitutional law from the early 1800s to the present'.[4] Though based on doctrinal and historical materials, the models are not simply descriptive, or purely imposed mental constructs, or intended to reflect either self-conscious pattterns of thought or unconscious explanatory structures. Instead they are heuristic and not mutually exclusive. Tribe's models are 'concerned with ways of achieving substantive ends through various governmental structures and processes of choice'.[5]

This substantive conception of constitutional law, and thus of constitutional models, has several implications. The first is the rejection of constitutional law as simply 'neutral' principles of structure.[6] Second, a

---

[2] See my 'General Course' for further discussion.
[3] *American Constitutional Law*, 2nd edn (Mineola, NY: Foundation Press, 1988).
[4] *Ibid.*, 2.   [5] *Ibid.*, 1673.   [6] *Ibid.*, 1673.

combination of structures rather than a single structure may best suit a particular context. Third, the 'optimal' structural embodiment of substantive ideals may change from one period to the next.[7]

Each of these implications is useful in the study of EU constitutional law. However, Tribe's method of analysis may perhaps be too ambitious in the present state of EU constitutional law scholarship. Most of the different models of the EU/EC constitution already sketched are concerned solely with the vertical organization of power, involving the EU and the Member States, though some recent work also takes account of other sets of relations, such as those encapsulated in European committees and agencies or relations between Member States. Only the models of ideals attempt to define criteria for the organization of power within the EU, but even they fail to build strong bridges between the vertical and the horizontal organization of power.

In effect, most of the existing models of the EU/EC constitution are models of legal orders rather than constitutional models. In other words, the structural and jurisprudential models concentrate almost exclusively on ascertaining whether the EU can be considered to be an autonomous legal order or a polity – that is, whether its legal framework 'deserves' to be called a constitution – rather than focusing on its content. When they go further, they are simply descriptive rather than normative. There are few, if any, real constitutional models of the EU. Existing models are concerned instead with explaining the process of European integration, identifying the normative challenge posed by EU/EC law to legal theory, or characterizing the *sui generis* features of the system.

Consequently, the present utility of Tribe's model for constitutional modelling lies in challenging us to go beyond existing models of the EU constitution. On the one hand, it forces us to try to integrate structures, ideals and theories of law in a more systematic way. On the other hand, it reminds us of the substance of constitutional law. Whatever else it may mean, constitutionalization is also a substantive process. To elucidate this substantive meaning is an important task of constitutional law scholarship.

So far we have seen that none of the existing models of the EU constitution is entirely satisfactory for our purposes. In addition, it is still very difficult to elaborate an EU analogue of Tribe's American model for modelling. I propose to draw on the sociological theory of structuration, as developed by Anthony Giddens.[8] The theory of structuration seeks to

---

[7] *Ibid.*, 1675.
[8] See A. Giddens, *The Constitution of Society* (Cambridge: Polity Press, 1984) and other writings.

combine agency and structure: for example, individual action and social practices, on the one hand, and normative and institutional structures, on the other hand. A basic proposition of structuration theory is the duality of structure, namely that 'the rules and resources drawn upon in the production and reproduction of social action are at the same time the means of system reproduction'.[9] This approach is especially apt in the study of EU constitutional law, because it emphasizes both structures and processes as distinct yet interconnected.

Most legal scholarship has concentrated on rules, institutions and other structures. Some remarks on the study of social processes may therefore be useful. Here I deliberately accentuate the processual character of social life, because it is so much less well known to lawyers than the rule-centred or structural paradigm.[10] This temporary imbalance, which represents a departure from structuration theory, will be remedied to some extent later in this chapter and then more fully, I expect, in subsequent publications.

The processual approach to social life is well developed in philosophy, anthropology and sociology. This perspective holds that the world is a process, that things are in a state of continual 'becoming'. The anthropologist Sally Falk Moore has summarized its basic postulate by saying that 'in this model social life is presumed to be indeterminate except in so far as culture and organized or patterned social relationships make it determinate'.[11]

Four elementary hypotheses regarding the EU will make this postulate more concrete. First, the EU is a social organization. Second, 'social organization is a dynamic process'.[12] Third, 'social organization is the process of bringing order and meaning into human social life'.[13] Fourth, 'social organization is the process of merging social actors into ordered social relationships, which become infused with cultural ideas'.[14]

Following this approach, we may distinguish three distinct but interrelated dimensions of the EU constitution. The first dimension refers to structures, namely constitutional principles. The second dimension concerns constitutionalizing processes. They include, but are broader than, those social processes which tend to transform (or block the

---

[9] Giddens, *Constitution of Society*, 19.

[10] For a discussion of the rule-centred and processual paradigms in the anthropology of law, see J. L. Comaroff and S. Roberts, *Rules and Processes: The Cultural Logic of Dispute in an African Context* (Chicago and London: University of Chicago, 1981), 5–17.

[11] S. F. Moore, *Law as Process: An Anthropological Approach* (London: Routledge, 1978), 48–9.

[12] M. E. Olsen, *The Process of Social Organization* (New York: Holt, Rinehart and Winston, 1968), 2.

[13] *Ibid.*, 2.   [14] *Ibid.*, 3.

transformation of) the EU constitution from a constitution in only a substantive sense to a constitution in both a substantive and a subjective sense. The third dimension consists of constitutional culture, a facet of legal culture. These three dimensions constitute my model of the EU constitution.

Constitutional principles

The first dimension of the EU constitution consists of constitutional principles. This may seem a truism, because legal scholarship usually focuses on norms. It should however already be clear that the approach to the EU constitution being proposed here does not follow the spirit of Grey's premise that 'the primary object of discourse in the study of constitutionalism should be constitutional norms, not entire constitutions'.[15] In other words, there is a difference between taking norms seriously and giving norms absolute – or even sole – priority.

Constitutional principles play an absolutely fundamental role in constitutional discourse. Norms must be set, however, within a broader context. One of the main arguments of this chapter is that we cannot understand the EU constitution adequately if we focus on norms alone. There is an intimate relationship between the normative dimension of the EU constitution and the other two dimensions, namely constitutionalizing processes and constitutional culture. Two further points, however, should be made about the broader context of EU constitutional principles.

First, in addition to their normative quality, EU constitutional principles are also to be considered as structures. They may be taken for granted, be considered to be legitimate or not, or be the object of political conflict. Nevertheless, they form part of the social field within which individuals and groups act, which informs or is part of this action, and to which it is often orientated. The general point applies to EU constitutional principles as to any other norms.

Second, structures and processes, or more abstractly structure and agency, form a duality. In part following Giddens, I have argued elsewhere that 'Structures represent outcomes of processes that have previously occurred; they are congealed at least temporarily in the form of institutionalised sets of social relations. Only a fine line separates structures and processes. They are dialectically related, each being in a sense

---

[15] Grey, 'Constitutionalism: An Analytic Framework', in J. R. Pennock and J. W. Chaplain (eds.), *Constitutionalism* (New York: New York University Press, 1979), 189–209 at 190.

simply a transformation of the other.'[16] In other words, EU constitutional principles, just as other norms, 'are simultaneously representations of previous outcomes as well as frameworks, influences and sometimes determinants of continuing conflicts and compromises'.[17]

In this light, we may view the constitutional principles of the EU from two perspectives. The first may be called the macro-sociological or even external perspective. The second is the micro-sociological or internal perspective. These two perspectives contribute different but complementary insights to our knowledge of the EU constitution.

It has been suggested that the five key concepts of constitutional government in a divided-power system are sovereignty, legitimacy, citizenship, federalism and rights.[18] Though helpful for many purposes, these concepts are too closely associated with – and, in fact, are drawn directly from – constitutional discourse premised on the nation state. In addition, some of them describe or postulate ideals, such as federalism or legitimacy, which in the EU context are missing in practice, inappropriate, or both.

In my view, the constitutional principles of the EU as seen from a macro-sociological perspective are: regional integration, a divided-power system, the Member States as 'Masters of the Treaty', the integrity of the EU and the rule of law. These principles vary in the source of their authority, in normative form or hierarchical status, and in the method by which they are enforced.[19] For example, the principle of regional integration, though mentioned in the Treaty of Amsterdam,[20] seems at first glance to be only an economic principle. Similarly, the principle that the EU is a divided-power system may appear to be merely a political statement.

It should not be surprising that many of these constitutional norms have been stated by the ECJ in its Opinions *ex* Article 300(6) (formerly Article 228(6)) EC. These Opinions are devoted to evaluating the compatibility of proposed international agreements with the European Community Treaty. Consequently they often delimit the fundamental general features of the EC, so as to present a profile or silhouette of certain features of the

---

[16] F. Snyder, *New Directions in European Community Law* (London: Weidenfield and Nicolson, 1990), 42.

[17] *Ibid.*, 61.

[18] See D. Castiglione and R. Bellamy, 'Constitutional Culture in Europe', 1 *RUSEL Comptes Rendus* (1995), 15 at 16.

[19] See the threefold classification of constitutional norms elaborated by Grey, 'Constitutionalism', 191.

[20] See e.g. Treaty of Amsterdam, Preamble, 1st, 2nd, 7th, 8th, 11th and 12th recitals; Title I, Art. A, second paragraph; Title I, Art. B, first indent; see also Art. 2 EC.

EC in order to distinguish it sharply from the outside world. It is evident that they are less concerned with the EU as such, because under Article 46 (formerly Article L) TEU the ECJ does not have jurisdiction over the Common Provisions or (with limited exceptions) over Titles VI and VII (formerly Titles V and VI) TEU.

The micro-sociological or internal perspective on EU constitutional law is that usually adopted by legal scholars. From this perspective, the constitutional norms of the EU are as follows:

(1) the single institutional framework, including the representation of interests;
(2) the separation of powers, which encompasses the notions of institutional balance, institutional autonomy and loyal cooperation between institutions;
(3) limited powers;
(4) implied powers;
(5) supremacy;
(6) direct effect;
(7) pre-emption;
(8) subsidiarity;
(9) non-discrimination;
(10) respect for fundamental rights;
(11) respect for national identities;
(12) duty of loyalty;
(13) respect for general principles of law.

The basic principles of the EU constitution thus may be identified from two perspectives. The macro-perspective tends to highlight more clearly those constitutional principles which form the sine qua non of the European Union. It also makes clear that these principles differ, for example, in their sources and in the extent to which they are recognized as legally binding. By contrast, the micro-perspective focuses on constitutional principles which either are expressed in the basic Treaties or have been elaborated in the judgments of the European Court of Justice. These perspectives complement each other in the analysis of the EU constitution.

Constitutionalizing processes

The second dimension of the EU constitution consists of constitutionalizing processes. By 'constitutionalizing processes', I refer to those social processes which might tend to confer a constitutional status on the basic legal framework of the European Union. These processes form part of 'the process of social organisation [which] occurs as social actors interact in patterned and recurrent relationships to create social ordering, which in turn becomes infused with cultural ideas'.[21]

Constitutionalizing processes in the EU are not only the work of the European courts. They also involve the European Council and the European Parliament as well as other institutions, such as committees, agencies and policy networks. Nor are they limited to the European Union institutions alone. They also engage courts, parliaments and administrations of the Member States. In addition, the legal profession is of special importance, though by and large the role of transnational law firms and groupings and the impact of EU law on local law practices has been neglected by EU constitutional lawyers. In fact, I suggest that we must cast our net much wider. Political and economic processes are likely to be much more important in the development of the EU constitution than is the law alone.

We can distinguish three groups of constitutionalizing processes in the EU. The first group consists of those processes which have fostered the development of legal institutions. These processes are regional integration, the (re-)institutionalization of norms, and institutional growth and expansion. The second group refers to those processes concerned with ensuring the effectiveness of law. It includes administrative negotiation of effectiveness, the development of a judicial liability system and, most recently, legitimation without democratization involving the European Council. The third group comprises a number of disparate processes which are concerned with deepening and delimitation. These processes include the creation of social solidarity, legitimation, democratization and differentiation, and the establishment and maintenance of boundaries. One may also add the search for values: constitutionalization as a substantive process. Only some brief examples can be given here.

Regional integration tends to require the development of legal institutions.[22] This may occur, for example, partly by means of the

---

[21] Olsen, *Process*, 62.

[22] There is broad agreement on this point among a range of scholars in different disciplines. See for example E. Mandel, *Power and Money: A Marxist Theory of Bureaucracy* (London and New York: Verso, 1992); J. Pelkmans and P. Robson, 'The Aspirations of the White Paper', *Journal of Common Market Studies* (1987), 203; P. Robson, *The Economics of International Integration*, 3rd edn (London: Allen & Unwin, 1987); W. Molle, *The Economics of European Integration – Theory, Practice, and Policy*, 2nd edn (Aldershot: Dartmouth, 1994); C. Joerges, 'The Market Without the State or the State Without the Market', European University Institute Working Paper No. 1996/2. See also the Kantian theory of right assumed by Mestmäcker: 'Whenever human beings are interacting with each other, there arises the

creation of treaties and their subsequent amendment, and partly by acts
of a less dramatic nature. In his introductory textbook Molle sets forth
a series of hypotheses regarding the institutional consequences of regional integration. They range from the statement that '[t]he higher the
form of integration chosen, the higher the institutional demands to be
fulfilled'[23] to assertions concerning the transfer of power from one level
of governance to another.[24] The validity of these specific hypotheses is
not our concern here; the point is that regional integration tends to imply
institution-building and institutional integration.

The kinds of institutions which are generated – or required – by regional integration are to some extent indeterminate. For example, the
institutions of the Third Pillar of the Maastricht Treaty were a mixture
of institutions drawn from EC economic law and institutions modelled
on those used previously in European Political Cooperation. The sources
of the institutions are unique to the EU. One can therefore say that, in
general terms, there is no necessary connection between economic integration and any specific institutional arrangements in the Third Pillar.
Even more indeterminate is the extent to which regional integration leads
to specific types of institutions and principles. For example, it is open to
question whether regional integration as such leads necessarily to human
rights protection, even in the Western European context.[25]

A second constitutionalizing process is the (re-)institutionalization of
norms. I draw the concept of re-institutionalization by analogy from
Bohannan's idea of double institutionalization of African 'customary law'

---

necessity to define the outer boundaries of their liberty and to provide for the judicial
resolution of conflicts that are associated with different perceptions of rights and duties',
Mestmäcker, 'On the Legitimacy of European Law', *Rabels Zeitschrift für ausländisches und
internationales Privatrecht* (1994), 615 at 620.

[23] Molle, *Economics*, 12.

[24] *Ibid.*, 8. For example, '[a]ll forms of integration require permanent agreements among
participating states with respect to procedures to arrive at resolutions and to the implementation of rules. In other words they call for partners to agree on the rules of the game.
For an efficient policy integration, common institutions . . . are created. However, for the
higher forms of integration, such as a common market, the mere creation of an institution
is not sufficient: they require a transfer of power from national to union institutions':
ibid., 14.

[25] See Frowein, Schulhofer and Shapiro, 'The Protection of Fundamental Rights as a Vehicle
of Integration', in M. Cappelletti, M. Seccombe and J. H. H. Weiler (eds.), *Integration
through Law* (Berlin and New York: Walter de Gruyter, 1986), vol. I, book 3, at 231; see also
J. H. H. Weiler and Lockhart, ' "Taking Rights Seriously" Seriously: The European Court
of Justice and its Fundamental Rights Jurisprudence', 32 *Common Market Law Review*
(1995), 51.

by colonial state courts.[26] With regard to the Tiv of Nigeria, Bohannan wrote:

> All social institutions are marked by 'customs' and these 'customs' exhibit most of the stigmata cited by any definition of law. But there is one salient difference. Whereas custom continues to inhere in, and only in, these in- stitutions which it governs (and which in turn govern it), law is specifically recreated by agents of society, in a narrower and recognisable context – that is, in the context of the institutions that are legal in character and, to some degree at least, discrete from all others.[27]

In Bohannan's view, 'the law rests on the basis of this double institution-alization... Legal rights are only those rights that attach to norms that have been doubly institutionalized'.[28]

I wish to suggest that re-institutionalization is one of the basic consti-tutionalizing processes of the EU. One of its aspects is 'juridification', the creation of legal norms from normative raw material which was previously not legal in character. A good example is the development of European so-cial law, in which soft law and agreements between the social partners have played a fundamental part.[29] Another aspect is the re-institutionalization of legal norms, that is, the statement or development as basic principles of EU law of legal principles drawn from other legal orders. One has only to consider the incorporation into EC or EU law of many constitutional or other legal principles of the Member States. The numerous examples in-clude proportionality, legitimate expectations, extra-contractual liability, state liability[30] and, most notably, human rights.

The history of the EC and the EU has been characterized simultaneously by the growth of institutions and the expansion of systemic (EC or EU)

---

[26] P. Bohannan, 'The Differing Realms of the Law', in P. Bohannan (ed.), *Law and Warfare: Studies in the Anthropology of Conflict* (Garden City, NY: Natural History Press, 1967), 43–56 at 45; reprinted from *American Anthropologist*, special publication, *The Ethnography of Law* (ed. L. Nader), vol. 67, no. 6, part 2, 33–42. I find this concept useful in analysing EU law, even though I do not agree entirely with Bohannan's view of the historical relationship between African customary law and the colonial state: see F. Snyder, 'Colonialism and Legal Form: The Creation of Customary Law in Senegal', 19 *Journal of Legal Pluralism* (1981), 49.

[27] Bohannan, 'Differing Realms', 45.   [28] *Ibid.*, 48.

[29] See Sciarra, 'Collective Agreements in the Hierarchy of Community Sources', in P. Davies, A. Lyon-Caen, S. Sciarra and S. Simitis (eds.), *European Community Labour Law: Principles and Perspectives. Liber Amicorum Lord Wedderburn of Charlton* (Oxford: Clarendon Press, 1996).

[30] See C. Harlow, 'Francovich and the Problem of the Disobedient State', 2 *European Law Journal* (1996), 199.

competences. This occurred initially by means of Article 308 (formerly Article 235) EC. More generally, as Weiler has shown, it involved various types of mutation of jurisdiction and competences.[31] Among the most dramatic examples is, first, the development of the Community's implied powers, notably in external relations. This was accomplished by the ECJ in a series of fundamental judgments, ranging from *ERTA*[32] until its recent retreat in *WTO*.[33] Another example, no less dramatic but perhaps less well known, is that of soft law, notably interinstitutional agreements.[34]

A second group of constitutionalizing processes in the EU concerns the effectiveness of law.[35] Constitutional norms do not have to be enforced by means of judicial review in order to be considered as constitutional.[36] Even though judicial review may be a – or even the most – common type of enforcement, we need to remember that constitutional norms can also be enforced, for example, by administrative or political means. In the Community, for example, the European Commission has sought to ensure the effectiveness of EC law through negotiation, including Article 234 (formerly Article 169) EC litigation, the use of soft law and structural reform. The European Court of Justice has created a judicial liability system, involving the direct effect of directives, the interpretative obligation, partial harmonization of national remedies and the remedy of damages against a Member State.

A third group of constitutionalizing processes is related to what we can call the deepening and delimitation of the EU. These processes are the creation of social solidarity, legitimation, democratization, differentiation, the establishment and maintenance of boundaries, and the search for values. A brief pointer regarding boundaries must suffice.

The boundaries of the EU are complex.[37] Boundaries determine membership. They distinguish insiders from outsiders. In an economic

---

[31] See J. H. H. Weiler, 'The Transformation of Europe', 100 *Yale Law Journal* (1991), 2403.

[32] Case 22/70 *Commission* v. *Council ('ERTA')* [1971] ECR 263.

[33] Opinion 1/94 [1995] ECR I-4577. Other important cases were Opinion 1/76 *Laying-Up Fund* [1977] ECR 741; Joined Cases 3, 4, 6/76 *Cornelis Kramer and Others* [1976] ECR 1279; Opinion 2/91 *Re ILO Convention 170* [1993] ECR I-1061.

[34] See generally F. Snyder, 'Interinstitutional Agreements: Forms and Constitutional Limitations', in Gerd Winter (ed.), *Sources and Categories of European Union Law* (1996), 453.

[35] See further F. Snyder, 'The Effectiveness of European Community Law: Institutions, Processes, Tools and Techniques', 56 *Modern Law Review* (1993), 19.

[36] See Grey, 'Constitutionalism', 195–6.

[37] See further F. Snyder, 'Integrità e Frontiere del Diritto Europeo: Riflessioni sulla Base della Politica Agricola Comune', RIDPC (1994), 579.

integration scheme, they separate those who benefit from trade creation from those who lose from trade diversion, and so on. They may be defined, for example, in terms of Member States, customs boundaries, national citizenship of individuals, residence of individuals, and in other ways. Consider the pyramid of privilege in EU trade relations, such as the different types of boundaries involved in the Europe Agreements, the Euro-Med Agreements and the Lomé Convention.[38] As these examples make clear, EU boundaries are problematic, flexible, permeable, often situationally defined and frequently negotiable. The maintenance of boundaries is a process. The key question for scholars of EU constitution law is therefore how boundaries are managed.

The ECJ has in fact played a fundamental role as gatekeeper in defining the boundaries of the EU for various purposes. Examples include: the extent to which international agreements, such as the GATT, have direct effect; the differentiated interpretation of legal texts according to their EC or international context; the extra-territorial application of EC competition law;[39] the question of 'fortress Europe' in relation to non-Community nationals; the issue of Japanese cars; and the rearrangement of trading boundaries during the continuing banana saga. The definition, negotiation and maintenance of boundaries are inherent in any postmodern constitution.[40] They also involve institutional and political choices that require further discussion.

Constitutional culture

'Constitutional culture' is an expression which is only gradually gaining currency among lawyers. Like its earlier analogue, 'political culture', it has been elaborated most fully so far by political scientists, including those interested in the EU constitution. Before sketching my conception of EU constitutional culture, it is useful to make several introductory points.

First, as contrasted to other major areas of the world, for example Asia, Europe can be said to be characterized by a single legal culture. Second, it is also true that, even with regard to legal culture, there is within Europe a great deal of diversity. Third, nevertheless one can in my view speak

---

[38] See further F. Snyder, *International Trade and Customs Law of the European Union* (Butterworths, 1998).

[39] See e.g. Joined Cases 89, 104, 114, 116, 125–9/85 *Wood Pulp Producers* v. *Commission* [1988] ECR 5193.

[40] See also Ruggie, 'Territoriality and Beyond: Problematising Modernity in International Relations', *International Organization* (1993), 139.

of a 'legal culture' which is developing within the European Union, and which has been powerfully influenced by the origins and development of the European Economic Community since the late 1950s.

There is a strong tradition of studies of legal culture in different European countries. But the study of legal culture within the European Union as such is at its beginning. The research questions remain for the most part still to be identified. It deserves to be stressed that it is possible to learn a great deal from what has already been done in various European countries, as well as from the studies of legal culture in other major cultural or legal areas. It is also important to note that these studies must rely very much on the work of sociologists, political scientists, anthropologists and those from other disciplines. Unless legal scholars are prepared to turn to these disciplines for help, the study of EU legal culture is likely to remain relatively neglected.

A classic definition of legal culture was given by Friedman in 1969. In his view, legal culture refers to

> the values and attitudes which bind the system together, and which determine the place of the legal system in the culture of the society as a whole. What kind of training and habits do the lawyers and judges have? What do people think of law? Do groups or individuals willingly go to court? For what purposes do people turn to lawyers; for what purposes do they make use of other officials and intermediaries? Is there respect for law, government, tradition? What is the relationship between class structure and the use or nonuse of legal institutions? What informal social controls exist in addition to or in place of formal ones? Who prefers what kind of controls, and why? . . . It is the legal culture, that is, the network of values and attitudes relating to law, which determines when and why and where people turn to law or government, or turn away.[41]

A legal culture exists whether people know about it or not, and whether they agree with it or not.[42] It thus closely resembles what Merryman calls a 'legal tradition'. He refers to 'a set of deeply rooted, historically conditioned attitudes about the nature of law, about the role of law in the society and polity, about the proper organisation and operation of the legal system, and about [how] the law is or should be made, applied, studied, perfected, and taught'.[43]

---

[41] L. Friedman, 'Legal Culture and Social Development', 4 *Law and Society Review* (1969), 29 at 34.
[42] Bohannan, 'Differing Realms', 51.
[43] J. H. Merryman, *The Civil Law Tradition* (1969), 2.

The concept of 'constitutional culture' is a variant of, but narrower than, that of 'legal culture'. For present purposes, by 'constitutional culture' I mean a legal culture oriented to the legal framework of the EU as a set of fundamental norms. It is not concerned solely, or indeed primarily, with judicial review.[44] Constitutional culture does not necessarily involve shared norms, based on common principles of justice and articulating an 'overlapping consensus'.[45] Instead it may express conflicting moral ideas and different traditions of constitutional democracy.[46]

The notion of a constitutional culture refers both to the actual provisions and the unwritten principles of the constitution. But it also involves the way in which the constitution is dealt with by the legislator, the administration, the judiciary and legal scholarship. The last is of particular importance. The role of legal scholarship in creating a specific EU legal culture has been relatively neglected, however, and deserves much closer attention.[47]

My working hypotheses are twofold. On the one hand, a constitutional culture which is specific to the EU is now emerging and being created at the individual, organizational and societal levels. On the other hand, its main features are not all fixed, nor are they by any means entirely coherent and free from contradiction.

EU constitutional culture may be conceived of as an onion, consisting of three layers: modern or postmodern legal culture, Western legal culture and a legal culture specific to the EU regional integration scheme. When we peel off the first layer, the second is revealed; and when we peel off the second, we can clearly see the third. The layers themselves are to some extent translucent, however, so one can sometimes see through each layer to the one below.

The first layer has been described by Friedman as composed of six characterisics: it is a culture of change; law is essentially instrumental; modern law is dense and ubiquitous; there is an emphasis on rights and entitlements; there is an emphasis on individualism; and globalization is

---

[44] Compare Robert F. Nagel, *Constitutional Cultures: The Mentality and Consequences of Judicial Review* (Berkeley: University of California Press, 1989).

[45] This is Rawls's conception.

[46] Castiglione and Bellamy, 'Constitutional Culture', 15; see also D. Castiglione and R. Bellamy, *Democracy and Constitutional Culture in the Union of Europe* (London: Lothian Foundation, 1995).

[47] An exception to the general pattern is H. Schepel and R. Wesseling, 'The Legal Community: Lawyers, Officials and Clerks in the Writing of Europe', 3 *European Law Journal* (1997), 165.

a key phenomenon.[48] We need to add the peculiar conjunction of universalism and fragmentation, of internationalization and localization, which appears to be concomitant with globalization.

The second layer consists of Western legal culture. In Wieacker's view, its essential features are personalism, legalism and intellectualism.[49] To this, we need to add the myth of the state: the idea that the state is the sole source of law.[50]

The third layer is profoundly influenced by the historical development of European regional integration since the 1950s. Of particular importance are the origins of the current EU, first in the early sectoral European Coal and Steel Community (ECSC), and then in the broader but still limited European Economic Community (EEC). These influences are manifested, for example, in the EU myths of origin. An example is the 'Community method' of neofunctionalist integration originally promoted by Robert Schuman and Jean Monnet. Though of course containing true elements, these accounts may also be conceived of as 'stories drawn from a society's history that have acquired through persistent usage the power of symbolising that society's ideology and of dramatising its moral consciousness'.[51]

The specific features of EU constitutional culture may be divided roughly and provisionally into two categories. The first category consists of 'the legacy of origins': those attributes that derive primarily from the specific historical experience of the EU. The second category is patterned on the model of the state: it comprises those features which the EU has assumed, or which are ascribed to it, and which are based on the historical model of the state in Western Europe. These two categories cut across what in my view is the great divide within contemporary EU legal culture: the profound distinction between elite or specific EU legal culture, on the one hand, and popular or general EU legal culture, on the other hand.

[48] L. Friedman, 'Law and Social Change: Culture, Nationality, and Identity', *Collected Courses of the Academy of European Law*, vol. IV, book 2 *The Protection of Human Rights in Europe*, 237–91 at 258–65.

[49] Wieacker, 'Foundations of European Legal Culture', 38 *American Journal of Comparative Law* (1990), 1.

[50] As to this and other myths of positive law, see N. Rouland, *Anthropologie Juridique* (1988), 410–18.

[51] R. Slotkin, *Gunfighter Nation: The Myth of the Frontier in Twentieth Century America* (New York: Atheneum, 1992), at 5, cited in Friedman, 'Law and Social Change', at 269 n. 83.

Consider first elite EU legal culture. Its main features, in my view, are as follows. First, the Member States are considered as the 'Masters of the Treaty', at least in the sense that they make the basic political decisions about the shape of the system. Second, the ideology of neofunctionalism is of central importance, not only as a thread running through the original EEC Treaty, but also as conceptual framework and working method which is shared by many officials of the EU institutions. Third, this legal culture emphasizes the importance of negotiation, in part a characteristic of regulatory law but unfortunately also a contributor to the EU's relatively weak popular legitimacy. Fourth, it emphasizes the role of divided power in the social construction of an ideology of the European Union legal system as closed, neutral, impartial and autonomous. An example is the view that the EU (formerly EC) represents a 'new legal order', in the words of the European Court of Justice in the landmark judgment in *Van Gend en Loos*.[52]

Fifth, despite the extension of its competences as a result of the Maastricht Treaty, the EU remains to a great extent a prisoner of its initially economic orientation. For example, there is still a debate about whether the EU (and EC) is best conceived as a single-purpose association rather than a general integration scheme. In addition, economic integration and economic rights are often considered (not always correctly) to have priority over social and political rights.[53] Sixth, the EU is marked by a strongly instrumentalist conception of law, a feature which is typical of contemporary Western states but which is heightened in the EU context by the historical legacy of economic orientation, task-focused administration organization and regulatory law. Seventh, some of the factors have converged to give the EU a very undemocratic character, at least if the degree of democracy is measured according to the usual criteria of the representative parliamentary democracies of its Member States.[54] Eighth, there has, at least in the past, been a certain orientation towards centralization, uniformization, or at least harmonization, as opposed to pluralism,

---

[52] Case 26/62 [1963] ECR 1.

[53] Compare R. Phelan, 'Free Movement of Services versus the Right to Life of the Unborn: The Normative Shaping of the European Union' 55 *Modern Law Review* (1992), and J. Coppel and A. O'Neill, 'The European Court of Justice: Taking Rights Seriously?', 29 *Common Market Law Review* (1992), 669, on the one hand; and Weiler and Lockhart, ' "Taking Rights Seriously" Seriously', 51 (Part I), 579 (Part II), on the other hand.

[54] See Mancini and Keeling, 'Democracy and the European Court of Justice', 57 *Modern Law Review* (1994), 175.

diversity and differentiation: the Common Agricultural Policy provides perhaps the best example.[55] A ninth feature is hierarchical organization. Thus, for example, the Maastricht Treaty is usually analysed by lawyers as being based on two opposing principles, supranationalism and inter-governmentalism; and cooperative relations between Member States have unfortunately been often viewed until recently as merely intergovernmental and necessarily anti-*communautaire*. Some of these elements are now changing, albeit sometimes very slowly.

Popular or general EU legal culture differs greatly. Its very existence is sometimes denied, for example by those who argue that the EU has only discrete national legal cultures. In my opinion this argument is misplaced. More research is needed on the impact of transnational sport, especially football; the limited impact of trans-European media and the barriers, including legal barriers, to further integration with regard to newspapers and television; and cinema. Further attention is required also to be given to the effects of globalization on the process of Europeanization of legal culture. Some research indicates that globalization and Europeanization are to some extent contradictory, even though both may be encouraged by EU law.[56]

Conclusion

In this chapter I have tried to outline a way of conceiving of the constitution of the European Union, one which engages with the concerns of ordinary citizens and which takes account of the social, political, economic and cultural contexts in which EU/EC law is produced and in which it operates. The model of the EU constitution proposed here consists of three interrelated dimensions: constitutional principles, constitutionalizing processes and constitutional culture. The next step is to elaborate this model in more detail and to explore its implications. It should be re-emphasized that the model is heuristic. It is intended to help us address the question as to whether, one day, the EU will have not only a constitution in the material sense but also a constitution in the subjective

---

[55] See F. Snyder, 'The Taxonomy of Law in EC Agricultural Policy: A Case Study', in Gerd Winter (ed.), *Sources and Categories of EC Law* (Dordrecht: Kluwer, 1995).

[56] See F. Snyder, 'Globalisation and Europeanisation as Friends and Rivals: European Union Law in Global Economic Networks', in F. Snyder (ed.), *The Europeanisation of Law: The Legal Effects of European Integration* (Oxford: Hart Publishing, 2000).

sense. The model does not, however, prejudge the answer to this question. Indeed the main contribution of the model may ultimately prove to lie in helping us to understand analytically why the EU has – and will always have – an unfinished constitution. We can then reflect on what 'unfinished' means, and possibly work towards a fundamental reformulation of our conceptions of the EU constitution.

4

Europe and the constitution: what if this is as good as it gets?

MIGUEL POIARES MADURO

Introduction

In *Alice in Wonderland* there is a moment when Alice gets to an intersection between two roads. At the top of a tree she sees a Cheshire cat and asks him: 'Which road should I take?' The cat answers: 'That depends on where you want to go.' As always in the works of Lewis Carroll, the answer is so logical as to be obvious but frequently forgotten. Constitutional lawyers are the cats of European integration. There are limits to what cats and lawyers can do. The central theme of this chapter is about knowing those limits as a starting point to provide meaningful normative proposals for European constitutionalism.

In this chapter, I argue that national constitutionalism is simply a contextual representation of constitutionalism whose dated and artificial borders are challenged by European constitutionalism. In themselves, constitutional ideals are not dependent on nor legitimized by the borders of national polities. As a consequence, there is often no a priori claim of higher validity for national constitutionalism vis-à-vis European constitutionalism. My first objective is to question the artificial supremacy of national constitutionalism and argue for a new form of constitutionalism. At the same time, I believe it will be possible to derive from a new analysis of constitutionalism a form of legitimation for the European Union

The first version of this chapter was written while at Harvard Law School as an EU–US Fulbright Research Scholar. I have benefited enormously from talks with Joseph Weiler and J. Shaw at Harvard Law School. I have also received many useful comments from Joaquim Pedro Cardoso da Costa, José Areilza, Damian Chalmers, Claike Kilpatrick, Neil Komesar, Francis Snyder, Stephen Weatherill and Francisco Lucas Pires. I would like to single out Francisco Lucas Pires whose death has deprived the constitutional law of the EU of one of its earlier and more creative advocates and thinkers. I would like to point out that my approach to constitutional law draws heavily on Neil Komesar's comparative institutional analysis in a manner which is not really reflected in the footnote references.

arising from its constitutional and democratic added value in facing the present atomization and de-territorialization of normative power. The deconstruction of constitutionalism required by European integration may actually promote an extended application of its ideals. We will see that, in many respects, the problems of the European Constitution are simply reflections of the limits of national constitutionalism that we have for long ignored.

It is becoming increasingly clear how artificial it is to conceive of national constitutionalism as the ideal form of constitutionalism.[1] As a consequence of the growing de-territorialization and atomization of power,[2] the conception of national constitutionalism centred in the power of the state and organizing society towards pre-defined social goals is in crisis. This conception has hidden, under an idealized construction of the 'common good', the true nature of constitutionalism: the balancing of diverse and often conflicting interests and fears.[3]

We need a different conception of constitutionalism which is not tied to abstract models and artificial boundaries. We should challenge the absolute conception of many constitutional values whose inherent paradoxes are frequently ignored.[4] A constitution may constantly redesign its borders without necessarily falling into relativism or nihilism.[5] Highlighting the artificial character of abstract models and concepts of constitutionalism does not undermine constitutionalism itself if we can derive from constitutional ideals criteria to help us balance between different constitutional authorities and principles. Whatever the solutions to Europe's

---

[1] J. Shaw talks about 'the unexamined conventions and traditions of modern constitutionalism, which crucially include an assumption that there is a single comprehensive form of constitutional dialogue', in 'Postnational Constitutionalism in the European Union', 6 *Journal of European Public Policy* (1999), 579 at 591.

[2] Gustavo Zagrebelsky talks about a pluralist revolution: *Il Diritto Mite* (Turin: Einaudi, 1992), especially 4–11 and 45–50.

[3] See Michele Everson, 'Beyond the *Bundesverfassungsgericht*: On the Necessary Cunning of Constitutional Reasoning', 4 *European Law Journal* (1998), 389 at 390; Shaw, 'Postnational Constitutionalism'; J. Cohen and C. Sabel, 'Directly-Deliberative Poliarchy', 3 *European Law Journal* (1997), 313.

[4] Zagrebelsky, *Il Diritto Mite*, 17, talks about the mitigation and 'relativization' of constitutional concepts as a result of intrinsic conflicts. As he states, at 171, 'conceived in absolute terms, principles will rapidly become enemies of each other' (my translation).

[5] The work of Stanley Fish is exemplary in this regard. He argues that constitutional concepts and principles are never absolute and lines are always being drawn, but refuses the idea that this recognition will lead to a form of relativism or nihilism. See *Doing What Comes Naturally: Change, Rhetoric, and the Practice of Theory in Literary and Legal Studies* (Durham: Duke University Press, 1989), and *There's No Such Thing as Free Speech, and It's a Good Thing Too* (New York: Oxford University Press, 1994).

constitutional problems, they will probably necessitate the taking of a variety of constitutional and democratic steps at the national and at the European level. Most of the proposals which have been put forward so far focus on democratic reforms of the European political process and decision-making or the rights of the European citizen with regard to the European institutions. One of the possible advantages of the approach taken in this essay is that it will promote new ideas about the role of European integration in the reform of national political processes and democracy and the particular rights of European citizens which are relevant in a context of a plurality of polities. This will also protect the plurality of democratic claims and constitutional authority of the national and European polities.

I will start with a brief review of the problems of European constitutionalism and the usual responses. The remaining sections of the chapter will focus on three paradoxes which are at the core of constitutionalism and which highlight the artificial character of the borders and concepts applied to national constitutionalism. I will review what I call the three paradoxes of constitutional law: the polity; the fear of the few and the fear of the many; and the question of who decides who decides. They will be related both to Europe's constitutional problems and to national constitutional limits. The aim is to demonstrate that the current European constitutional problems are not unique but actually reflect constitutional problems which already exist in the context of national constitutionalism. As a consequence, I will restate my claim that there is no a priori higher claim of legitimacy of national constitutions in relation to the European Constitution. Furthermore, the paradoxical character of constitutional concepts determines that there are no ideal solutions and that different polities and/or institutions may come closer to constitutional ideals in different real-life settings. I will attempt to identify the constitutional criteria necessary to make these institutional and polity choices. The approach taken will allow me to show the added value of European constitutionalism even with regard to purely national constitutional problems.

The existential crisis of the European Constitution

The European Constitution suffers from an existential crisis, reflected in a growing dissatisfaction with the current state of affairs at the level both of constitution-making and of constitutional interpretation. There are growing tensions arising from a Constitution which was largely

developed as a function of economic integration. The constitutionalization of the Treaties created a constitutional body without discussing its
soul. Therefore, the European Constitution appears as a simple functional
consequence of the process of market integration without a discussion of
the values it necessarily embodies: it has been taken as a logical constitutional conclusion without a constitutional debate. The legitimacy of the
process of constitutionalization is therefore under challenge, highlighting
the democratic and constitutional deficits of European integration:

> The spillover of market integration rules into all areas of national reg-
> ulation raises a conflict between the functional legitimacy of market
> integration and the democratic legitimacy of national rules. The goal
> of market integration is no longer capable of explaining and legitimat-
> ing the reach of EU law in national legal orders.
>
> The increased competencies of the European Union have led to
> claims of a democratic deficit since powers previously under the control
> of national parliaments are transferred to the European Union level and
> subject to a lower degree of parliamentary participation and majoritar-
> ian decision-making coupled with higher concerns over transparency
> and accountability.
>
> Euro-sceptics argue that there is no underlying European political
> community (no demos) that can support the existence of a European
> Constitution. On the other side of the spectrum, European federalists
> argue for an exercise of constituent power (*pouvoir constituant*) from
> the European people(s) creating and legitimating a true European
> Constitution.
>
> Finally there are increased fears of conflict between national legal
> orders (mainly national constitutions) and the EU legal order. Both
> national and European constitutional law assume in the internal logic
> of their respective legal systems the role of higher law. In this way, there
> is no agreement as to the 'kompetenz/kompetenz' between national
> legal orders and the EU legal order.

The recent decisions by national constitutional courts demonstrate a 'clear
and present danger' of constitutional conflict. In effect, there is talk of a
counter-revolution, grounded in a revolt against European constitutionalism. But is the counter-revolution a claim for reform of the European
Constitution or a rejection of the idea altogether? And why is the debate
spreading to public opinion? Is it out of concern for the existence of a
European Constitution or out of concern about what that Constitution is?

Three approaches can be detected in the debates on European integration. One of the most frequently heard theses, usually supported by the European Parliament, is the claim for a formal European Constitution which has gained momentum with current debate on the future of Europe: the replacement or complementing of the Treaties by a legal text establishing Europe's constitutional principles, fundamental rights and political organization. This is expected to clarify the present constitutional system, give a voice to European citizens (*le pouvoir constituant*) and create mechanisms to control the increased powers transferred to the Union. This constitutional alternative is often linked with the usual response to Europe's democratic deficit: that which argues for a reinforcement of European institutions (stronger political leadership) and their democratization (mainly through an extended application of the principle of majority decision-making). In other words, to the erosion of national powers and representative democracy we should respond with increased EU powers and an enhanced role for the European Parliament and majoritarian mechanisms. In this way it will also be possible to reinstate political control over market integration (economic integration would be followed by political integration). This constitutional model answers to the challenges to national democracy by developing European democracy but, in doing so, replaces the national polity with the European polity.

The most common objection raised to the previous proposals is that there is no European polity. A polity requires a community with a high degree of cultural, ethnic or historical cohesion, which is not the case with the European Union. Instead, this type of community is still identified with the national state. Here, the problem of European constitutionalism is not identified with the absence of a written constitution and a traditional majoritarian democratic system but with the absence of a demos capable of legitimizing such a Constitution. This view is at the origin of the arguments in favour of limits to the growth of EU powers, a return to intergovernmentalism and, where necessary, a role for national parliaments at the European level. It is an analysis which still sees national democracies as the highest source of constitutional legitimacy. As a consequence, the final authority between national and European 'constitutionalism' belongs to national constitutions.

There is a third alternative, albeit less popular than the two more classical views described above. It is a conception of European constitutionalism deriving from a particular ideal of constitutionalism and its limits on power coupled with a historic understanding of the process of

European integration. This alternative supports the erosion of national powers arising from European integration but claims that this should not correspond to an increase of powers for the European Union. The ultimate goal of the European Constitution should be to limit power and protect individual freedom. This vision arises from ordoliberal and neo-liberal conceptions of federalism and its application to Europe following the Second World War. Federalism is seen as a new form of separation of powers to supplement the traditional (and not totally efficient) horizontal separation of powers. The goal is the creation of a free market economy which is constitutionally protected. There is no need for a transfer of powers to the European Union, since free market transactions, protected through the rules of free movement and free competition, constitute the true legitimating source of the European Constitution. According to this vision what we need is a system of rules limiting state and, in general, public and private power in the market.[6] This vision of European integration conceives the constitutional functional result of European market integration not as giving rise to a constitutional deficit but as the last and ideal stage of constitution-making. This constitutional 'solution' is not exclusive of European integration and it is becoming a standard answer to the current democratic problems detected in national institutions (in particular, the political process): the best way to save the state is to have less of it.[7]

A starting paradox is that all of the alternatives discussed are argued on similar democratic grounds. They depart from the same legitimating factor but reach quite different conclusions on the model of governance that ought to be adopted in the European Union. The reason lies in their open or hidden assumptions regarding, for example, the relevant polity to be taken into account (Europe or the nation state) and the different constitutional ideals and fears that should govern the relations within that polity: namely, the balance between the interests of the many and those of the few or that between majority decision-making and individual rights. A discussion of these concepts and their paradoxes will help us to highlight some of the limits of constitutionalism and democracy at the national level and review the impact of European integration for constitutionalism and democracy in general.

[6] See the discussion in my *We the Court, the European Court of Justice and the European Economic Constitution* (Oxford: Hart Publishing, 1998), especially ch. 4.

[7] C. Sabel and Dorf, 'A Constitution of Democratic Experimentalism', http://www.columbia.edu/~cfs11/Recon.html, at 2.

Before advancing I need, however, to disclose three assumptions which underlie my analysis of the three paradoxes of constitutionalism. First, in this essay I will assume a link between democracy and constitutionalism. They will be taken to be two sides of the same coin (one focusing on the democratic organization of power, the other on the limits to that power). When I use the word 'constitutionalism', in this context, I am referring to constitutional democracy. This will also help to deal with the fact that most of the critiques on the European Constitution concentrate on its possible lack of democratic legitimacy. The second assumption is that the best form of legitimation for national and European constitutionalism derives from representation and participation. In this, I do no more than follow a basic concern which democratic theories have always reflected.[8] The third assumption is probably the most contentious one. The major differences between democratic theories tend to arise in the conception of the institutions and processes which are thought to be necessary to provide representation and participation and in the notions of the individual and political communities that precede or result from such processes and institutions. My view is that the broader goals of political communities derive from the co-ordination and satisfaction of individual preferences as judged by individuals themselves. This means that I oppose organic or communitarian conceptions of the polity whereby the political system is devoted to the pursuit of goals which are independent from the aggregation of individual preferences. This is a liberal and individual-centred conception of democracy which I assume even at the epistemological level. In my view, not only outcomes but also processes are to be measured in terms of individual representation and participation. As a consequence, the democratic character of the political form of organization of the polity is not assessed on the basis of whether its results meet the interests of individuals (which would always be measured by criteria independent of the individuals' preferences) but on whether such process grants effective representation and participation to all affected individuals.

[8] In this regard I follow closely the criteria developed by Robert Dahl (*Democracy and Its Critics* (New Haven and London: Yale University Press, 1989), especially 108–15) or what Bobbio (*Il Futuro della Democrazia* (Turin: Einaudi, 1984), 13) has coined the 'minimum definition of democracy'. The fashionable deliberative and discourse-based theories of democracy are also mainly about participation. See e.g. Jürgen Habermas, *Between Facts and Norms* (Cambridge: Polity Press, 1998), for instance at 110, 166–7; Roberto Gargarella, 'Full Representation, Deliberation and Impartiality', in Jon Elster (ed.), *Deliberative Democracy* (Cambridge: Cambridge University Press, 1998), 260; and Jon Elster, 'Deliberation and Constitution Making', in *ibid*.

Paradox I – the polity

Constitutions are understood as founded on a contract, an agreement or any other form of social consensus, through which popular sovereignty is exercised. Members of a polity define their common interests, empower common institutions and establish the rules and limits to the exercise of public and private power. The Constitution both defines and presupposes a polity or political community whose members are bound, in solidarity, by the Constitution. It is from this political community and its people that the democratic process draws its legitimacy and that of the majority decisions reached in the democratic representative process. The basis of the polity is normally referred to as 'the people'. Constitutional and democratic theory scholars normally presuppose that 'a people' already exists.[9] But what makes a people? And who has the right to be considered as part of the people? A polity may be determined in different ways (including liberal or communitarian conceptions). That determination will, in turn, define citizenship (or vice versa), giving a right to representation and participation in constitution-making and the political process.

The European integration process disturbs this constitutional construction by introducing into the picture different polities or by assuming a Constitution without a traditional polity; a Constitution without a people. What, if any, is the polity behind European constitutionalism and how does it fit with the traditional conception of polities in constitutional law? One of the usual critiques of the European Constitution departs from the 'absence' of a 'European people': the 'no demos' thesis.[10] There is no European demos (people), therefore there can be no European Constitution. The debates about the democratic deficit also have much to do with the uncertainty as to the relevant polity to be taken into account in measuring European democracy. A majority can exist only with reference to a certain polity. A majority in national terms may well be a minority in European terms and vice versa. Those advocating more majoritarian decision-making in the European Union are, in effect, transferring the application of the democratic criterion from the national to the European level. In other words, they are moving the constitutional centre from the national to the European polity. On the contrary, those opposing a transfer of powers to the European Union often do so on the basis that

---

[9] Dahl, *Democracy and Its Critics*, at 3.
[10] J. H. H. Weiler, 'Does Europe Need a Constitution?'; and J. H. H. Weiler, Haltern and Mayer, 'European Democracy and Its Critics', 18 *West European Politics* (1995), 4.

there cannot be a truly democratic European political process once, in their view, there is no European demos to support it.

Much of the criticism of the constitutional developments of the European Union is based on a simple assumption: national constitutionalism is superior to European constitutionalism because democracy and constitutionalism can only take place in the presence of a demos and this only exists at the level of nation states.[11] It is a view that correlates constitutionalism with a demos and the demos with the nation state. It conceives of the political community as based on a people bound by a high degree of cultural, historical and ethnic identity and cohesiveness. But there are several possible critiques to this view. The first important critique is that a polity does not necessarily require a demos as traditionally understood at the national level. It is possible to conceive of the European polity as based on a civic understanding of the European demos independent of belongingness to an ethno-cultural identity.[12] What forms the European polity is our voluntary agreement to share certain values and a form of political organization open to anyone wishing to enter into this social contract. The second important critique derives from constitutionalism itself: why should participation and representation be limited by the requirement of belongingness to an ethno-cultural identity? It is the paradox of the concept of polity in its relation with constitutionalism and democracy. Is not a national demos a limit to democracy and constitutionalism? In fact, participation in national democracies is not granted to all those affected by the decisions of the national political process but only to those affected

---

[11] This is the view underlying the German Constitutional Court *Maastricht* decision (English translation published in 33 *International Legal Materials* (1994), 395, see especially para. C-I-3). For a discussion of the decision, see Weiler, 'Does Europe Need a Constitution?'; and Steve Boom, 'The European Union after the *Maastricht* Decision: Will Germany be the "Virginia of Europe"?', 43 *American Journal of Comparative Law* (1995), 177. According to Jacqué ('La Constitution Communautaire', RUDH (1995), 397 at 409), the German Constitutional Court might change its view with the development of European political parties and European public opinion. It is also possible to argue that such already exists in Europe. For a view in this regard (though not an absolutely clear one) see Peter Häberle ('Existe un Espacio Público Europeu?', *Revista de Instituciones Europeas* (1995), 113, especially 121ff.) who identifies an emerging European public sphere based on a European common culture.

[12] See Weiler, 'Does Europe Need a Constitution?'; and Weiler, Haltern and Mayer, 'European Democracy and Its Critics'. Weiler has consistently advocated a European polity which is not dependent on a community defined on the basis of ethnic, cultural or historical criteria, speaking instead of a civic polity. In the same sense, see also Lucas Pires, *Introdução ao Direito Constitucional Europeu* (Coimbra: Almedina, 1997), 68–9; and Gomes Canotilho, *Direito Constitucional e Teoria da Constituição*, 2nd edn (Coimbra: Almedina, 1998), 1221–5.

who are considered as citizens of the national polity.[13] It is not the existence of democracy at national level that is contested but the extent of that democracy.[14] There is a strong problem of inclusion faced by national polities.[15] National polities tend to exclude many who would accept their 'constitutional contract' and are affected by their policies simply because they are not part of the demos as understood in the ethno-cultural sense mentioned above. But the dependence of democracy and constitutionalism on these ethno-cultural polities is in contradiction with the founding principles of constitutional democracies which aim at full representation and participation.

National polities have a twofold deficit: on the one hand, they do not control many decision-making processes which impact on those national polities but take place outside their borders; on the other hand, national polities exclude from participation and representation many interests which are affected by their decisions. The borders of national democracy no longer correspond to the scope of action of the 'modern citizen'.[16] They have probably never corresponded, but it becomes increasingly obvious how artificial are the jurisdictions of democracy, and the lack of correspondence between the democratic polities in which we participate and the democratic polities that affect us. National constitutional democracies cannot cope with our desire to be involved in different polities and do not legitimize the different decision-making processes that affect our lives.

David Held has highlighted this global challenge to nation state democracy and the need for a new model of democracy (which can be extended to constitutionalism). In his words:

---

[13] Christian Joerges comments in this way on the German Constitutional Court conception of Community law exposed in the *Maastricht* judgment: 'Foreign sovereign acts, so the Court argues, must not claim superior validity to democratically legitimised law. What if we turn this argument around? Constitutional states must not unilaterally impose burdens on their neighbours ... "No taxation without representation" – this principle can claim universal validity even against constitutional states.' See 'Taking the Law Seriously: On Political Science and the Role of Law in the Process of European Integration', 2 *European Law Journal* (1996), 105 at 117 (footnote omitted).

[14] The difference between the existence of democracy and the extent of democracy is highlighted by Elster, 'Deliberation and Constitution Making', 99.

[15] Dahl points out that polities have a twofold problem: '1 – The problem of inclusion: Which persons have a rightful claim to be included in the demos?; 2 – The scope of its authority: What rightful limits are there on the control of a demos?', *Democracy and Its Critics*, 119. See also David Held, *Democracy and the Global Order* (Cambridge and Oxford: Polity Press, 1995), especially chs. 1 and 10.

[16] As noted by Lucas Pires, national constitutional democracies are no longer able to satisfy the needs of the new 'multiple and supranational individual' who corresponds to the 'modern citizen', *Introdução*, 67.

the problem, for defenders and critics alike of modern democracy systems, is that regional and global inter-connectedness contests the traditional national resolutions of key questions of democratic theory and practice. The very process of governance can escape the reach of the nation-state. National communities by no means exclusively make and determine decisions and policies for themselves, and governments by no means determine what is appropriate exclusively for their own citizens.[17]

There are thus both pragmatic and normative arguments in favour of a broader form of constitutionalism and democracy 'overseeing' national constitutional democracies.[18] First, nation states can no longer (perhaps never could) contain the impact of outside policies inside their borders and therefore need to acquire forms of constitutional control over decision-making taking place outside those national borders. Second, nation states never fully fulfilled the democratic and constitutional ideals of full representation and participation. It is no longer possible to sustain the illusion of a symmetric relationship between national political decision-makers and the recipients of political decisions.[19]

Two important consequences arise from the discussion so far: first, there is no valid general claim of democracy for national constitutionalism with regard to European constitutionalism; second, constitutionalism and democracy should not be understood only with reference to their nation-state ideal. This is not to say that the ideal polity for constitutionalism and democracy is always that where the broadest representation and participation can be achieved. The paradox of the polity means that smaller jurisdictions may often provide less extensive but better representation. In other words, the simple expansion of the scope of the polity does not determine an increase in democracy and constitutional legitimation. This is so because constitutionalism and democracy are also about the quality of representation and participation.[20] It is not only the scope but also the degree and intensity of representation and participation that need to be promoted. There is a frequent trade-off between these two aims. Small communities may increase the degree and intensity of

---

[17] Held, *Democracy and the Global Order*, 16–17 (footnote omitted).

[18] The use of the word 'overseeing' is not to be understood as defining a form of hierarchical control and supremacy, as will be made clearer below.

[19] Held, *Democracy and the Global Order*, 224.

[20] Further, from a liberal perspective constitutionalism also guarantees to individuals (separated or aggregated in smaller groups) the possibility of original constitutional self-exclusion in certain areas from the forms of political organization that require democracy and representation. This raises complex questions that cannot be addressed here.

representation and participation by diminishing information and orga-nization costs. They also increase the relative value of each individual participation.[21] Therefore it would not also be correct to state that when-ever European constitutionalism would provide a broader representation it would have a higher claim of legitimacy. Many questions remain open as to which polity and when will provide the best basis for constitutionalism and democracy. But my argument is precisely that there is no abstract ideal polity for constitutionalism and that this is a consequence of the constitutional paradoxes involved in the concept of the polity.

Constitutional questions have always been addressed within a pre-existing polity (normally the nation state). It is that polity that has served as the yardstick of constitutionalism. Relations within the polity are reg-ulated by constitutional law. Relations among polities, instead, have been dominated by a different set of actors (the states) and a different set of rules (international law). Previously, constitutional questions addressed the source of legitimacy within a polity, and democracy was limited to that polity. European integration makes this picture more complex by introducing competing polities and a larger polity. But this may be seen as bringing an added value to democracy and constitutionalism. First, we are no longer prisoners of our original polity and can choose to live among a variety of polities. While benefiting from national communities as our original polity we are also granted a new form of social contract that includes the (still limited) right to choose among those different national polities in the European space. Second, we also gain rights of represen-tation in the other national polities with regard to their decisions which affect our interests: many of the rights granted by EC market integration rules and the principle of non-discrimination on the basis of nationality can be conceived of as such. As I have argued elsewhere, EU economic law should be conceived of as providing the European citizen not only with economic rights but with political rights to have their interests taken into account in non-domestic national political processes.[22] In this sense, EU rights promote the constitutional ideals of full representation and partici-pation. Moreover, the competition between the different national polities

---

[21] The democratic value of small communities can be easily explained through the costs involved in decision-making. On these see Buchanan and Tullock, *The Calculus of Consent* (Ann Arbor: University of Michigan Press, 1965), 63ff.

[22] For an example, see my *We the Court*, especially 169–73 (or see in: 'Reforming the Market or the State? Article 30 and the European Constitution: Economic Freedom and Political Rights', 3 *European Law Journal* (1997), 55). In the same sense see Joerges, 'Taking the Law Seriously', 117.

generated under the larger European polity may promote an overall im-
provement of all national polities even from their internal perspective. On
the downside, the introduction of the new European polity increases the
costs of decision-making and, as a consequence, may decrease the quality
of representation and participation. We may also be prevented from exercising some of our preferences as they now have to be compatible with
those of a larger jurisdiction. The relative value of our representation and
participation is reduced within a larger polity.

The paradox of the polity implies a challenge to the supremacy of
national constitutionalism over European constitutionalism by stressing
how much the critiques of European constitutionalism ignore the constitutional and democratic limits of national polities. Furthermore, it
highlights how the debates on European constitutionalism need to be related to the paradoxical concept of the polity and how constitutionalism
and democracy may require different polities in different circumstances
depending on a comparative analysis of their representation and participation relative value in different contexts.

Paradox II – the fear of the few and the fear of the many[23]

Constitutionalism is normally presented as a two-edged concept: empowering and limiting power. All major constitutional arguments and
doctrines gravitate around a complex system of countervailing forces set
up by constitutional law to promote the democratic exercise of power
(assuring that the few do not rule over the many) but, at the same time,
to limit that power (assuring that the many will not abuse their power
over the few). Constitutionalism is all about these difficult balances between values or institutions that it, simultaneously, advances and fears:
the balance between the common values of the polity and the individual
preferences of its members; the balance between the democratic will of
the majority and the rights of the minority. There are two basic fears underlying constitutional discourse and organization: the fear of the many
and fear of the few. The core of constitutional law is the balance between

---

[23] Expressions such as this one (as well as those of minoritarian and majoritarian biases,
to be employed below) are borrowed from Neil Komesar. They form the basis of what
he has coined the two-force model which is applied to the judicial review of the political
process. See *Imperfect Alternatives – Choosing Institutions in Law, Economics and Public
Policy* (Chicago and London: Chicago University Press, 1994); and 'A Job for the Judges:
The Judiciary and the Constitution in a Massive and Complex Society', 86 *Michigan Law
Review* (1981), 657.

the fear of the many and the fear of the few. Constitutional law sets up the mechanisms through which the many can rule but, at the same time, creates rights and processes for the protection of the few. Separation of powers, fundamental rights and parliamentary representation are all expressions of these fears.[24]

Traditionally, the many have been associated with the decisions taken by the majority through the political process while the protection of the few is associated with individual rights. The function of judicial review of legislation has frequently been argued on substantive or procedural conceptions of minority protection.[25] This classical picture of constitutional law has been challenged by the multiplication of social decision-making forums and the insights brought by new institutional analyses. Interest group theories of the political process have demonstrated, for example, how democratic decision-making may, in effect, be controlled by a few against the interests of the many.[26] It is no longer possible to associate a particular institution with a particular fear of the few or of the many.

However, many of the current constitutional analyses still depart from idealized notions of institutions as a simple reflection of their abstract models constitutionally defined. Changes in the composition and distribution of interests, the multiplication of alternative forms of participation and the dependence of representation and participation on information and transaction costs are frequently ignored in much of the standard constitutional law literature. Even more frequent is the tendency to concentrate the analysis on a single institution and/or on only one of the fears mentioned. This ignores the fact that constitutionalism requires the fears of the few and the fears of the many to be understood as two sides of the same coin. Often, constitutional lawyers assume that normative goals can

---

[24] R. Bellamy ('The Political Form of the Constitution: The Separation of Powers, Rights and Representative Democracy', in R. Bellamy and D. Castiglione (eds.), *Constitutionalism in Transformation: European and Theoretical Perspectives* (Oxford, Blackwell, 1996), 24) highlights three principles which have defined constitutionalism: rights, separation of powers and representative government. However, in his view, the first has come to predominate in recent years: 'Rights, upheld by judicial review, are said to comprise the prime component of constitutionalism, providing a normative legal framework within which politics operate': at 24.

[25] For the former see Ronald Dworkin, *Taking Rights Seriously* (Cambridge, MA: Harvard University Press, 1977). For the latter see John Ely, *Democracy and Distrust: A Theory of Judicial Review* (Cambridge, MA: Harvard University Press, 1980).

[26] Other theories have contributed in the same sense. Bruce Ackerman's 'dualist democracy', for example, equates both the political process and the courts with the promotion and/or protection of democratic decisions. See *We the People, I – Foundations* (Cambridge, MA: Harvard University Press, 1991).

be translated into 'real life' in a sort of causal relationship that ignores the institutions that will interpret and specify such goals. When they do pay attention to institutions it is common for constitutional scholars to concentrate their normative assessments in one institution, arguing for a different institutional alternative simply on the basis of the institutional malfunctions (related to a fear of the few or a fear of the many) detected in the institution reviewed. This obvious but diffuse problem of legal analysis has been identified by Neil Komesar as 'single institutionalism'.[27] For example, most analyses of the judicial review of legislation focus exclusively on the malfunctions detected in the workings of the political process. Once a malfunction is highlighted in the political process, the claim is made for the courts to step in and 'correct' (review) the decisions of that political process. However, it may well happen that in many cases in which the political process operates badly the courts operate even more badly. As Komesar has consistently argued, institutional choices should be made by comparing alternative institutions and not solely on the grounds that a particular institution suffers from serious institutional malfunctioning. Single institutionalism could also be referred to as single constitutionalism, since it represents a form of constitutional analysis which ignores the constitutional paradoxes to which I have been referring. In other words, it identifies a constitutional problem and proposes an alternative without enquiring about the potential constitutional problems hidden in that alternative. This is in great part due to the fact that, while the present alternative is reviewed in a 'real life setting', the proposed alternative is assumed to correspond perfectly to its constitutional ideal. This is the case with much of the constitutional analysis of the European Union. Normally, authors tend to identify a constitutional deficit in a current institution (for example, the Council) and propose a transfer of decision-making to an alternative institution (for example, the European Parliament) without comparing the relative ability of these institutions in the specific settings under analysis (assuming, for example, that the European Parliament will always reflect the democratic ideal). In doing so, they ignore the constitutional paradox of the fear of the few and the fear of the many. My argument here is not only that the analyses of the European Constitution ought to be more sophisticated. I expect that the nature of Europe's constitutional discourse will force constitutional scholars to uncover new forms of fears of the few and of the many. This must depart from an understanding of the institutional choices inherent in the interpretation and application of

---

[27] *Imperfect Alternatives.*

the law, the introduction of a contextual analysis of those institutions and a more sophisticated conception of the interests which are assumed to be reflected in the decisions of those institutions. It further means that the identification of one of those fears in an EU institution cannot constitute, by itself, a sufficient claim for an institutional alternative.

An example will make these ideas clearer and also help to highlight its normative power in reconstructing legal analysis and, in this specific case, the debate on the European Constitution. I will review the classic critiques of the European democratic deficit and highlight how they have been dominated by single institutionalism or single constitutionalism. They focus on particular types of fear of the few, ignoring both the fear of the many and other forms of the fear of the few. This, it will be argued, is not only a failure in constitutional analysis but tends to hide the value that European constitutionalism may have in correcting less-known forms of those fears and promoting new mechanisms of participation and representation.

There are at least two facets of the European democratic deficit: one relates to the 'insufficient degree' of majoritarian decision-making in the Council; the other refers to the low level of parliamentary control over that decision-making. Both correspond to fears of the few but they are of different types. The first can be seen in the well-known thesis of the 'joint-decision trap' developed by Scharpf.[28] Unanimous decision-making tends to support suboptimal policies because policies cannot be created, abolished or changed so long as there is a single Member State preferring the status quo.[29] This can also be presented as another aspect of the democratic deficit: 'the ability of a small number of Community citizens represented by their Minister in the Council to block the collective wishes of the rest of the Community'.[30] However, from the fact that there are serious risks of malfunctions and fear of the few under unanimity does not follow that majority decision-making will produce more representative or efficient outcomes. There is nothing to suggest that decisions taken by majority voting will have a more balanced representation of the affected interests. Decisions taken by a majority of states or a majority of the population will not take into consideration the distribution of costs and benefits in all states or all the population but only in the states or people that comprise that majority. What changes under unanimity or majority

[28] Fritz Scharpf, 'The Joint-Decision Trap – Lessons from German Federalism and European Integration', 66 *Public Administration* (1988), 239 at 255.
[29] *Ibid.*, 257.
[30] Joseph Weiler, 'The Transformation of Europe', 100 *Yale Law Journal* (1990), 2403 at 2467.

rules is only the distribution of the costs and benefits arising from unequal representation in the decisions. Under unanimous voting the risk is that a decision will be taken only if it favours all states independently of the intensity of their needs, and that it will be maintained even though the benefits that it brings to one state are lower than the costs imposed on the others (minoritarian bias or a form of fear of the few). Under majority voting the risk is that a decision is taken or maintained even though the cumulative benefit it gives to the majority of states is lower than the cumulative costs burdening the minority of states (majoritarian bias or a form of fear of the many). We move from minoritarian bias to majoritarian bias. The same occurs if instead of a majority of states we talk of a majority of European citizens. Scharpf falls into the trap of single institutional or single constitutional analysis by reviewing only the malfunctions arising under unanimous voting.[31]

The democratic deficit literature which concentrates on the limited role of the European Parliament in the decision-making process focuses on two problems: first, there is a transfer of power from a directly representative institution (parliaments) to an indirectly representative institution (governments acting in the Council); second, there is a transfer of power from an institution where all individuals are (approximately) proportionally represented to an institution where (it is said) there is low proportional representation and some minorities may block the will of the majority. Both of these concerns correspond to fears of the few but, in this case, the majority is defined cross-nationally (it is individuals not states who constitute the 'measure' of the majority). The risk is that a non-directly representative and non-majoritarian political process may be dominated by the interests of a minority. It would suffer from minoritarian bias. The focus is on democratic representation through parliaments. This is certainly a necessary condition for the democratic legitimacy of the Union.[32] The question is: to what extent?[33] As stated, underlying the democratic deficit literature is the concern with the fear of the few. However, if the

---

[31] At the same time, he also appears to confuse the aggregation of individual preferences with the aggregation of governmental preferences.

[32] See e.g. K. Lenaerts and de Smijter, 'The Question of Democratic Representation', in J. A. Winter, D. Curtin, A. E. Kellermann and B. de Witte (eds.), *Reforming the Treaty on European Union – The Legal Debate* (The Hague: Kluwer Law International, 1996), 173 at 175. These authors recognize, however, that the democratic deficit will not be resolved on the basis of a simple transfer of parliamentary democratic representation to the European Union level. Indirect representation of this kind is also envisaged through national parliaments for example. See especially at 178.

[33] See Renaud Dehousse, 'Constitutional Reform in the European Community: Are there Alternatives to the Majoritarian Avenue?', 18 *West European Politics* (1995), 118 at 122.

powers of the European Parliament become dominant in the European legislative and political process (which is increasingly the case in the post-Amsterdam era) the opposite fear is raised: that of the control of the political process by the majority even against an overwhelming interest of a minority.[34]

The dilemma between the fears of the few and those of the many is visible in the discussions on institutional reform. The conception of these fears tends to depart, however, from a conception of the European political process as exclusively dominated by state actors. This is a consequence of the functional model which is based 'on the idea that the controllers of the public realms of the Members States are able to represent the totality of the national interests of the participating people, and hence that the public interest of the EU . . . is nothing more than the aggregate of the public interests of the Member States, mediated through the collective willing of the public-realm controllers'.[35] The fears of the many and of the few are dealt with in a context of state representation. The impact of other actors in the European political process and the importance of alternative forms of participation in the European context (such as the market or the judicial process) are often ignored. In the same way, though many recognize in abstract that individual and group interests are no longer divided across national lines few take this into account when discussing specific problems of European constitutionalism.

The transfer of power to the European Parliament is normally argued to prevent the fears of the few already mentioned. However, the fear of the

[34] It is the balance between these two fears that dominates the discussions on majority decision-making versus unanimous decision-making. This is a very contentious point in constitutionalism which I cannot address here. Buchanan and Tullock, for example, have worked extensively on this problem and distinguished between constitutional choices and political choices. Ideal decisions should be based on a non-coercion principle and be made by unanimity (thus achieving a kind of Pareto optimum where no one would be harmed by the decision). But unanimous decisions also involve many costs of decision-making. Therefore, the distinction is made between constitutional decisions which require unanimity and other decisions which can be taken according to majority decision-making. See Buchanan and Tullock, *Calculus of Consent*. For an application to the European Union see Vibert, 'Non-coercion, Decision Rules and Europe's Constitutional Debate', in Schmidtchen and Cooter (eds.), *Constitutional Law and Economics of the European Union* (Cheltenham and Lyme: Edward Elgar, 1997), 258. On this topic in the European Union see also Pistone, according to whom societal core decisions to be taken by consensus are more and more frequent and lead to increased discussion of the mandatory character of majority decisions even at the national level. See 'Il Trattato di Unione Europea e la Legittimità delle Decisioni Democratiche a Maggioranza', 27 *Il Federalista* (1985), 178 at 178–9 (referring to Gerda Zellentin, 'Überstaatlichkeit statt Bürgernahe?', 1 *Integration* (1984)).

[35] Philip Allott, 'The Crisis of European Constitutionalism: Reflections on the Revolution in Europe', 34 *Common Market Law Review* (1997), 439 at 477.

few (minoritarian bias) can also increase with a transfer of power to the
European Parliament. Moving from intergovernmental decision-making
to European Parliament decision-making may not reduce the risks of minoritarian bias in Europe's political process. What changes is the type of
minoritarian bias or fear of the few. A transfer of power to the European
Parliament will shift representation from an institution where representation is aggregated mainly through the different national governments
to an institution with a much larger and more distant constituency of representation. The problem is that the larger the constituency to be taken
into account in representation the higher tend to be the transaction and
information costs of participating in the political process. This is not simply related to the lack of public visibility of the European Parliament; it
involves a more complex set of factors. The higher the number of represented people the more difficult it will be to organize dispersed interests
due to the low stakes of individual members and the information and organization costs involved. In areas where the interests of the majority tend
to be dispersed, national levels of representation may perform better in
organizing and mobilizing the majority. The information and transaction
costs of participating in the European political process at the level of the
European Parliament may be higher than participating in the European
political process through the national governments. As a consequence, in
issues where the European majority interests are quite dispersed it may be
easier for a minority of concentrated and organized interests to capture
the European Parliament political process than the intergovernmental political process.[36] In these cases, we still have risks of minoritarian bias or
fears of the few, only they arise from the actions of cross-national interest
groups and not particular Member States. Thus, depending on the issues
and the interests at stake, the European Parliament may actually be subject
to a higher risk of minoritarian bias than the intergovernmental process.
What varies is the type of minoritarian bias or, if you prefer, the few to be
feared.

There is no single solution or abstract model of constitutional democracy that can be adopted. What is needed is a more sophisticated constitutional analysis which understands the different versions of the fears
of the few and of the many and adopts a comprehensive comparative institutional analysis of Europe's constitutional problems. This will allow
us to highlight, for example, that even from a purely European point of
view national institutions may perform closer to our constitutional ideals.

---

[36] In the latter, national governments may act as catalytic elements of the cross-national
majority.

In other words, even if one accepts the European polity as the relevant polity it does not follow that a European institution will perform better in representing all the affected interests in the European polity. As the discussions on the European Parliament and majority decision-making were intended to show, there may be circumstances in which greater national input will help prevent European institutional malfunctions and bring about greater participation and more representative decisions from the point of view of the larger European polity. But the opposite may also occur: European integration and institutions may help improve the constitutional democratic character of national institutions even from a purely national perspective.

The inclusiveness promoted by European constitutionalism in national polities will also help to correct instances of purely national minoritarian and majoritarian biases which are often ignored because they are deeply embedded in national institutions and excluded from the sphere of public deliberation.[37] Most instances of discrimination against (or under-representation of) foreign nationals in national political processes are, at the same time, instances of capture of the national political process by a national interest group against the interests of a dormant national majority. The typical example is trade protectionism which tends to occur where concentrated national interests try to conserve their economic privileges

---

[37] This can be described as a consequence of the relation between lifeworld and system developed by Habermas in *Theory of Communicative Action*, vol. II (Cambridge: Polity Press, 1989). Systems are 'genetically' embodied with certain values and assumptions that are excluded from communicative action (that is, discourse). What happens is that systems tend to take control over lifeworld (where communicative action and rationality dominate) and in this way reduce the area of normative action subject to discourse and deliberation. In other words, they reduce the scope for democracy. This can be conceived to be one of the negative side-effects of constitutional dogmatics and its apparent neutrality. A good discussion of the problems posed by the constitutional status quo and its artificial neutrality can be found in Cass Sunstein, *The Partial Constitution* (Cambridge, MA and London: Harvard University Press, 1993) (see especially 1–10). As Sunstein states, right at the beginning, 'the status quo, like everything else, should be subject both to deliberation and to democracy'. Whether one agrees or not with the specific challenge brought by Sunstein to the status quo is another issue. Another way of looking at the problem of different degrees of democratic deliberation is through the theory of dualist democracy and constitutionalism developed by Bruce Ackerman. He conceives of a two-track democracy: the higher law-making track (corresponding to constitution-making) is that where we would be closer to an ideal form of full participation in deliberation. In a sense, European constitutionalism forces us to bring traditional national constitutional paradigms to the higher law-making track and, in doing so, broadens the scope of deliberation. See Ackerman, *We the People*; and 'Neo-Federalism', in Jon Elster and Rune Slagstad (eds.), *Constitutionalism and Democracy* (Cambridge: Cambridge University Press, 1988), 153.

at the expense of foreign competitors *and national consumers*. Because of the concentrated interests and high stakes of the small minority they can easily dominate the national political process even against the interests of the dispersed majority of consumers whose low per capita stakes and high transaction and information costs prevent them from being aware of their interests and exercising pressure in the political process. The obligation for national political processes to take into account foreign interests may bring those issues back into the sphere of public deliberation and promote a broader and more active representation of domestic interests. This explains why many cases of EU law are raised by nationals against their own state. EU law is often used by individuals as a new form of voice in the national political process. The Sunday trading saga[38] is a good example of how EU law reintroduces certain issues into the national public sphere, leading to a new political agreement within the national polity. In this way, EU law raises the voice of some domestic actors in national political processes.

The fears of the few and of the many can also be detected in alternative forms of participation and representation, such as those involved in the regulatory model[39] and the European market,[40] which ought to be subject to the same constitutional analysis. Again, none of these institutional alternatives fits perfectly with an ideal constitutional model of full

---

[38] Regarding legislation prohibiting Sunday trading which was challenged under Article 30 of the EC Treaty. Article 30 (now 28) has been called, in that context, the 'European defence' of domestic actors against national policies. See R. Rawlings, 'The Eurolaw Game: Deductions from a Saga', 20 *Journal of Law and Society* (1993), 309 at 313.

[39] For an analysis of the possible benefits of the regulatory model in the European Union, see Renaud Dehousse, 'Europe Institutional Architecture After Amsterdam: Parliamentary System or Regulatory Structure?', 35 *Common Market Law Review* (1998), 595, especially 600–1 and 625. On the regulatory model, its legitimation and its own democratic deficits, see also G. Majone (ed.), *Regulating Europe* (London: Routledge, 1996); M. Shapiro, 'The Problems of Independent Agencies in the United States and the European Union', 4 *Journal of European Public Policy* (1997), 262; C. Joerges and Vos (eds.), *EU Committees – Social Regulation, Law and Politics* (Oxford: Hart Publishing, 1999). Broadly, on the virtues and problems of deliberative democracy, see Cohen and Sabel, 'Directly-Deliberative Poliarchy'; Elster, *Deliberative Democracy*.

[40] On the democratic virtues and problems of the market see my *We the Court*, especially 136–43; and my 'Striking the Elusive Balance between Social Rights and Economic Freedoms', in Philip Alston (ed.), *The European Union and Human Rights* (Oxford: Oxford University Press, 1999). The departing point for a constitutional analysis of the market is a recognition (often made but rarely taken seriously by lawyers) that 'the market and the State are both devices through which co-operation is organized and made possible' (Buchanan and Tullock, *Calculus of Consent*, 19): in other words, social decision-making institutions.

representation and participation. What I have done is to highlight their diversity and to advance a method and criteria to be used in the complex institutional and constitutional choices before us. The departing point will continue to be the old constitutional fears of the many and of the few. Only now this debate takes place in a context of competing polities and must take into account the cross-national nature of representation of interests and the requirements of comparative institutional analysis.

Paradox III – who decides who decides?

Constitutional law has usually been considered as the higher degree and ultimate source of legitimacy of the legal system and its rules. Independently of one's conception of constitutional law as a *Grundnorm*, a set of rules of recognition, positivized natural law, a higher command of a sovereign supported by a habit of obedience, or other, constitutional law has always been conceived of as the higher law of the legal system, criterion of legitimacy and validity of other sources of the law. European integration 'attacks' this hierarchical understanding of the law. In reality, both national and European constitutional law assume in the internal logic of their respective legal systems the role of higher law. According to the internal conception of the EU legal order developed by the European Court of Justice, Community primary law will be the 'higher law' of the Union, the criterion of validity of secondary rules and decisions as well as that of all national legal rules and decisions within its scope. Moreover, the Court of Justice is the higher court of this legal system. However, a different perspective is taken by national legal orders and national constitutions. Here, Community law owes its supremacy to its reception by a higher national law (normally constitutions). The higher law remains, in the national legal orders, the national constitution and the ultimate power of legal adjudication belongs to national constitutional courts. In this way, the question of who decides who decides has different answers in the European and the national legal orders[41] and, when viewed from a perspective outside both national and Community legal orders, requires a conception of the law which is no longer dependent upon a hierarchical construction. Such a form of legal pluralism has already been convincingly

---

[41] Rossa Phelan has made a detailed analysis of the different viewpoints on the relationship between the national and the European legal orders depending on whether it is observed from the perspective of EC law, national constitutional law or even public international law. See *Revolt or Revolution: The Constitutional Boundaries of the European Community* (Dublin: Sweet & Maxwell, 1997).

argued by Neil MacCormick.[42] However, the *Maastricht* decision of the
German Constitutional Court and the challenges to a Community legal
act in German courts regarding the Bananas regulation[43] have again raised
fears of actual conflicts between national courts and the ECJ disrupting
the European Union legal order and ultimately the process of European
integration.

In my view, the question of 'who decides who decides' has long been
around in constitutionalism. It is a normal consequence of the divided
powers system inherent in constitutionalism. In fact, it can be considered
as an expected result of the Madisonian view of separation of powers as
creating a mechanism of checks and balances. The conflicts surrounding
the exercise of judicial review, for example, are linked to the following
question. When a court strikes down a piece of legislation according to
its interpretation of a constitutional norm which could be the object of
different interpretations, two opposing positions can be argued: one, that
the court has done nothing but apply the higher law; another, that the
court has overstepped its role since the indeterminacy of the constitutional
norm meant that it was for the legislator to choose one from among several possible interpretations of that norm. Of course, in the operation of
national constitutions and where constitutional judicial review exists, it is
expected that the legislator will accept the court's decision and therefore
it is stated that it is the latter which has the 'right to decide who decides'.
But that is more a result of the historical development of separation of
powers than a logical conclusion to be derived from the foundations of
constitutionalism. Moreover, the reality is that the political system can
still impact upon the judiciary (for example, by changing the members of
the constitutional court)[44] and, in this way, still has an important share of
the power 'to decide who decides'. I am not going to address the complex
questions involved in judicial review and separation of powers. What I
want to stress is that the paradox of 'who decides who decides' is inherent in the values of constitutionalism as one of its guarantees of limited

---

[42] Neil MacCormick, 'Beyond the Sovereign State', 56 *Modern Law Review* (1993), 1.

[43] See, for example, M. Kumm, 'Who is the Final Arbiter of Constitutionality in
Europe?', Harvard Jean Monnet Working Paper 10/98, www.law.harvard.edu/Programs/
JeanMonnet/papers/98/98-10-.html. Among other relevant issues (mainly, the direct effect
of the GATT rules in the German legal order), the argument was made by some German
companies which traditionally imported bananas from Latin American countries that
the EC Regulation discriminated against those importers in favour of intra-EC banana
producers (mainly from Canary Isles and Madeira) and importers from ACP countries.

[44] An exemplary case was Roosevelt's 'repackaging' of the American Supreme Court to change
the classical economic due process interpretation of the American Constitution.

power. If the question of 'who decides who decides' was constitutionally allocated to a single institution, all the mechanisms of countervailing powers and checks and balances would be easily undermined. Therefore, in a multi-level or federal system it is the vertical or federal conception of constitutionalism (as a form of limited government at the state and federal level) that requires the decision on 'who decides who decides' to be left unresolved. The open question should be left open.

Are conflicts therefore unavoidable? Should the conflicts between EU law and national constitutional law be subject to a *primus inter pares* (for example, international law[45] or a new Constitutional Court composed of EU and national constitutional judges[46])? Cannot different legal orders coexist in the same sphere of application under different claims of legitimacy?[47] And if they can, how can conflicts be avoided or dealt with?

The general tendency may be for national courts to comply with the 'European Constitution' but, as shown, there is still a challenge to the absolute supremacy of EU law on the part of several national high courts. This is visible either in the description that national constitutionalism makes of itself or in the dependence of EU law for effectiveness upon national law and national courts. National law still holds a veto power over EU law[48] and that is important even when it is not used. It is well known that many developments in EU law can be explained by the European Court of Justice's perception of the possible reactions by national courts. A hierarchical alternative imposing a monist authority of European law and its judicial institutions over national law would be difficult to impose in practical terms and could undermine the legitimacy basis on which European law has developed.[49] Though the grammar used by EU lawyers

---

[45] Neil MacCormick, 'Risking Constitutional Collision in Europe?', 18 *Oxford Journal of Legal Studies* (1998), 517. Although MacCormick suggests subjecting such conflicts to the arbitration of international law as a possible direction he does not really take that path and prefers to remain faithful to a totally legal pluralistic solution where the question of conflict is left open.

[46] J. H. H. Weiler, 'The European Union Belongs to its Citizens: Three Immodest Proposals', 22 *European Law Review* (1997), 150.

[47] Phelan (*Revolt or Revolution*), for example, argues that 'revolt or revolution' is unavoidable unless Community law partly redraws its claim of supremacy over national law. For a critical review of Phelan's position see MacCormick, 'Risking Constitutional Collision'; and my 'The Heteronyms of European Law', 5 *European Law Journal* (1999), 160.

[48] See D. Chalmers, 'Judicial Preferences and the Community Legal Order', 60 *Modern Law Review* (1997), 164 at 180.

[49] In the words of Chalmers, 'the regime is able to develop provided it does not significantly disrupt the egalitarian relations enjoyed between national courts and the Court of Justice': *ibid.*

in describing the process of constitutionalization may assume a top-down approach, the reality is that the legitimacy of European constitutionalism has developed in close cooperation with national courts and national legal communities which have an increasing bottom-up effect on the nature of the European legal order.[50]

We have to start reasoning in the realm of what could be called counter-punctual law. Counterpoint is the musical method of harmonizing different melodies that are not in a hierarchical relationship. The discovery that different melodies could be heard at the same time in a harmonic manner was one of the greatest developments in musical history and greatly enhanced the pleasure and art of music. In law we too have to learn how to manage the non-hierarchical relationship between different legal orders and institutions and to discover how to gain from the diversity and choices that are offered to us without generating conflicts that ultimately will destroy those legal orders and the values they sustain. There is much to be gained from a pluralist conception of the EU legal order. In a world where problems and interests have no boundaries, it is a mistake to concentrate the ultimate authority and normative monopoly in a single source. Legal pluralism constitutes a form of checks and balances in the organization of power in the European and national polities and, in this sense, it is an expression of constitutionalism and its paradoxes. But, to take full advantage of this legal pluralism, we need to conceive of forms of reducing or managing the potential conflicts between legal orders while promoting exchanges between them and requiring courts to conceive of their decisions and the conflicts of interests at hand in the light of a broader European context. This will also highlight the transnational character of many of these conflicts which is often ignored by national constitutional law.

Catherine Richmond has proposed an attractive framework for the 'legal indeterminacy' entailed in the non-hierarchical relationship between national and European legal orders. She argues that each legal order has its own viewpoint over the same set of norms[51] and that each is to take into account the changes in that set of norms arising from the other legal orders: 'each time a norm is created or amended in one particular legal order, the cognitive arrangement of norms must, from our one particular viewpoint, be shuffled around in order to accommodate the

---

[50] Kamiel Mortelmans, 'Community Law: More than a Functional Area of Law, Less than a Legal System', 1 *Legal Issues of European Integration* (1996), 23 at 42–3.

[51] In the suggestive expression of Josephine Shaw: 'each national constitution creates a different "gateway" for the EU legal order'. 'Postnational Constitutionalism'.

change'.[52] However, no legal order should be forced to abandon its own viewpoint (or, if you prefer, its own cognitive framework). In her words:

> A state of legal indeterminacy is only stable, however, as long as no *normative* challenge is made to it which challenges the *political* basis of the cognitive model adopted . . . Therefore it is in all parties' interest to preserve the indeterminacy in the Community, enabling each to latch on to the model of legal authority that is politically most comfortable.[53]

Identity is lost if it is not self-determined. On the other hand, such self-determination should not dispute the self-determined identity of the other legal orders. In my view, one of the consequences ought to be that each time a legal order changes the set of norms shared with the broader European legal community it ought to do so in a manner that can be accommodated by the other legal orders (a good example being the introduction of fundamental rights protection in the Community legal order). The EU legal order should be conceived of as integrating the claims of validity of both national and EU constitutional law. Any judicial body (national or European) would be obliged to reason and justify its decisions in the context of a coherent and integrated EU legal order. I do not share the view that the best form of safeguarding legal pluralism is to recognize, pragmatically and normatively, the possibility for national constitutional authorities to derogate from EU law so long as that would not itself be recognized by EU law and would be valid under national constitutional law but not EU law. For Kumm, who has argued powerfully in favour of such a view,[54] the fact that the deviations would take place under national law and not EU law would mean that the integrity and uniformity of EU law would be safeguarded. But this would be so from a purely formal perspective. Further, the fact that the deviations would be legitimized on purely national grounds and 'not affect' EU law might promote the use and abuse of national constitutional exceptions without any form of EU control. Ultimately, it could lead to a 'race to the bottom' between national courts in the uniform application of EU law.

I argue that national deviations can still be possible but they need to be argued in 'universal' terms, safeguarding the coherence and integrity of the EU legal order. The idea is to promote the universality of national decisions on EU law and integrate them into a coherent system of interpretation of EU law by national courts. In other words, national decisions

---

[52] Catherine Richmond, 'Preserving the Identity Crisis: Autonomy, System and Sovereignty in European Law', 16 *Law and Philosophy*, 377 at 417.
[53] *Ibid.*   [54] Kumm, 'Final Arbiter'.

on EU law should not be seen as separated national interpretations and applications of EU law but as decisions to be integrated into a system of law requiring compatibility and coherence. This may raise fears of corrosion of EU law since it appears to promote and multiply national deviations from the European rule of law. However, this assumption must be confronted with the dynamics of law and legal reasoning. If a national constitutional court is aware that the decision that it will take will become part of European law as interpreted by the 'community' of national courts, it will internalize in its decisions the consequences in future cases and for the system as a whole. This will prevent national courts from using the autonomy of their legal system as a form of evasion and free-riding and will engage the different national courts and the ECJ in a true discourse and coherent construction of the EU pluralist legal order. At the same time, we should improve European legal pluralism by raising in each legal order the awareness of the constitutional boundaries of the other legal orders. And, in here, an important role is to be played by the changes in constitutional thinking which I have been arguing for, particularly the abandoning of single constitutionalism which has dominated the conceptions of national constitutionalism.

The conception of European legal pluralism or counterpunctual law advocated here safeguards the constitutional value of the paradox of who decides who decides by preserving the identity of each legal order while at the same time promoting its inclusiveness through what, according to Luhmann and Teubner, could be described as a process of reflexivity. Not only identity but also communication needs to be fostered between national and European legal orders. In this case, 'the fact that we define our identity by exclusion from the other does not ultimately exclude because there is no way of knowing where the next redefinition will go'.[55] This discourse between different legal orders and different institutions resulting from the emerging European polity is a further promotion of constitutionalism, broadening its deliberative elements beyond the exclusive deliberative communities involved in each national institution.

Conclusion

I have tried to show the hidden assumptions of national constitutionalism and how many of them are artificial. It is artificial to assume the national

---

[55] Bańkowski and Christodoulidis, 'The European Union as an Essentially Contested Project', 4 *European Law Journal* (1998), 341 at 351–2.

polity as the natural jurisdiction for full representation and participation. It is artificial always to take the parliamentary system as the default form of representation and its decisions as a simple expression of the 'volonté générale'. It is artificial to conceive of interests as homogeneously divided according to national borders and, within those, according to particular institutions. It is artificial to make institutional choices on the basis of single institutional analysis. Finally, it is artificial to think that constitutionalism can allocate a final authority as to who decides who decides when constitutionalism is precisely about dividing (and, in this way, limiting) authority. As a consequence of the limits of national constitutionalism, there is no a priori higher claim of validity for national constitutionalism vis-à-vis European constitutionalism.

I have also stressed that many of the perceived European constitutional problems are simply reflections of three paradoxes that are at the core of constitutionalism: the paradox of the polity; the fear of the few and the fear of the many; and the question of who decides who decides. I have related those paradoxes to the limits of national constitutionalism and the problems of its European version. The reconstruction of the tools of constitutionalism to be employed in framing the European Constitution must depart from those paradoxes. In this process, European integration may promote the reformation of national constitutionalism, challenging old habits such as single constitutionalism. The diversity of interests and forms of institutional representation and participation is not compatible with single constitutionalism and its focus on the political process as the default form of representation. We have to develop a more complex constitutional analysis which can help us in making the difficult choices identified in this chapter. In making these choices we should assess the different institutional alternatives according to a common constitutional criterion, creating a constitutional language that will allow us not only to assess better institutional alternatives such as the political process or the courts, but also to integrate in this discourse phenomena such as 'regulatory models' and decision-making by the market. The overall consequence is an extension of the scope of constitutionalism, allowing us to face the growing atomization and de-territorialization of power. As Zagrebelsky has noted, we may be moving from the 'sovereignty of the State' to the 'sovereignty of the Constitution'.[56]

European constitutionalism will continue to be in crisis. However, there are good reasons to look also at the 'sunny side of the street'. Some of the

---

[56] Zagrebelsky, *Il Diritto Mite*, 9.

problems of European constitutionalism are old problems of constitutionalism that constitutional lawyers have, to a large extent, ignored. As
constitutional lawyers, we have to take seriously the task of facing these
problems without some of the traditional medicines that may now be
shown to have been artificial panaceas that have been killing the patient
by hiding the disease.

5

The European Union as a polycentric polity: returning to a neo-medieval Europe?

MARLENE WIND

Introduction

> Between the cooperation of existing nations and the breaking of a new one
> there is no stable middle ground. A federation that succeeds becomes a
> nation; one that fails leads to secession; half-way attempts...must either
> snowball or roll back.[1]

Federate or perish. That is how Stanley Hoffmann characterized the options for Europe in a famous comment made in 1966. In the eyes of Hoffmann the European Community would never be able to survive as an 'in-between organization' in constant turmoil. It had either to put on traditional federal clothing or to dissolve itself altogether. Hoffmann's comment is almost forty years old but could just as well have been taken from the ongoing debate about the future of Europe. It resembles remarkably the words of the German foreign minister Joschka Fischer in his widely cited speech at Humboldt University in May 2000.[2] Fischer argued that 'The consequence of the irrefutable enlargement of the EU is...erosion or integration.' Confronted with two enormous challenges, 'enlargement as quick as possible' and 'Europe's capacity to act', Europe is forced in a federal direction – at least if one seriously wants to avoid erosion of the entire European project.

It is not the first time that enlargement is used as an argument for further integration, but Fischer's proposal is far from straightforward. He sees flexibility, or 'enhanced cooperation' as some prefer to call it, as an inroad to a more federal Europe. The EU should, Fischer argues, skip the 'Monnet method' where all members have to integrate simultaneously and follow the same goals, and opt instead for a mechanism where only those Member States that are able and willing to integrate further can do so.

[1] Hoffmann 1966.   [2] Fischer 2000.

The question is, however, whether federation is the logical consequence of flexibility. In this chapter I argue that this is far from being the most likely outcome. A more frequent use of flexible integration will rather result in a more heterogeneous Union that in its basic nature will escape traditional concepts like 'state' or 'federation'. Flexibility, particularly the variable geometry version of it,[3] may thus constitute a useful conceptual tool that can counter the often restricting conception of Europe as always either a potential state or a purely international organization. Some of the questions to be raised are: (1) What is flexibility when seen in the historical context of the European integration process? (2) Why is the emergence of a constitutionally less coherent Union so difficult for many Community lawyers and other analysts to accept? (3) How has the concept of the state and the idea of a harmonious legal order coloured the way we look at Europe today? (4) What are the likely constitutional implications of invoking flexibility as a means of integrating a still more diversified European Union?

Concepts on the move

Not only among practical politicians but also among the academy of Europeanists there seems to be great conceptual anxiety when it comes to dealing with phenomena that do not fit well into our pre-established categories. As we saw in the Hoffmann/Fischer debate above, political systems that do not fit into a federal or traditional nation-state model are regarded as inherently unstable and will sooner or later either evaporate altogether or merge into one of our ready-made frameworks.

Philip Schmitter seems to be an exception to the rule however. He has long acknowledged the need for a new vocabulary when talking about the European future.[4] In a comment on the future of the nation state in Western Europe, he argues that if conceptual innovation is to result, it is scholars (and other idealists!) who have to provide the necessary tool-kit. Or to put it differently, in order to loosen up pre-established images, scholars need to be in the forefront when it comes to launching conceptual alternatives. As Schmitter notes, 'nothing ever disappears in political life until its replacement has already been discovered and is functioning effectively'.[5] While it seems somewhat difficult to evaluate the 'effectiveness' of what at this stage will be nothing but mental maps of an emerging European order, one needs at least, as Schmitter puts it, to have 'some

[3] See p. 105 below.   [4] Schmitter 1996.   [5] *Ibid.*, 212–13.

alternative set of viable practices in mind, no matter how ideologically misguided they were and subsequently disillusioned they become'.[6] As he continues:

> whatever is going to replace the SNS (sovereign nation state) in Europe must already exist, even if it has not yet been acknowledged as such or has yet to reach the magnitude to make it a viable substitute. Unless and until a sufficient number of actors recognize that there exist alternatives ... beneath and beyond the existing SNS and ISS (the inter-state-system), it is highly likely that both will survive no matter how badly they perform.

May it then be that alternatives to our well-known state model already exist out there and what is lacking is a *language* for describing them? According to Neil Walker this is indeed the case. As he puts it, 'the drift away from the constitutional state as the center of legal authority seems to have lacked the language to advance the debate, whether in explanatory or normative terms'.[7]

One of the main purposes of this chapter is to propose new categories for conceiving of political organization in Europe. This is done first by linking the current debate of flexibility with the concept of legal polycentricity and by taking a brief look at the way in which we have conceptualized the state and the state-system in European history.[8] As opposed to Joschka Fischer's federal vision, this analysis uses flexibility as a key to unlock our understanding of the increasingly diversified character of the European Union. The aim of what follows is thus to situate the debate on flexibility within a broader constitutional and historical context. First, however, we will have to get a better idea of the way in which flexible integration has been used in the European integration process.

The Union as a system of exceptions and opt-outs?

'Flexibility' as an instrument of integration was first *formally* blue-stamped with the adoption of the Amsterdam Treaty in 1997. For the first time in the history of the European Community, the flexibility mechanism was written into the general principles of a treaty document. Inscribing flexibility into the Treaty has been seen by many analysts as an almost revolutionary step – some have even described it as the first step towards a dissolution of the entire Union. The argument is that it breaks the traditional Community orthodoxy under which no *permanent* derogations

---

[6] *Ibid.*, 213.   [7] Walker 1999, 23.   [8] See pp. 118–23 below.

to the Community *acquis* have been acceptable.[9] While flexibility as a *temporary* mechanism has always been part of the Community toolbox when it has come to helping new, less advanced Member States to adapt to the Community *acquis*, it was never the intention that members should be granted permanent exceptions to the common rules and principles.

As in most other Community matters however, severe disagreements flourish about how one should interpret the *long-term* implications of this new invention. Is flexibility, as La Serre and Wallace have put it, a 'Placebo or a Panacea'?[10] Some analysts have seen the adoption of the flexibility provisions in Amsterdam as nothing but an attempt to make a virtue out of the necessity experienced in the Maastricht negotiations. Here the desire to incorporate more far-reaching policies into the Community structure, i.e. the EMU, put strong pressure on finding a more pliant formula for integration. Due to the increasing reluctance of some Member States, combined with a certain fatigue with the foot-dragging members among those countries that seek further integration, the Community simply had to accept a less harmonious structure where some are on board and others are left behind.

But this is not the only way to look at it. Some have given the flexibility mechanism a more creative interpretation. They have seen it, not as the lowest common denominator solution, but as a means of facilitating integration by relaxing the formerly strict Community discipline in order to let Member States integrate, not only at different speeds but also at different levels. In this more positive narrative, it is hypothesized that the more integrationist members, by cooperating more closely in some important areas like, for instance, the EMU and foreign and asylum policy, could become the new motors of the 'integration train'. This interpretation would probably be close to that of Herr Fischer discussed above. Differentiated integration is in this narrative seen as of crucial importance for avoiding the enlargement with the new Central and East European states turning the Community into nothing but a loose free-trade zone. It is not difficult to imagine how enlargement without a significant reform of the Community institutions might undermine the already established decision-making system and not least the Community's ability to act. If the concessions already made in the Nice Treaty turn out to be insufficient and if no agreement can be reached at the intergovernmental conference in 2004, flexibility could even turn out to be a substitute for institutional reform. Few observers would see this outcome as ideal but it might nevertheless be the only way out if the situation is deadlocked.

[9] Wessels and Jantz 1997.   [10] La Serre and Wallace 1997.

In sum, in spite of the fact that flexibility as such is not a new invention in the history of the Community, it was not until the Maastricht intergovernmental conference on Political and Monetary Union that flexibility as an instrument of integration gained constitutional significance. It was not until Maastricht that permanent derogations to the Treaty were accepted (and later codified in the Amsterdam Treaty) as a tool for mediating among those Member States which wanted either a more or a less integrated Europe.[11]

A historical sketch

As indicated above, flexibility is far from being a new phenomenon: in fact it is quite the contrary. It has always been there, though primarily as a means of managing the accession of new Member States in the enlargements of the Community in 1972, 1981, 1986 and 1995.[12] It has also been a predominant feature in the ongoing enlargement process with Central and Eastern Europe that will be finalized with their accession on 1 May 2004. New Member States have thus always been in need of transitional periods when the Community *acquis* was to be adopted. It is, however, important to distinguish between different types of derogations. *Traditional*, or what most analysts refer to as 'multi-speed' flexibility, represents those *time-based* 'exceptions' to the general Community *acquis* that are found in accession agreements with most new Member States. Another example of an older flexibility arrangement would be the provision that has allowed Luxembourg and Belgium to cooperate more closely on a common currency, something they did long before the establishment of the Community. This arrangement thus comes closer to what I will refer to below as *variable* or *permanent* flexibility, where some Member States can cooperate more closely on a more enduring basis. In the more traditional category we also find acceptance of allowing the UK to maintain its special imports of New Zealand butter; Greece and Portugal's special treatment regarding a delayed implementation of the Community environmental legislation; Denmark's second home rule; Sweden's ability to maintain its 'snooze'; and so on.[13] The important thing to note about the above-mentioned arrangements, however, is that they serve a purely managerial function. They are for the most part ad hoc exceptions to concrete

---

[11] Shaw 1997, 6; J. Janning 1997.   [12] See Nomden 1997; Shaw 1997; Stubb 1996.

[13] Koen Nomden has moreover referred to Art. 36 of the Rome Treaty as a flexibility instrument. Art. 36 allows Member States with very good excuses to maintain exceptions to the internal market rules on imports. See Nomden 1997.

adaptation problems. They are, moreover, small and often temporary and do not therefore bring the common objectives of the Community into question. It is thus more than likely that these types of arrangements will continue to be a quite effective – though not necessarily sufficient – mechanism to solve adaptation problems in the years ahead.

As noted already, the debate on differentiated integration has, however, been given a different twist in the past years and it is this 'new twist' which is the most interesting part of the present discussion. With the Maastricht, Amsterdam and, in particular, the Nice Treaty, flexibility is no longer 'just' an instrument at hand to solve practical problems in connection with enlargement of the Union. Flexibility has – by being written into the general provisions of the treaty – been accepted as a mechanism of a more *enduring* nature that may turn out in the long run to create a Union that looks very different from the one we know today.

The idea of using flexibility as a mechanism for integration where not all members play by the same rules was very controversial when it was put forward. It was first suggested in a report by the German CDU/CSU in 1994. The report was written by two (then) leading German Christian democrats, Karl Lamers and Wolfgang Schäuble.[14] They argued that in order not to lose momentum in the integration process as the Community was enlarged, *differentiated integration* should be accepted and even institutionalized as a means of letting the more capable Member States deepen their integration in some cardinal areas while leaving less capable and more reluctant Member States behind. More specifically, Lamers and Schäuble proposed a so-called *Kerneuropa* which was identifiable with Germany, France and the Benelux countries. The fear was that, if the Community was enlarged without being integrated simultaneously, a reversion to a *competitive* instead of a *cooperative* dynamics between, in particular, France and Germany would be the likely result. The *Kerneuropa* should thus integrate deeper than the rest in areas of, for instance, monetary and fiscal policy, defence and wider political union. This, it was suggested, would create a new momentum in the overall integration process to the benefit of all.[15]

The report was not very well received however. Originally, the *Kerneuropa* was proposed as a *multi-speed* arrangement where the more able countries would take the lead and the more reluctant would follow later. The provocative feature of the Lamers/Schäuble plan was, however, that it explicitly pointed out which countries were the natural candidates to

---

[14] Gillespie 1997; La Serre and Wallace 1997.   [15] Gillespie 1997, 50.

participate in the core, and thus a priori excluded the remaining Member States – even an old member like Italy. The report was thus accused of creating a Europe of first and second division members where it would be up to the first division alone to decide about subsequent inclusions of new 'inner-circle candidates'.[16] A second problem which worried many was that the *Kerneuropa* as launched by Lamers and Schäuble gradually might undermine the *acquis* because different rules were likely to develop within the different 'divisions' and areas of cooperation.

While former Chancellor Kohl did not explicitly endorse the Lamers/Schäuble proposal he was clearly sympathetic to its main argument. This became obvious when he, in commenting on John Major's speech in Leiden in 1994 (where Major insisted on maintaining unanimity in all Community decision-making), emphasized that: 'the slowest ship could not be allowed to dictate the speed of the convoy'.[17] There is little doubt that the slow ship in this specific context was the UK. For Kohl, as well as for Lamers/Schäuble, flexibility had a double purpose. It was regarded as a means of speeding up the integration process but it was also a threat of exclusion: 'If you don't want to go along with us – we will proceed without you.'

The 1994 German paper on flexible integration was however not the first (nor the last) to discuss possibilities in differentiated integration as a means of bringing about new dynamics. Willy Brandt had already, in 1974, talked about the need for a two-speed integration process in Europe.[18] Brandt argued that because Member States have such diverse economic starting points a *non-differentiated* treatment in relation to the Community *acquis* might harm rather than strengthen the solidarity between them. Behind the proposal was the idea that 'the economically stronger Member States would have the obligation to come to the aid of the weaker, and that the slow speed group should take part in but not have the right to veto the actions of the leading group'.[19]

Supplementing the German contributions to the flexibility debate, the former French Prime Minister Edouard Balladur presented his ideas on

[16] Curtin 1995, 241.   [17] Gillespie 1997, 51.   [18] 30 *Europa Archiv* (1975).
[19] Curtin 1995, 242. The ideas of flexibility were also mentioned in the Tindemans report from 1976. Leo Tindemans, who was the prime minister of Belgium, chose in his analysis to focus less on the development of a federal Europe and more on the need to reform the existing Community institutions. The most controversial part of the report was the call for a 'two-speed' Europe where Member States would integrate according to their own will and ability. The Tindemans report never gained any true stronghold among the heads of state and disappeared into the archives like so many other Community reports. See Dinan 1994, 94–5.

the matter in the mid-1990s. What Balladur talked about was not a 'two-speed' Europe, nor was it a Europe split up in divisions, but a Europe of *concentric circles* or *variable geometry*.[20] The novelty in the Balladur proposal, compared to the Lamers/Schäuble report, was that the circles were separated on *subject matter* rather than on which Member States should be in and which should be out. It thus opened up the perspective for a more overlapping or 'polycentric' European order where some Member States would be part of the inner circle in some policy matters and part of a second or even a third circle in others. It should, moreover, be up to the individual state – if it met the objective requirements of the circle it desired to enter – to decide whether or not to opt in. As in the Lamers/Schäuble proposal, the driving force would be the inner circle however. A second circle was then to consist of those Member States that were either unwilling or unable to meet the often more ambitious standards of the inner circle. Finally, Balladur saw a broad outer circle consisting of those Member States which had only applied for membership, for instance, and those with only very long-term prospects of membership.[21]

While the Brandt and the more recent Lamers/Schäuble and Balladur proposals represent what one could call a 'positive approach' to flexibility where differentiation serves the purpose of keeping the integration process on the 'right track', John Major's 'pick and choose' or 'open partnership' approach (the official term in his 1994 speech in Leiden) points in a somewhat different direction.[22] Major's vision – first promoted by Ralf Dahrendorf in 1979 – was clearly a return to a Europe of traditional diplomacy, where each nation's commitment only reached as far as the national interest. It was simultaneously clear, however, that the British were not happy to let a core Europe, consisting of France, Germany and the Benelux countries, move ahead through enhanced cooperation. What the UK really preferred was a pick and choose option *together* with a veto that could prevent the others from moving ahead if they should find it necessary.[23] Some observers have argued that the UK almost obtained their demands in Amsterdam where a veto on flexibility was in fact written into the Treaty.

If we, for a second, disregard this latter 'pick and choose' strategy, it is quite obvious that the most important difference between a traditional flexibility mechanism and the one suggested in particular by Balladur

---

[20] Gillespie 1997, 50.   [21] See Nomden 1997, 4.

[22] What is referred to here is John Major's William and Mary Lecture at the University of Leiden, the Netherlands, 7 September 1994: 'A European Future that Works' (unpublished manuscript).

[23] La Serre and Wallace 1997, 11.

is that, while the former is a temporary or 'ad hoc' instrument to facilitate periods of transition, the latter implicitly accepts differentiated
integration as a permanent part of the integration process. This type of
permanent flexibility was, however, already well known in areas that used
to be *outside* the Treaty, like the WEU, Schengen, the European Monetary
System and so on. After the adoption of the Maastricht Treaty in 1992,
many observers asked themselves whether the all-embracing Community
structure would fall apart due to the institutionalization of permanent exceptions and partial memberships in different Community policy areas.
Several observers also feared that the three-pillared structure of the Treaty
might disrupt the prospect of a unitary legal order due to the intergovernmental character of pillars two and three. As we shall see below, Deirdre
Curtin has few doubts: 'Such a system inevitably would introduce different legal rights and obligations of membership among the Member States
breaking with the backbone of the system hitherto, the unitary nature of
the institutional system and creating even more complicated procedures
of decision making differing from policy area to policy area.'[24] As I will
show this seemingly pessimistic picture need not, however, be the only
viable outcome.

We can now distinguish three different types of flexibility:[25]

(a) A classical 'multi-speed' version where the common objectives are
preserved and where the Community rules in principle apply evenly
to all. This type of flexibility accepts that Member States (especially
acceding ones) which may be facing very difficult domestic problems
need to be granted temporary exceptions to the standard Community
requirements. The multi-speed provision thus allows for these often
less-developed Member States only gradually to adopt the full body
of Community rules and regulations.

   The most important conclusion to be drawn from multi-speed
forms of integration is, as Shaw has put it, that 'there is nothing constitutionally disruptive about them'.[26] Multi-speed integration has
always been there and does not as such break the ideal of a uniform
and coherent constitutional structure. The only thing it really does is
that it gives room for often less-developed Member States to adopt
the full *acquis* at a slower speed.

   It is also possible, however, to say that multi-speed flexibility *simultaneously* represents the most ambitious *and* the most constitutionally
ideal way of integrating. It is ambitious because it explicitly assumes

[24] Curtin 1995, 243.   [25] Stubb 1996, 97–131.   [26] Shaw 1997, 4.

that the possible twenty-seven members of the Community *eventually* will be able to play by exactly the same rules. It is, however, exactly this premise that also makes it most ideal – from a constitutional point of view.

(b) The second option, which was promoted by Balladur, is clearly the most interesting from a political point of view and has often been referred to as a so-called 'variable geometry' model. It opens the door for a more permanent kind of differentiated evolution of the Community and therefore also for a union that is non-state-like. In order to avoid this type of integration disrupting the Union's constitutional basis and thus creating small sub-communities with their own rules and norms, rights and obligations, the bulk of states will have to embrace some basic constitutional principles like the internal market *acquis*, the rule of law, human rights, etc.

(c) In a Europe à la carte a common *acquis* only exists as lip-service to the national interest. A Europe of only pick and choose will represent a return to traditional diplomacy and is – if implemented – most likely to result in a much less integrated Union than the one we know today. As we shall see below in the analysis of the Maastricht, Amsterdam and Nice Treaties, however, several examples of a Europe à la carte have already materialized.

Flexibility in the Maastricht Treaty

Whether one would agree with the sceptics that flexibility was nothing but a passive response to an already deadlocked situation or whether one prefers a more positive interpretation where flexibility is seen as a new avenue for speeding up the integration process, it all started in Maastricht with the acceptance of the three-pillared structure of the European Union Treaty (TEU). Here the supranational Community (Pillar One) was supplemented with two areas of a purely intergovernmental character, Common Foreign and Security Policy (Pillar Two) and Justice and Home Affairs (Pillar Three). The TEU thus not only integrated into the Union two intergovernmental pillars where the Commission, the Parliament and the Court of Justice were almost completely expelled from influence, but also included some new policy areas that concerned only some of the existing Member States. While, from a narrow constitutional point of view, it seems somewhat odd to include policy areas in a Community structure that concern only certain of its members, there was no initial intention to 'communitize' these intergovernmental pillars in the

Maastricht negotiations. Nor were the new fields like the WEU and Schengen forced on those members which had already chosen to stay outside.[27] It was nevertheless decided that the new policy areas could make use of the Community's institutional set-up, civil servants, etc.

At the conclusion of the Maastricht negotiations, it was agreed that those Member States which did not meet the convergence criteria which were required for entering the third phase of the EMU could not join the EMU. Countries that did not meet the economic requirements could become members at a later stage when their domestic finances had improved. As noted earlier, we are dealing here with a traditional multi-speed flexibility arrangement. This type of flexibility was, however, not the only type that came to apply to the EMU. At the Maastricht negotiations Britain had refused to follow suit and, after the Danish 'no' to the treaty in 1992, it became quite clear that it was impossible to form a common position either on Schengen or on the EMU. However, instead of deadlocking the negotiations (or renegotiating the Treaty) in striving for a uniform structure, a permanent flexibility arrangement was created. It now became acceptable to stay outside an agreement – not just for those Member States that *could not* (for instance, Greece) but equally for those that *would not* (Denmark and the UK) enter the third phase of the EMU. The radically new feature of these ad hoc derogations was, in other words, that some members – Denmark and the UK – which both met the criteria for full membership, were granted an 'opt-out' of a permanent or, at least, optional character.

A different construction was found for the Social Chapter in Maastricht which the Conservative British Government refused to endorse.[28] Instead of writing the Social Chapter into the Treaty while granting the UK a special status, the eventual result was a Social Protocol signed by only eleven members. According to Curtin, however, this 'remains an acute and anomalous construction'.[29] And as La Serre and Wallace note, there was a critical problem with this Protocol simply because 'it worked too well for the British Conservatives in portraying an image of triumphant exceptionalism, one which might be extended to other domains'.[30]

---

[27] Denmark, Ireland, Sweden, Finland and Austria were not originally members of the WEU.

[28] La Serre and Wallace 1997, 11ff.

[29] Curtin 1993, 29. Special declarations and Protocols were, of course, equally granted to Denmark at the Edinburgh summit in 1992.

[30] The British government actually attempted to extend these exceptions to other areas like fisheries.

It was, in other words, feared not only that Britain might claim this right to exceptionalism again, but equally that other Member States might be inspired by it.

Considering all the more or less permanent derogations contained in the final treaty documents, Maastricht thus ended up 'hijacking' parts of the *acquis communautaire* – at least if we follow Curtin.[31] As she sees it, this kind of 'protocolization' may in the end imply that there will no longer be any genuine institutional framework for the Community. While it was never the intention of the Maastricht negotiations 'to replace the existing Communities in any way [but] merely to bring certain extra-Community activities under the general umbrella of the European Union',[32] this actually happened, Curtin argues, without making these new areas accountable to the already existing democratic rules of the game. As we are to see below, however, Curtin's vision of constitutionalism is not very clear and can certainly be criticized.

From Maastricht to Amsterdam

The march towards an even more diversified European Union continued in the Amsterdam Treaty where 'enhanced cooperation' was written into the treaty as a general principle for the first time in the history of the European Community.[33]

It has often been argued that the involuntary architects of a more flexible integration strategy were the Danes, due to the turbulence resulting from the Danish referendum on the Maastricht Treaty in 1992.[34] As a small country, Denmark has never liked any of the Union's flexibility provisions however. Making it possible for some countries to move ahead without the agreement of all is analogous to dropping the veto power, and thus the influence, of the more reluctant Member states.

After Maastricht and the Danish 'no' there seemed however to be a growing awareness among the political elites in all Member States that the following IGC on enlargement and institutional reform had to take public opinion and the interests and desires of the ordinary citizen more into consideration. The Council decided at the Corfu Summit in July 1995 to establish a think tank or a so-called Reflection Group to work out a general document that could function as a basis for the 1996 IGC. Among many

---

[31] Curtin 1993, 21.   [32] *Ibid.*, 23.
[33] The general provisions are included in Arts. 43, 44 and 45 of the TEU as a new Title VII under the heading: 'Provisions on Closer Cooperation'.
[34] Kraup and Rasmussen 1998, 46.

other issues, the report by the Reflection Group gave the flexibility issue a central position. It was now no longer a question of whether there should be openings in the amended treaty for a more flexible Union, but rather what should be their scope.[35] Several of the Reflection Group's proposals were adopted in Amsterdam, though in a somewhat revised form.

The Group's basic premise was that the Union should continue to be structured around a common core formed 'by the maintenance and development of the acquis communautaire on the one hand, and the consolidation of a single institutional framework on the other'.[36] Like the later amended treaty, the Reflection Group – unsurprisingly – emphasized that an undermining of the common constitutional framework should be avoided and that an à la carte flexibility strategy was unacceptable. This was not quite how it turned out however, but there is little doubt that fear of undermining the common constitutional basis was one of the main concerns both in the report of the Reflection Group and in the final Treaty documents. There was at this stage general agreement that flexibility was not to develop into an escape clause for deadlocked decision-making in the Council.[37]

In the end the Amsterdam Treaty came to contain both important general clauses that allow for enhanced cooperation and provisions relating to the particular pillars. Of the general clauses, Art. 44 in particular is interesting in the sense that it spells out that only the Member States involved in enhanced cooperation shall take part in the adoption of decisions. Those countries that choose to stay outside the common decision may take part in the negotiations, but they do not have voting rights. The costs following from the implementation of a joint action, other than administrative costs which fall on the Community institutions, shall be met by the involved Member States themselves however.

---

[35] See Nomden 1997.   [36] *Ibid.*, 5.

[37] Art. 43 of the Amsterdam Treaty stated the following about when to make use of flexibility: Closer cooperation must (1) be aimed at furthering the objectives of the Union and at protecting and serving its interests; (2) respect the principles of the Treaties where the objectives of the Treaties cannot be attained by applying the relevant procedures laid down; (3) concern at least a majority of Member States; and (4) be open to all Member States, i.e. Member States that do not participate in closer cooperation can become parties to it at any time, provided that they comply with the basic decision and with the additional decisions taken within the framework of closer cooperation. In addition, closer cooperation must not affect either (5) the *acquis communautaire* and the measures adopted under the provisions of the Treaties, or (6) the competencies, rights, obligations and interests of those Member States that do not participate in closer cooperation. Finally, closer cooperation must comply with additional criteria laid down in the first and third pillars.

While some feared that this might lead to wide-ranging flexibility, it should be added that an important veto option was preserved – *and* even written into the treaty documents. If a Member State found that enhanced cooperation threatened its vital interest, it was allowed to veto such an initiative altogether. This veto option was later removed however. All in all, the flexibility arrangements in Amsterdam turned out to be more of symbolic than real value. The important thing in Amsterdam was thus that flexibility was put into the Treaty in the first place, signalling that Member States are willing to accept a future Union that has a less uniform character.

From Amsterdam to Nice

Flexibility was never really put to the test before the next IGC which resulted in the Nice Treaty. The 2000 IGC was set up to deal with enlargement and, in particular, the 'leftovers' from the Amsterdam Treaty. One of the key issues for which a solution had not been found in Amsterdam was: how did one prepare the EU institutions for the addition of not five but ten new countries? The Nice Treaty thus ended up dealing with questions that always provoke intense and endless discussion when new members are about to enter: how does one define the new balance of power in a new, enlarged Union? How should the votes in the Council and the Parliament be divided, and should the EU continue with a rotating Presidency after the new (and often smaller) members have joined? Then there is the debate over the European Commission: should it be reformed? Will there be jobs enough for twenty-seven Commissioners in an enlarged European Union? This latter question was eventually postponed until the European Convention set out to draft a European Constitution by the end of 2003. In Nice it was, however, agreed what the power balance between new and old members should look like and it was also decided that the Union should have a charter of basic rights, though it was up to the Convention and a 2004 IGC to decide about its legal status.[38] Flexibility was also on the agenda and, towards the end of 2000, there turned out to be broad agreement among the heads of state that it should be easier for some states to take the lead in the integration process. The situation was, however, somewhat paradoxical since the provisions for enhanced cooperation in the Amsterdam Treaty had never been in force. Thus a mechanism that had never been tested was to be revised.

---

[38] In Nice it was also decided to add more policy areas to be decided by majority voting.

In preparing the Nice Treaty the new Commission headed by Romano Prodi initiated the establishment of a group of 'wise men' who were to reflect on the themes that should be on the agenda for the negotiations.[39] One of the issues that figured prominently was indeed flexibility. The wise men argued that flexibility would be even more important in an enlarged European Union than at present. They warned against a Europe à la carte but also stressed that a small vanguard should be allowed to move ahead with integration if they so desired. In May 2000 the German foreign minister Joschka Fischer delivered his speech at Humboldt University in which flexibility was a key issue and, in June, in a talk to the German Bundestag, Jacques Chirac followed suit. He talked about the possibility of a *pioneer group* moving ahead with integration while leaving the more reluctant members behind. The argument that kept popping up in the negotiations in the autumn of 2000 before the Nice summit was that, if it was not made easier to invoke enhanced cooperation, the most eager Member States would just start cooperating outside the Treaty, skip the European institutions and establish their own small secretariat. Such a development would obviously make it more difficult for the less eager to control what was going on. At the final summit in Nice the governments thus agreed to make it easier to employ the flexibility mechanism. The most important thing that they decided was that, even in an enlarged European Union, it should take only eight countries to move ahead with further integration. In Amsterdam the provision was that a majority of the Member States should be behind such an initiative. Added to this was another important development. In Nice it was moreover decided that it should no longer be possible to veto an initiative of enhanced cooperation. This means that the emergency brake is gone and flexible integration will be possible if only eight countries are behind it. It is important to note, however, that the Member States also agreed that enhanced cooperation should not disrupt the *acquis communautaire*.[40] There thus seems to be a certain fear that a Europe à la carte might replace a Europe of variable geometry.

Even though the outcome of the flexibility provisions can seem somewhat limited and even though, at this point, it is quite hard to predict the overall consequences for the Community if the mechanism is further

---

institutionalized, there is little doubt that the traditional rigid concept of integration has been supplemented by a new form that breaks the old orthodoxy of constitutionalism. Whereas traditional theoretical approaches to integration, such as intergovernmentalism, functionalism, neofunctionalism and federalism, etc., all implicitly or explicitly rest on a very static model, with the nation state hiding somewhere in the background, flexible integration – if employed in its variable geometry form – confronts this traditional image head on.

In the remaining part of this analysis, concrete discussion of flexible integration will be linked to a more speculative analysis of polycentricity. In support of Schmitter, we will try to be a little innovative in our search for a better description of the 'European Beast'. The flexibility discussion will thus draw on some of the more adventurous recent debates in legal theory as well as work developed by so-called critical theorists in political science.[41] The aim will be partly to problematize the classical legal dogma that legal systems need to be unified, coherent and hierarchical, partly to question the parallel conventional political science image of the hierarchical, territorial state as the only viable building block in international society. The ambition is not to provide a final model of a future European Union, but rather to contribute to the attempt to redraw our inherently conservative mental maps of what a political system ought to look like.

From unity to polycentricity – a resurrection of the Holy Roman Empire?

> Let's have the courage to say it. Tomorrow's Union will no doubt be made up of two distinct levels: a Union of common law, comprising the fifteen present members and those with the vocation to join it; at the heart of this Union of this first circle, a second circle, more limited, but durable, made up of a small number of states at the center of which will be France and Germany, nations prepared and willing to go further or faster than the others on subjects such as the currency or defense.[42]

One inroad to understanding the concerns that many observers have when it comes to accepting a European Union where flexibility has gained a central position is through studying the editorials of mainstream

---

[41] For a good introduction to critical and post-structuralist international relations theory see Booth, Smith and Zalewski 1996.
[42] Agence Europe, 15 March 1996.

Community law journals, in particular the *Common Market Law Review*. Scrutinizing the editorials from the time when flexibility was first introduced thus gives one a quite telling picture of how many legal analysts think, not only about the recent treaty developments, but also about the European future.

For most legal observers flexibility is not their favourite cup of tea. As the *Common Market Law Review* editorial that appeared after the conclusion of the Amsterdam Treaty[43] phrased it, 'significant doubts must now be raised as to whether the constitutional structure and coherence of the European Union can be preserved'. Flexibility, as the editor sees it, constitutes a very dangerous development primarily because it has now been generally accepted that the so-called 'community discipline' no longer applies evenly to everyone. The Union has, in other words, turned into a Community of exceptions and 'opt-outs' and is now characterized by many centrifugal forces that, according to the editor, blur its unity and 'general design':

> Not only are there a number of protocols and declarations which disfigure the unity of the Treaty, and not only is the 'pillar' structure maintained, but within each pillar, including the 'Community pillar', a number of exceptions, escape clauses, special regimes of flexibility, and special provisions concerning the jurisdiction of the Court blur the general design of the European Union. This makes the construction indecipherable even for experts, not to mention the man in the street.[44]

Similar concerns were raised by several lawyers in the wake of the Maastricht Treaty. Deirdre Curtin, for instance, became famous for talking about the new Union Treaty as one of 'bits and pieces' and for saying that the entire Community had turned so inherently fragmentary and diffuse that it represented a 'democratic retrogression'.[45] The problem is that parliamentary and juridical control were excluded from the intergovernmental pillars two and three, a fact that might undermine the transparency and democratic legitimacy of the Union.[46]

---

[43] Editorial Comment 1997. See also the more optimistic comment by the editor, 34 *Common Market Law Review* (1997), 767–72.

[44] Editorial Comment 1997, 1108.   [45] Curtin 1993, 21–2. See also Curtin 1995.

[46] As Curtin puts it: 'from the point of view of liberal democracy the danger of democratic retrogression is real if matters are taken out of the national systems and intergovernmentalized, but not within the Community system (with its concomitant parliamentary and judicial control). This is largely because governmental decisions in international matters are only very weakly accountable in modern democracies.' See Curtin 1993, 20.

But the democratic deficit is not the only problem with the recent treaty amendments. What many legal observers find even worse, whether in Maastricht, Amsterdam or Nice, is a gradual disintegration of the *acquis communautaire*. The agreement to let the UK and Denmark stay out of the EMU possibly even permanently, the UK's original refusal to accept the Community Social Chapter and Denmark's four exceptions all indicate a weakening of the *acquis* which may have serious consequences. Renaud Dehousse has seen these trends as disturbing and has referred to the Maastricht Treaty as a 'Union without unity' or a 'house half-built... suddenly abandoned by its builders'.[47]

Many analysts have thus regarded it as somewhat paradoxical that a 'protocolization' of the Community was allowed in the first place, considering that the Preamble to the Union treaties continues to talk about a 'new stage in the process of creating an ever closer union among the peoples of Europe', where one of the central objectives is to *preserve and extend* the *acquis communautaire*.[48] But what does it in fact mean to talk about unity and coherence of the Community structure which so many lawyers call for? Curtin defines constitutional coherence in this manner: 'a logically structured entity absorbing (or expanding) the existing Communities and all its achievements and building further on the basis of that – solid – *foundation*. It implies a single institutional framework and uniform applicability and enforcement of Union law.'[49] What is left of such a 'single institutional framework' after the initial steps towards a more flexible Union is, as Curtin sees it, 'mere lip-service to an ideal'. Maastricht is 'single only in the sense that the intergovernmental pillars do not have institutions of their own'.[50] A similar description of the 'Amsterdam Monster' has been presented by Philip Allott: 'The Amsterdam Treaty will mean the co-existence of dozens of different legal and economic sub-systems over the next ten years, a sort of nightmare resurrection of the Holy Roman Empire.'[51]

It is quite clear that the above reflections on Community development over the past ten years not only represent a few more or less technical expert comments on the amended treaties. They also implicitly or explicitly raise some very fundamental constitutional concerns related to the long-term architecture of the Union. To many Community lawyers and others occupied with a uniform and uncontradictory development of the

---

[47] Dehousse 1994, 12–13.   [48] Curtin 1993, 45–6.
[49] *Ibid.*, 22. Emphasis by the author.   [50] *Ibid.*, 28.
[51] Allott, cited in Shaw 1997.

constitutional structure, the preservation of a homogenous Community is clearly the centre of attention and therefore quickly comes to overshadow the otherwise more positive, pragmatic aspects of the flexibility mechanism.[52] As Weiler has put it: 'The holiest cow of all has been the preservation of the acquis communautaire and, within the acquis, the Holy of Holies is the constitutional framework of the Community.'[53]

There is little doubt that many lawyers have the *nation state* as their ideal when they talk about law and legal systems. It is quite obvious that in talking about constitutional unity, coherence and so on, a lot of theoretical luggage is already taken on board. What is implied in raising the question of fragmentation as a consequence of flexibility in the first place are, in other words, some very specific ideas about what a 'true' constitutional order *ought* to look like. The underlying image is a nicely organized hierarchical polity with no internal contradictions and with all rules and norms applying universally to everyone.[54] It is also the image of a polity where there are no doubts as to who is the final arbiter of constitutionality in all Community matters.[55]

In such a vision, an increased use of flexibility would necessarily imply fragmentation or an 'intergovernmentalization' of the Community. However, one can also raise the question of whether this way of thinking about law and legal/political systems has prevented us from conceiving of a European polity where things are less nicely organized. Some so-called pluralist legal theorists have in recent years emphasized this point and have warned strongly against a direct duplication of the traditional state model in the European Union.[56] The Swedish legal theorist Anna Christensen has described the link between a harmonious legal system and the state in the following manner: 'The Western legal system is connected with the state in such a way that there can be only one legal system in one and the same state. The legal system emanates from the state. We have even created a mythical figure to personify the state will.'[57] Thomas Wilhelmsson has defined conventional legal thinking in this manner:

> Traditional legal theory constructs the legal order as a harmonious and systematic whole. Legal doctrine transforms the legal order into a legal system. The elements of this system are constructed to appear as consistent.

---

[52] Shaw 1997, 8.   [53] Weiler 1997, 98.
[54] MacCormick 1993; Petersen and Zahle 1995.   [55] MacCormick 1995.
[56] See for instance MacComick 1993; MacCormick 1995; Petersen and Zahle 1995; G. Teubner (1996), 'The King's Many Bodies: The Selfdeconstruction of Law's Hierarchy', manuscript; Christensen 1995; Bellamy and Castiglione 1997.
[57] Christensen 1995, 235.

> The perceived unity of legal order is secured by reference to a basic external
> legitimation of the law, 'the ideational source of law', such as God, reason,
> nature etc.

But, as he continues: 'This construction of law as a unified system has
always been a fiction.'[58] It is not that fictions are not important or should
not be taken seriously in any social analysis. However, what these critical legal theorists suggest is that we should stop forcing a hierarchical
structure on a Community that is not – and probably never will be – a
hierarchical unitary polity in the true state-centric sense of the term. The
Danish legal theorist Henrik Zahle has contributed to the development of
a theoretical language that can account for political systems like that of the
EU which, as he sees it, has a much more decentralized structure than that
favoured by the ECJ, most Community lawyers or any political federalist.
Zahle employs the term 'polycentricity' to describe such a system in its
extreme form:

> in a polycentrical order there are no fixed hierarchical relations, and the
> relations of internal deviation that can be proved in a conflict do not exist
> in a stable form. This conflicting ambition within the individual orders,
> this instability is not new, but has perhaps been less noticed earlier, and
> the breaking up of fundamental divisions and relations has increased the
> uncertainty . . . between national law and international law, between private
> law and public law, between state law and informal non-authoritative law,
> between cooperative law, private law and state law.[59]

A polycentric approach would thus reject that the hierarchical nation state
is the only *or* the best model to describe the European Union as it looks
today or may come to look in the future. One might instead try to see the
Community as consisting of an ongoing dialogue or negotiation between
multiple networks and levels – each claiming its interpretation to be the
valid one. This is also, as MacCormick has pointed out, an acceptance
of the fact that not all legal problems can be solved legally.[60] It is an
acceptance that courts and legal systems can only go so far. When some
delicate cases appear before the courts, judges will have to refuse to solve

---

[58] Wilhelmsson 1995, 125.
[59] Zahle 1995, 196. See also Griffiths 1995. He defines legal pluralism as follows: 'The new
paradigm, as far as the social scientific study of law is concerned, is legal pluralism: the
legal order of all societies is not an exclusive, systematic and unified hierarchical ordering
of normative propositions depending on the state but has its sources in the self-regulatory
activities of all the multifarious social fields present [in society]' (p. 202).
[60] MacCormick 1995, 265.

them by legal means alone. Judges will simply have to acknowledge the cases' inherently political character and leave it to the politicians to make a final choice.[61]

Flexible integration and Europe as a polycentric polity?

As we saw above there is little doubt that with the last treaty revisions, the Member States have escaped from former principles of coherence and opened up previously unknown avenues for differentiated integration inside the Community structure.[62] The worry of the editor of the *Common Market Law Review* and several others mentioned above was that such a development might turn out to threaten the constitutional framework of the Union. The fear is far from unfounded if various derogations will transform the Community into small subsystems with their own legal logic rules and norms. Those who are less occupied with uniformity and coherence have a different view however. Could one not, as La Serre and Wallace argue, see enhanced cooperation as a 'miracle solution that would allow the Union to have the best of both worlds. It would provide a means of organizing diversity in an increasingly heterogeneous Europe, while at the same time preserving an integration dynamic. Thus the old contradiction between "widening" and "deepening" would be resolved.'[63]

This does not mean, however, that we should disregard the constitutional effects of flexibility altogether. Before we draw any conclusions it may be beneficial just for a moment to consider our modern heritage and

---

[61] Philip Schmitter has launched parallel ideas reflecting on the increased use of flexibility in the European Union. Institutional flexibility thus tends to blur the lines between identity and jurisdiction and may result neither in a federal polity nor in a renationalization, but in a system that Schmitter has referred to as a 'condominium' where there is a variation in both territorial and functional constituencies. Schmitter 1996, 136.

[62] Observers often forget that, even though there may be rather strict limitations to the application of flexibility in the Amsterdam Treaty structure, there have been several other important examples of enhanced cooperation *outside* the Treaty. A good example was the so-called EURO-Group. It was established under strong protests from the non-EMU members in 1997, that is, those members that did not at the outset take part in the final phase of the EMU, in particular Denmark and the UK, but also Sweden and Greece. The purpose of the Group is to co-ordinate the macro-economic policies of the EMU members on an informal basis. The out-countries – which are only allowed to participate when the issues discussed are considered to be vital to them *by the in-countries* – fear that this high-profile body may supplant the so-called ECOFIN Council consisting of the finance ministers of the Union.

[63] La Serre and Wallace themselves do not end on such a positive note however. See La Serre and Wallace 1997, 5.

try to relate that to the ongoing debate. Several things suggest that we need to rethink fundamentally the manner in which we conceive of legal and political systems in order to get out of the current conceptual deadlock. In this we can draw not only on legal theory but certainly also on recent writing within political science.

Revisiting sovereignty

Most of us have been brought up with the image of the modern state. Inherent in this image was the idea not only that political systems have to be hierarchically organized but also that this system should have a final arbiter of law – a sovereign – over which no other authorities can decide.[64] This historical image of the European nation state has, however, been transformed from an *empirical fact* that shaped life in Europe from the Thirty Years War onwards to an *ontological claim* on which much modern theorizing is based.[65] The state is thus no longer a question, a historical object of analysis that needs to be explained and situated in a concrete social context, but has been turned into a mythical entity that is taken for granted and left largely unproblematized. The result has been that we have a tremendously hard time conceiving of political systems where territory, identity and power are separated, functionally and/or spatially. We thus continue ending up with the federal or the national model as the only conceivable outcomes of international transformation. The study of the European integration process is a glaring example in this respect. But clearly these two archetypes are not the only ones out there (Weiler 1999). Though many modellers of world politics tend to forget it, Europe *did not* always consist of nicely hierarchically organized enclaves.[66] The question is thus whether we can use the past to open our eyes to the present and the future. What, in other words, did Europe look like before the territorially based European states system emerged and captured our minds? What type of rule, what type of authoritative relations did we have?

With the emergence of the European states system after the Thirty Years War in 1648, the 'sovereign' only gradually turned into the ultimate source of authority from which all legal rules should originate. What characterized the world (or at least Europe) before the end of the Thirty Years War and the treaties of Münster and Osnabrück which made up the peace settlement at Westphalia was *not* rulers with exclusive powers, that is, rulers encapsulated by well-defined territorial boundaries, capabilities

---

[64] Trubeck 1972.   [65] Bartelson 2001. See also Wind 2001.   [66] Wind 2001.

and functions as we now know them, but rather diffuse overlapping power relations.[67] This was feudalism together with the spiritual 'unity' of Roman law. As John Ruggie has delineated the medieval system:

> The feudal state, if the concept makes any sense at all, consisted of chains of lord–vassal relationships. Its basis was fief, which was an amalgam of conditional property and private authority. Property was conditional in that it carried with it explicit social obligations. And authority was private in that the rights of jurisdiction and administration over the inhabitants of a fiefdom resided personally in the ruler. Moreover, the prevailing concept of usufructure meant that multiple titles to the same landed property were the norm. As a result, the mediaeval system of rule reflected a patchwork of overlapping and incomplete rights of government which were inextricably superimposed and tangled, and in which different juridical instances were geographically interwoven and stratified, and plural allegiances, asymmetrical suzerainties and anomalous enclaves abounded.[68]

Europe was thus structured in a way that bore little resemblance to the state system we know today. It was not until the middle of the seventeenth century that 'the characteristics of possessiveness and exclusiveness associated with the modern concepts of sovereignty'[69] got institutionalized in most parts of Europe. 'Diplomats' (or just messengers of a certain ruler) regarded themselves as representatives of Christendom and the Roman Church *and not* as servants of the ruler who had appointed them.[70] The medieval system of rule thus represented, as Ruggie has put it, 'a heteronomous organization of territorial rights and claims'.[71]

This does not mean, however, that sovereignty as a territorial right to exclusion of other powers had gained general acceptance by the seventeenth century. In Germany (or what we now call so) the concept of sovereignty had no meaning whatsoever until the late eighteenth century:

> It comes as no surprise to find that in Germany the concept and the vocabulary of sovereignty were still much obscured. Until well into the eighteenth century, when the foreign term *Souveränität* was perforce introduced, the German language possessed no word for the concept; not until the area felt the impact of Napoleon at the beginning of the nineteenth century did the

---

[67] See Tilly 1975; Anderson 1983, 37–8; Giddens 1985, 38–41, 80–2.
[68] Ruggie 1986, 142.   [69] Camilleri 1990, 13.
[70] Der Derian 1987; Wight 1977, 28–33, 141–2.
[71] Ruggie 1986, 143. Or, as Martin Wight has put it: 'If the medieval society provides an example of a states-system at all, which I am inclined to deny, it is a uniquely complicated dualistic or double-headed suzerain state-system.' Wight 1977, 29.

meaning of this word come fully to correspond to that of the French and
English term.[72]

What can we then learn from this? First and foremost it is extremely problematic, not least when trying to conceive of change in the international
system, that the state and the concept of sovereignty – in the bulk of modern legal and political science literature – have been conflated with an
ontological proposition.

Would it then, one could ask, be possible to extend the metaphor of
pre-modern Europe to the diversity we experience in Europe today? Could
the image of overlapping authorities in the medieval world broaden our
understanding of what legal and political systems *can* look like?

Some legal scholars have taken up this idea by arguing that the harmonization of standards, laws and regulations in the Community and the
role that the European Court has played in establishing 'a new legal order'
could be seen as an attempt to unify European law on a grand scale in
the Roman image. As Thomas Wilhelmsson has put it: 'The nationally
disintegrated law is seen as a parenthesis between the medieval strongly
homogenous European legal culture based on Roman and canonic law
and a new integrated EC law.'[73] It could perhaps be tempting to buy into
this seductive narrative; however, the entire idea of unity, hierarchy, and
coherence in the law is an inherently modern one that did not exist in the
Holy Roman Empire. The 'unity' of Roman law was, in other words, very
different from what we understand by unity and coherence today. The
Roman Empire was highly polycentric and consisted of many layers and
interlocking compartments of legal norms and rules. These coexisted side
by side, linked together in a common norm system, yet semi-autonomous
and self-defining.

May it then be that what we are currently witnessing in Europe is the
emergence of a similar polycentric system with unity in diversity? If we relate the more concrete discussion of flexibility to this conceptual analysis,

[72] The German language contained in fact several different words for 'rule'. Until the middle
of the eighteenth century one could find a word for rule like 'Machtvoll-kommenheit',
emphasizing, as Hinsley puts it: 'absolute and technocratic *plentitudo potestatis*'. Another
word for power or force of government was *Staatsgewalt*. A word meaning 'the dignity
of the government or the ruler' was *Majestät* and there were other words for positions of
superiority like *Obergewalt and Landeshocheit*. But, as Hinsley notes, there was no word
for sovereignty: 'The foreign word *Souveränität* was beginning to be introduced; but it
was not until the establishment of the Rhine Confederation in 1806 that princes who had
hitherto possessed *Landeshocheit*, under the nominal sovereignty of the Emperor, were
granted the *pléntitude de la souveraineté*.' Hinsley 1966, 137–8.

[73] Wilhelmsson 1995, 128. My emphasis.

it would be fundamentally wrong to conclude that the Community at the beginning of the twenty-first century is sliding back into a bundle of loosely allied states.[74] Very few political leaders, if any, would allow enhanced cooperation to develop into a simple metaphor for increased intergovernmentalism. Nor does it necessarily imply a slide towards a federal state as suggested by Joschka Fischer however. It is much more likely that we will be facing a Europe that, in its authoritative structures, differs fundamentally from anything seen previously in our modern era. Following this logic one should see the Community as constituting the first truly 'multi-centred polity' since the emergence of the European state system.[75] Instead of a new hierarchically organized sovereign construct modelled after the nation state, we may be confronting a situation where different authoritative orders and circles overlap, compete and collaborate.[76] This does not imply that we should sacrifice all attempts to preserve institutional coherence in the Community in the future and let flexibility flourish wherever the (mainly large) member states so desire. Perhaps we should turn the issue upside down. It is true that the Treaties as they have been revised recently may leave a lot to be desired, but if we look at the Community's most fundamental constitutional principles such as human rights, democracy and the rule of law, these are not that easy to undermine and will most likely also in the future constitute a solid common basis for integration. Many things suggest that this is what will happen. The current draft for a new European constitution to be negotiated and amended in 2004 indicates that there will indeed be a legally solid basic rights charter that everyone will have to abide by. There is also broad agreement among political leaders that no matter how imaginative some politicians may be in promoting new areas of cooperation with only a few Member States, these arrangements will not be allowed to create their own institutions and secretariats and in that way submerge the European institutions.

Does this then mean that there exist no contradictions between the preservation of a constitutional core and flexible integration of a more enduring character? The editor of the *Common Market Law Review* and several other learned scholars pointed to the problem of non-uniformity and constitutional messiness of the Treaties as a consequence of flexibility. They also raised the important issue of the lack of transparency and thereby implicitly of increased problems with democratic legitimacy.

[74] Everson and Snyder 1997, 207.
[75] See MacCormick 1993.   [76] Bellamy and Castiglione 1997.

There is little doubt that a treaty document that contains fewer protocols and derogations is easier to read than one which is overflowing with all kinds of exceptions. It is also obvious that a Community where rules apply differently to the same group of actors will be much more complex and thus more difficult to hold democratically accountable. However in a Europe with twenty-seven and perhaps more countries (if Turkey and the Balkans are accepted as candidates), national peculiarities and pragmatic compromises will most likely have a very high priority. The big question will then be whether European citizens will be more satisfied in the long run with a flexible Europe which preserves common constitutional principles, but which equally guarantees an acceptance of difference. If one answers this question in the negative the future of Eastern enlargement seems bleak indeed. As MacCormick has framed it: 'What is possible is not independent of what we believe to be possible. The possibility of such developments in the practical world depends upon their being grasped imaginatively by the people who make the practical world work.'[77]

The American historian Tony Judt has argued that, as he interprets things, the prospects for European unity have rarely been bleaker than in the post-Maastricht era. He even refers to it as 'the Grand Illusion'.[78] Judt argues that with the accession of several new Eastern members, 'flexibility' and a multi-speed Europe, the Community is most likely to end up as a new League of Nations. What characterized the League was that states simply opted out of those decisions they did not like and went along only with those that served their short- and long-term interests.[79] If this 'pick and choose' image were to be the necessary consequence of a more flexible Europe, differentiated integration should clearly be abandoned. But is this really a reasonable prediction? It is clear that flexible integration differs quite fundamentally from the traditional image of how the European integration process was 'meant' to proceed – in a harmonious fashion with Community rules and regulations applying equally to all. It is, however, hard to see how a Union of up to thirty members will be able to maintain the momentum if differentiated integration is expelled from its now-central position in the 'Euro-speak' directory.[80]

---

[77] MacCormick 1993, 18.   [78] Judt 1996.   [79] *Ibid.*, 6–8.
[80] The most important target in the years ahead may then be, not to avoid flexibility altogether, but to make sure that it stays inside rather than outside the Community treaties.

References

Anderson, B. (1983), *Imagined Communities. Reflections on the Origin and Spread of Nationalism* (London: Verso)

Bartelson, J. (2001), *The Critique of the State* (Cambridge: Cambridge University Press)

Bellamy, R. and D. Castiglione (1997), 'Building the Union: The Nature of Sovereignty in the Political Architecture of Europe', 16(4) *Law and Philosophy* 421

Booth, K., S. Smith and M. Zalewski (eds.) (1996), *International Theory: Positivism and Beyond* (Cambridge: Cambridge University Press)

Camilleri, J. A. (1990), 'Rethinking Sovereignty in a Shrinking, Fragmented World', in R. Walker and Mendlovitz (eds.), *Contending Sovereignties, Redefining Political Community* (London: Lynne Rienner)

Christensen, A. (1995), 'Polycentricity and Normative Patterns', in H. Petersen and H. Zahle (eds.), *Legal Polycentricity: Consequences of Pluralism in Law* (Aldershot: Dartmouth), 235

Curtin, D. (1993), 'The Constitutional Structure of the Union: A Europe of Bits and Pieces', 30 *Common Market Law Review* 17

(1995), 'The Shaping of a European Constitution and the 1996 IGC: "Flexibility as a Key Paradigm"', 50 *Aussenwissenschaft*, 237

Dehousse, R. (1994), 'From Community to Union', in R. Dehousse (ed.), *Europe After Maastricht: An Ever Closer Union?* (Munich: Law Books in Europe)

Der Derian, J. (1987), *On Diplomacy* (Oxford: Blackwell)

Dinan, D. (1994), *Ever Closer Union?* (London: Macmillan)

Editorial Comment (1997), 34 *Common Market Law Review* 1105

Everson, M. and F. Snyder (1997), 'Editorial: Regulating Europe?', 3(3) *European Law Journal* 207

Fischer, J. (2000), 'From Confederacy to Federation: Thoughts on the Finality of European Integration', in C. Joerges, Y. Mény and J. H. H. Weiler (eds.), *What Kind of Constitution for What Kind of Polity?* (Harvard Law School)

Giddens, A. (1985), *The Constitution of Society* (London: Macmillan)

Gillespie, P. (1997), 'The Promise and Practice of Flexibility', in B. Tora (ed.), *Amsterdam: What the Treaty Means* (Dublin: Institute of European Affairs)

Griffiths, J. (1995), 'Legal Pluralism and the Theory of Legislation', in H. Petersen and H. Zahle (eds.), *Legal Polycentricity: Consequences of Pluralism in Law* (Aldershot: Dartmouth)

Hinsley, F. H. (1966), *Sovereignty* (London: C. A. Watts & Co.)

Hoffmann, S. (1966), 'Obstinate or Obsolete? Reflections on the Nation-State in Western Europe', 95 *Daedalus* 862

Janning, J. (1997), 'Dynamik in der Zwangsjacke – Flexibilität in der Europäische Union nach Amsterdam', 1(2) *Integration*

Judt, T. (1996), 'Europe: The Grand Illusion', 11(7) *New York Review of Books* 6

Kraup, O. and H. Rasmussen (1998), *Amsterdam-traktaten. Så den kann forstås* (Copenhagen: Fremad)

La Serre, F. de and H. Wallace (1997), 'Flexibility and Enhanced Cooperation in the European Union: Placebo rather than Panacea?', *Research Policy Papers* No. 2, revised version (September 1997)

MacCormick, N. (1993), 'Beyond the Sovereign State', 56 *Modern Law Review* 1
  (1995), 'The Maastricht *Urteil*: Sovereignty Now', 1(3) *European Law Journal* 219

Nomden, K. (1997), 'Flexibility: A Key Element in the Future European Integration?', manuscript, later published in Dutch in *Internationale Spectator* (December 1997)

Petersen, H. and H. Zahle (eds.) (1995), *Legal Polycentricity: Consequences of Pluralism in Law* (Aldershot: Darthmouth)

Ruggie, J. (1986), 'Continuity and Transformation in the World Polity: Toward a Neorealist Synthesis', in R. Keohane (ed.), *Neorealism and its Critics* (New York: Columbia University Press)

Schmitter, P. (1996), 'If the Nation State were to Wither Away in Europe, What Might Replace It?', in S. Gustavsson and L. Lewin (eds.), *The Future of the Nation State* (Stockholm: Nerius & Santerus)

Shaw, J. (1997), 'The Tension Between Flexibility and Legitimacy in the Domain of the Treaty Establishing the European Community', paper presented at the Maastricht Conference on Managing the New Treaty on European Union, 27/28 November 1997

Stubb, A. (1996), 'A Categorization of Differentiated Integration', 34(2) *Journal of Common Market Studies* 283
  (2000), 'Dealing with Flexibility in the IGC', in E. Best, G. Marks and A. Stubb (eds.), *Rethinking the European Union – IGC 2000 and Beyond* (European Institute of Public Administration)

Tilly, C. (1975), 'Reflections on the History of European State-making', in C. Tilly (ed.), *The Formation of National States in Western Europe* (Princeton: Princeton University Press)

Trubeck, D. (1972), 'Max Weber on Law and the Rise of Capitalism', 3 *Wisconsin Law Review* 720

Walker, N. (1999), 'Flexibility within a Metaconstitutional Frame: Reflections on the Future of Legal Authority in Europe', Harvard Law School Working Paper No. 12/99

Weiler, J. H. H. (1997), 'The Reformation of European Constitutionalism', 35(1) *Journal of Common Market Studies* 97
  (1999), *The Constitution of Europe* (Cambridge: Cambridge University Press)

Wessels, W. and B. Jantz (1997), 'Flexibilisierung: Die Europäische Union vor einer neuen Grundsatzdebatte? Grundmodelle unter der Lupe', in H. Rudolf (ed.), *Die Reform der Europäischen Union – Positionen und Perspektiven der Regierungskonferenz*

Wight, M. (1977), *Systems of States* (Leicester: Leicester University Press)

Wilhelmsson, T. (1995), 'Legal Integration as Disintegration of National Law', in H. Petersen and H. Zahle (eds.), *Legal Polycentricity: Consequences of Pluralism in Law* (Aldershot: Dartmouth)

Wind, M. (2001), *Sovereignty and European Integration. Towards a Post-Hobbesian Order* (London: Palgrave)

Zahle, H. (1995), 'The Polycentricity of the Law or the Importance of Legal Pluralism for Legal Dogmatics', in H. Petersen and H. Zahle (eds.), *Legal Polycentricity: Consequences of Pluralism in Law* (Aldershot: Dartmouth)

PART III

6

Beyond representative democracy: constitutionalism in a polycentric polity

RENAUD DEHOUSSE

Introduction

For many years, discussions on the legitimacy of the European institutions have revolved around the place of the parliamentary branch in the institutional system. The alleged weakness of the European Parliament and the inability of most national assemblies to influence the behaviour of their executive significantly were perceived as the core of the Union's 'democratic deficit'. The European Parliament itself was not slow in raising the issue. From the mid-1980s onwards, it has repeatedly emphasized that while the competences transferred to the European Community were mostly of a legislative nature, its own legislative powers remained weaker than those of national legislatures, which situation was said to result in a weakening of the democratic quality of European decision-making.[1]

Interestingly, this parliamentary vision of democracy has featured prominently in the positions taken by institutions that did not share the European Parliament's vested interest in promoting its own role. Thus, in the discussions on institutional reform since the mid-1980s, many national governments have regularly advocated an increase in the powers of the European Parliament – a position which apparently had the support of large sectors of the population in countries like Germany[2] or Italy. Similarly, in its now-famous ruling on the Maastricht Treaty, the German Constitutional Court identified in the institutional weakness of the European Parliament the main shortcoming in the democratic credentials of the European Union:

> Where [the European Union] assumes sovereign tasks and exercises sovereign powers to carry them out, it is first and foremost for the national

[1] Resolution on the democratic deficit, OJ 1988, C 187/229.
[2] F. Larat, 'L'Allemagne et le Parlement Européen', 5 *Critique Internationale* (1999), 30.

135

peoples of the Member States to provide democratic control via their national parliaments. Nevertheless, as the Community's tasks and powers
are expanded, so the need grows to add to the democratic legitimacy and
influence imparted through the national parliaments by securing the representation of the national populations of the Member States in a European
Parliament, as a source of additional democratic underpinning for the policies of the European Union.[3]

This apparent concession to orthodoxy was all the more remarkable, given
that the *Bundesverfassungsgericht* ruled out any possibility for democratic
government ever to emerge at the European level, on the grounds that
the European polity lacks the ethnical and cultural homogeneity that is
indispensable for the proper functioning of any democratic system. Why
bother about institutional engineering if it is unable to ensure the results
that one seeks to achieve anyway?

This convergence in the political discourses on European democracy
shows how deeply anchored a model representative democracy is in the
Western European political culture. To assess the relevance of this model
in the EU context, it is however useful to identify clearly a number of
underlying assumptions. First, in its most basic understanding, the system is based on what one could call an *input-oriented* form of democratic legitimation:[4] people elect their representatives, the latter take decisions affecting the fate of the polity, and they must be accountable for
their choices before voters. Central to this assumption is the fact that
all political choices can somehow be reduced to the will expressed by
citizens through their votes. Secondly, laws passed by representative bodies are par excellence the instruments whereby such political choices are
made. In this vision inherited from Jean-Jacques Rousseau, legislative bills
are the expression of an axiomatic 'general will'. Thirdly, there is often
an implicit equation between the 'general will' and the common good:
what legislators decide is supposed to serve the interests of the whole
polity.

Applying such a model to the governance of the European polity is,
however, problematic. Indeed, I would argue that this model is analytically weak, and normatively ill-adapted to the specificity of the European
Union.

---

[3] Case Nos. 2 BvR 2134 and 2159/92, 12 October 1993, reprinted in A. Oppenheimer (ed.), *The
    Relationship between European Community Law and National Law: The Cases* (Cambridge:
    Cambridge University Press, 1994), 524–75 at 553.
[4] F. Scharpf, 'Democratic Policy in Europe', 2 *European Law Journal* (1996), 136.

The vision of representative democracy that is used in discussions on the legitimacy of European institutions often seems to have more to do with eighteenth-century models of democracy than with the governance of complex post-industrial societies. It fails to take account of the many problems this form of government has been confronted with at national level. To mention but a few: we have known since Schumpeter that it is wrong to assume that the people themselves decide issues through the election of representatives:[5] elections are better described as a way to choose – or, better said in our times of growing dissatisfaction with politics, to get rid of – those who govern, and this choice is far from being merely influenced by competing visions of the common good. Likewise, phenomena such as the emergence of large-scale bureaucracies, technological development and the growing importance of expert advice in public policy make it difficult to argue that all decisions affecting the fate of the polity are taken by people's representatives. The decision-making process is generally much more complex: in many countries, legislation to be adopted by parliaments is almost always drafted by the executive, and is often conditioned by expert advice or by complex negotiations involving representatives of organized interests. Political parties, the role of which was not contemplated in liberal constitutions, also play an important mediating role. In other words, the somewhat ethereal vision of representative democracy which is referred to in discussions on the would-be European democracy has little to do with the way this model actually operates in our times.[6]

Applying the representative model at European level is also problematic from a normative standpoint. Its use often rests on an implicit assumption: if it works at home (a risky statement, as was just said), it will also work at the European level. Indeed, the institutional reforms since the mid-1980s, with their steady increase in the powers of the European Parliament, seem to be inspired by the idea that parliamentary democracy is a valid model at the European level as well as at national level. This, however, fails to take into consideration the fact that moving from the national to the supranational level entails a change in the level of analysis. Because the European Union is not a state, but some sort of union of states, it would be fallacious

---

[5] J. A. Schumpeter, *Capitalism, Socialism and Democracy* (London: Allen & Unwin, 1942).

[6] Interestingly, parliaments themselves now seem to realize that the complexity of contemporary society requires a redefinition of their traditional role. See Working Group of European Union Speakers on the Quality of Legislation, *The Complexity of Legislation and the Role of Parliaments in the Era of Globalization*, mimeo (Lisbon, 1999).

to imagine that such a transposition can be done mechanically.[7] On the contrary, the exercise is fraught with problems. Recent analyses have high-lighted the limits inherent in an input-based approach to the question of democracy in the European Union. In a conglomerate where people's primary allegiances tend to remain with their state,[8] the legitimacy of supranational institutions remains problematic. The development of a democratic debate is hampered by the absence of a common language and of pan-European media.[9] Moreover, and more fundamentally, the heterogeneity of the European polity is such that the adoption of a purely majoritarian system, in which decisions can be taken by a majority of rep-resentatives of the people, is difficult to conceive. The lack of any strong collective identity makes it difficult to believe that minorities would easily accept that their fate be decided against their will.[10] Already now, it is far from rare to hear the EU being accused of ignoring the traditions or the interests within the Union, in spite of the many safeguards that exist in the decision-making process to protect Member States' interests. This kind of tension would be likely to grow exponentially if some strict majoritarian rule were to be adopted. Ultimately, majority rule would end up feeding centrifugal forces.

Does it follow that the best way to ensure the democratic functioning of the EU is simply to return to a pure intergovernmental system, in which no decision could be taken but with the explicit consent of all Member States, as is often argued in these days of creeping Euro scepticism? That would be a simplistic conclusion. Even leaving aside the transaction costs inherent in pure intergovernmental models, it ignores the fact that nego-tiations in a multi-veto system cannot reach an optimal outcome unless negotiators depart from their 'democratic' mandate, namely the prefer-ences of their fellow citizens.[11] It also overlooks the fact that at national

---

[7] I have developed this point in an earlier essay: 'Comparing National Law and EC Law: The Problem of the Level of Analysis', 47 *American Journal of Comparative Law* (1994), 201.

[8] A.-P. Frognier and S. Duchesne, 'Is there a European Identity?', in O. Niedermayer and R. Sinnott (eds.), *Public Opinion and International Governance* (Oxford: Oxford University Press, 1995), 194–226.

[9] D. Grimm, 'Does Europe need a Constitution?', 1 *European Law Journal* (1995), 282; T. Meyer, 'European Public Sphere and Societal Politics', in Mario Telo (ed.), *Démocratie et Construction Européenne* (Brussels: Presses de l'Université Libre, 1995), 123–31.

[10] R. Dehousse, 'Constitutional Reform in the European Community: Are there Alternatives to the Majoritarian Avenue?', *West European Politics* (1995), 118–36; Joseph H. H. Weiler et al., 'European Democracy and its Critique', in Jack Hayward (ed.), *The Crisis of Representation in Europe* (London: Frank Cass, 1995), 4–39; F. Scharpf, 'Legitimacy in the Multi-Actor European Polity', in M. Egeberg and P. Laegreid (eds.), *Essays for Johan Olsen* (Oslo: Scandinavian University Press, 1999), 260–88 at 276–8.

[11] Scharpf, 'Legitimacy', 282.

level too, the state machinery can easily be captured by specific interests, or even be simply concerned with interests of its own. What is conveniently presented as *the* national interest often corresponds more to the interests of specific groups of people, rather than the public good. France's traditional tough stance on agricultural issues in trade discussions may serve farmers' interests, but does it really serve those of industrial producers or of consumers? Likewise, Britain's attitude in the BSE crisis appeared to be motivated more by a concern for the fate of beef producers than by the interests of consumers.

This is not without analogy to the motive given by James Madison to justify the establishment of some kind of constitutional democracy at continental level. Rejecting Montesquieu's idea that the public good was easier to achieve in a small, homogeneous republic, Madison argued that it was easier to ignore the interests of minorities in smaller polities: 'the fewer the distinct parties and interests, the more frequently will a majority be found of the same party; and the smaller the number of individuals composing a majority, and the smaller the compass within which they are placed, the more easily will they concert and execute their plans of oppression.'[12] To protect republican government, he wrote, the remedy is to extend the 'sphere' of the polity. By taking in 'a greater variety of ideas and interests', this change of scale will 'make it less probable that a majority of the majority of the whole will have a common motive to invade the rights of other citizens'.[13] Applied to contemporary Europe, such an approach might lead one to view the integration process as adding value in terms of democracy. For a British trade unionist in Mrs Thatcher's Britain, or for a French industrialist interested in greater freedom of trade, the Europeanization of social policy or of trade relations, respectively, might have appeared as a way to secure a policy less hostile to their preferences, rather than as a loss of collective sovereignty. Indeed, behind calls for European interventions, we often find groups of people who somehow have failed to secure from public authorities the kind of decision they wanted.

Reflections on European constitutionalism must therefore avoid two kinds of evils. Statism – the tendency to reason as if one could simply transpose at supranational level solutions experienced at national level – is likely to lead to conclusions that might threaten the stability of the whole system. At the same time, however, one should take account of the fact that the EU is in many respects unlike traditional international

---

[12] J. Madison in A. Hamilton, J. Madison and J. Jay, *The Federalist Papers 1787* (reprint, New York: Bantam Classic, 1982), 42–9.
[13] *Ibid.*

organizations, be it only because it decides on a wide range of issues that affect people's daily life. Advocating a return to the good old days when national sovereignty, embodied in national parliaments, was the answer to all legitimacy concerns will not help, as a large number of issues appear to require transnational cooperation. Some sort of democratic input into European decision-making is therefore needed – urgently, one might argue, given the lack of enthusiasm displayed by citizens of all Member States in Euro-elections. The best way to achieve this objective, I would argue, is to go beyond classical discussions on the kind of institutional arrangement that should exist at the end of the integration process, and to pay greater attention to the evolution of European governance. Normative analysis should be grounded on a careful analysis of reality, if it is to avoid the pitfalls of excessive abstraction.

The growth of bureaucratic governance

As indicated above, so far normative discussions on how to improve the legitimacy of European institutions have essentially focused on the powers of the European Parliament. In many respects, this is but a corollary of a tendency to regard harmonization, i.e. the approximation of substantive rules, be they contained in laws or in administrative regulations at domestic level, as a key instrument in EU policies. Harmonization being primarily a legislative exercise, it was only natural to pay so much attention to legislative procedures. However, this emphasis on legislative procedures overlooks a fundamental transformation under way in the governance of the European Union. Now that the legislative framework for the internal market is nearly complete, there seems to be a slowdown in the Community's legislative activities. Figure 1 shows that the number of primary legislative proposals has declined in recent years.

It would be wrong to conclude from this that the overall volume of Community regulatory activity is declining. Indeed, the overall volume of Commission rule-making, most of which takes place in the comitology framework, remains rather high, as shown in Figures 2 and 3.

The Commission has long – and by far – been the main producer of Community regulations. Moreover, in 1997, the number of directives adopted by the Commission exceeded for the first time that of directives adopted by the Council.

In other words, in terms of sheer numbers, the importance of secondary (non-legislative) rule-making appears to be considerable. The combination of these two elements – the decline of purely legislative

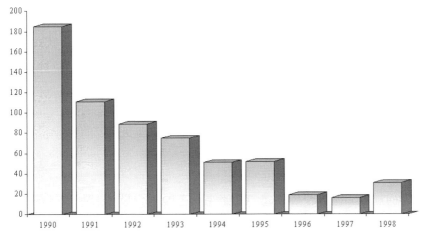

Figure 1 Proposals for primary legislation introduced by the European Commission
Sources: Reinforcing Political Union and Preparing for Enlargement, Commission
Opinion for the Intergovernmental Conference 1996, 1995, p. 87, for 1990–5; COM (95)
512 final for 1996; SEC (96) 1819 final for 1997;
http://europa.eu.int/comm/off/work/1998/index_fr.htm for 1998

activity, and the respectable size of secondary rule-making – suggests that
we should reconsider the traditional emphasis on legislative procedures
in discussions on the legitimacy of European institutions. The legislative
phase is but one (admittedly important) part of the decision-making process. A growing number of salient political issues are likely to arise in the
post-legislative phase, be it in rule-making or the concrete application of
Community rules. Should a given product be authorized? What kind of
precautionary measures are needed to protect human health in the case
of scientific doubts related to our alimentary habits? The management
phase may gain even more importance in the future, as the Amsterdam
Treaty has enhanced the powers of the European Community to deal with
what is known as 'risk regulation' in areas such as human health, consumer
policy and environmental protection.[14] As risk regulation decisions are
often made on the basis of complex scientific evidence, they cannot always, or indeed most of the time, be made *in abstracto,* once and for all,
in legislation, but rather require individual, ad hoc decisions, taken by
administrative bodies.

[14] R. Dehousse, 'European Institutional Architecture after Amsterdam: Parliamentary System
or Regulatory Structure?', 35 *Common Market Law Review* (1998), 595; P. Ludlow, *Preparing
Europe for the 21st Century: The Amsterdam Council and Beyond* (Brussels: CEPS, 1997).

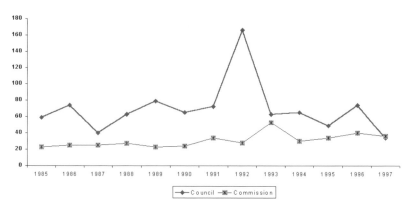

Figure 2 Number of Directives adopted by the European Institutions
Source: General Report of Activities of the EC and data retrieved from CELEX, the
interinstitutional computerized system on Community law, excluding instruments not
published in the Official Journal of the European Communities and instruments listed
in light type (routine management instruments valid for a limited period).

For years 1993 to 1997, directives adopted by the European Parliament and Council
in accordance with the co-decision procedure are included in the category 'Council'.

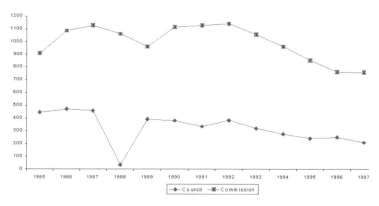

Figure 3 Number of Regulations adopted by the European Institutions
Source: General Report of Activities of the EC and data retrieved from CELEX, the
interinstitutional computerized system on Community law, excluding instruments
not published in the Official Journal of the European Communities and instruments
listed in light type (routine management instruments valid for a limited period).

For years 1993 to 1997, regulations adopted by the European Parliament and
Council in accordance with the co-decision procedure are included in the category
'Council'.

If this analysis is correct, a growing number of important decisions at European level are likely to be taken by bureaucratic structures of some kind. In practice, as the EU largely remains a system of decentralized administration, in which legislative rules are implemented by the Member States' administration, this suggests that the role of intergovernmental committees, known as comitology in the Euro jargon, is bound to increase in the years to come. However, the way those committees operate may be the source of a variety of legitimacy problems. First, the system is striking in its opacity. Who does what and how is nearly impossible to tell for a lay audience. This lack of transparency may undermine the authority of Community decisions: citizens may find it difficult to accept decisions based on recommendations fron obscure bodies, the composition and functioning of which remain a mystery. Secondly, it is not clear that the social prestige of committee members will be sufficient to command obedience. While scientific experts may derive some authority from their technical knowledge, bureaucrats are the focus of widespread mistrust in European countries. Thirdly, the little we know of the way comitology works may also become a source of concern. The convergence of concerns, interests and language among experts which is said to be the hallmark of comitology seems to enable the system to operate fairly smoothly.[15] However, while positive from the standpoint of efficiency, this consensus may undermine the legitimacy of the system, as it can easily be depicted as one more instance of power in the hands of a closed circle of elites. The risk of collusion is quite real: can experts be regarded as neutral in areas where research is largely financed by industry? Can we really assume that they will not be influenced by their national origins? The BSE crisis has shown that issues of this kind are far from moot. They must therefore be addressed squarely if one is to put comitology on firmer grounds for legitimacy purposes.

How may this objective be achieved? Generally speaking, five different types of arguments are traditionally used to legitimize bureaucratic processes.[16] Given the specificity of the Community regulatory process, it would be wrong to assume that they can be mechanically transposed to the European level. However, they provide good yardsticks for assessing the legitimacy of bureaucratic decisions taken at that level.

---

[15] C. Joerges and J. Neyer, 'From Intergovernmental Bargaining to Deliberative Political Processes: The Constitutionalisation of Comitology', 3 *European Law Journal* (1997), 273.

[16] I am using here (in a slightly adapted fashion) a terminology borrowed from R. Baldwin, *Rules and Government* (Oxford: Clarendon Press, 1995), 41–5.

- The 'legislative mandate' approach is the most traditional. Parliament is seen as the main repository of legitimacy and the administration must strive to achieve the objectives that are set out in governing legislation.
- In the 'accountability or control' model, legitimacy is grounded in the fact that the administration is somehow under control, i.e. that it is held accountable for its decisions by a representative body (generally the legislature) or by courts.
- The 'expertise' claim stresses that, as a result of their technical character, many decisions cannot be taken by the legislature: expert judgement is needed to judge the respective merits of competing options, and experts must be granted sufficient discretion.
- The 'procedural' approach emphasizes the fairness of decision-making processes. It demands that consideration be given to the interests of persons affected by administrative decisions. Procedures designed to associate such persons with the decision-making process are therefore viewed as essential. They tend to vary according to the kind of decisions that are taken. Under 'due process' requirements, administrative bodies must consider the interests affected by individual decisions. As regards rule-making, the same concern for fairness may lead to the adoption of rules guaranteeing transparency and participation or consultation rights.
- 'Efficiency' is also often claimed as a ground for legitimacy, particularly in recent times, as the ability of government structures to deliver results is becoming increasingly important. While there are many ways of defining efficiency, two meanings are particularly relevant for our purposes: decision-making efficiency (the ability to take decisions when needed) and substantive efficiency, i.e. the ability to take the 'right' decisions.

Obviously, these approaches are not necessarily mutually exclusive. Accountability and control can be used to monitor the effective implementation of legislative mandates or the compliance with the procedural requirements of the 'due process' model. Likewise, the resort to experts is often advocated on efficiency grounds, and can be balanced through various accountability techniques. Nevertheless, there are clear differences among various claims. The degree of discretion required in the 'expertise' model is at odds with the idea of exhaustive legislative mandates. Similarly, the vision of the public interest inherent in the 'legislative mandate' approach often assumes the existence of a collective body – the people – whose interests are represented by Parliament, while the 'procedural' model is informed by a more polycentric vision of the polity, in which the coexistence of a wide variety of interests, which must all be given due consideration, is acknowledged.

At this stage, my concern is not to endorse any one of these models, but rather to discover how suitable they may be, given the specific character of Community decision-making. To streamline somewhat the discussion, I will take as a starting point the limits of an approach that would rest exclusively on the 'expertise' model. Involving experts at various levels of the decision-making process is undoubtedly necessary, particularly when the decisions to be taken have a technical dimension. Providing much-needed expertise is clearly an important achievement of the European committee system. It can even be argued that the quality of deliberations among experts will not only contribute to the quality of the regulatory process, but also to its legitimacy, as was suggested by Joerges and Neyer.[17] Yet, this does not suffice. For one thing, there is no guarantee that experts' 'deliberations' are actually exclusively inspired by the public good: all sorts of considerations, ranging from their vision of their country's interests to possible links with the industry they are supposed to regulate, may influence the positions they take within committees. Moreover, even assuming that their attitude is *in fact* influenced by purely disinterested concerns, would this suffice to ensure the legitimacy of their decisions? I do not think so: granting experts 'carte blanche' is likely to be unpopular in a period of widespread mistrust of technocrats of all kinds. Rightly or wrongly, lay people may also have views on the decisions to be taken, and insist that they too should be considered. Some sort of control over their deeds is therefore necessary.

Our reflections should therefore focus on the remaining approaches. Various versions of the 'legislative mandate' and the 'accountability' models have been invoked by those who argue that the European Parliament, now that it has acquired the status of a co-legislator in many areas, should have more power over delegated legislation. Both types of arguments are part of the same, *supranational* avenue: the European Parliament, it is said, being the institution most representative of the European people at large, should play a greater role in overseeing comitology. In contrast, as was just indicated, the *procedural* model rests on a radically different vision of legitimacy, one which would require the opening of comitology to representatives of all interests affected by its decisions. Each of these two options will now be reviewed in turn.

---

[17] Joerges and Neyer, 'From Intergovernmental Bargaining'.

The supranational avenue: legislative mandates and parliamentary control

Since the introduction of legislative co-decision in 1993, the European Parliament has insisted on being treated as a Council co-equal in supervising Commission implementing decisions. It has opposed particularly vigorously management and regulatory committees, which it regards as a way of circumventing its newly acquired legislative powers: in the four years since co-decision was introduced, comitology was an issue in about two-thirds of the dossiers that were subjected to the conciliation procedure. Disagreement over the proper implementing procedure was also at the root of the Parliament's rejection of the directive on voice telephony – the first time that the Parliament used its co-decision prerogatives to reject a Council common position.

There are several ways in which the European Parliament could become more closely involved with the decisions currently being taken within the comitology framework.

The first, 'legislative mandate', approach would suggest that the current balance between legislation and administrative decisions be altered in order to ensure that the most salient policy decisions are taken as legislative measures. A return to legislative policy-making is a technique widely advocated in order to combat the growing influence of bureaucracies.[18] Surely, it would be historically incorrect to describe comitology as having robbed the European Parliament of its legislative prerogatives, as comitology predates Parliament's rise to the status of a fully fledged legislature. However, MEPs have consistently called for a clearer demarcation between decisions that can be taken through comitology and those that require a proper legislative procedure,[19] a position that underlies Parliament's support for a clear hierarchy of Community acts. The European Court of Justice itself has suggested that 'the *basic elements* of the matter to be dealt with' must be adopted in accordance with the legislative procedure laid down by the Treaty, while 'the provisions implementing the basic regulations' may be adopted according to a different (i.e. comitology) procedure.[20]

However, there seem to be clear functional limits to what can be achieved along these lines. As indicated above, it is not always possible for

[18] T. Lowi, *The End of Liberalism*, 2nd edn (New York: Norton, 1979).
[19] K. St Clair Bradley, 'The European Parliament and Comitology: On the Road to Nowhere?', 3 *European Law Journal* (1997), 230.
[20] Case 25/70 *Köster ECR* [1970] 1161.

legislation to anticipate all the problems that may arise in the implementation phase. Parliaments may lack the time or the necessary expertise to solve all problems in advance, and they may find it expedient to delegate part of the problem-solving task to implementing agencies. Moreover, the borderline between policy choices and implementation 'details', between legislation and administration, is often blurred when scientific or technical choices must be made. Prior to the BSE crisis, who would have thought that animal feed was an issue that would gain considerable public attention?

Parliamentary control over the executive, another traditional oversight instrument, seems equally difficult to adapt to the specific features of Community governance. While at national level parliamentary control over the administration is a by-product of its control over the cabinet via the institution of ministerial responsibility, no such thing exists at European level. Although the Parliament has gained considerable control over the Commission in the post-Maastricht years, functionally comitology committees are not under the Commission's authority.[21] The vertical chain of command thought to exist at national level (parliament–executive–bureaucracy) is broken at European level, where delegated legislation is, at least partly, in the hands of networks of national experts. The European Parliament's role must be adapted to this network-based reality if it is to be of more than symbolic relevance.

The Parliament's response to that structural difficulty has been to put pressure on the Commission, as the latter plays a leading role in implementation procedures and appears to be extremely influential in comitology committees. The Plumb–Delors agreement of 1987 stipulated that the Parliament would be notified by the Commission of most draft implementing measures. These were then to be forwarded to the responsible parliamentary committee so that it could voice its concerns whenever necessary. Clearly, the effectiveness of such an agreement depends primarily on the Commission's willingness to keep the Parliament informed and to take its views into account. In both respects, the first years of the agreement have been rather disappointing: many drafts have not been sent to the Parliament and, in all but a handful of cases, parliamentary committees have failed to react.[22] The strengthening of the Parliament's

---

[21] Even though the Court of Justice has recently ruled otherwise, at least as regards access to committee documents. See Case T-188/97 *Rothmans International BV* v. *Commission*, ECR [1999] II–2463.

[22] Bradley, 'European Parliament', 237; R. Corbett *et al.*, *The European Parliament*, 3rd edn (London: Catermill, 1995), 254–5.

grip over the Commission in recent years has led to a formal recognition of its right to be informed of committees' proceedings.[23] Even if this were to occur, however, a question would still remain: how should the Parliament process this information, and react if need be? Here, two problems must be addressed: lack of time and expertise. Can the Parliament effectively scrutinize the hundreds of decisions adopted each year by committees, given its heavy agenda and complex organization? Will MEPs have the relevant expertise?

Entrusting supervision to parliamentary committees, as was decided in the wake of the Plumb–Delors agreement, is a sound division of labour. Members of committees are likely to be better equipped than many of their colleagues to make sense of the technical issues addressed in draft implementing measures; further, decentralization is needed to deal with the masses of documents involved. But what kind of relationship should be established between parliamentary committees and their counterpart(s) in the web of comitology committees?

Interestingly, the Parliament's ambitions seem to have increased in parallel with the emergence of its legislative profile. The Parliament has at times expressed an interest in being more closely involved with the work of committees, e.g. by including its own observers in the committees.[24] This proposal raises a delicate but fundamental issue: in a system where influence appears to be directly related to the degree of expertise enjoyed by the various participants in the debate,[25] what can be the impact of elected representatives, namely politicians? True, the European Parliament could set up its own expert networks to control the work of committees. But in terms of legitimacy, the 'value added' of another layer of experts would be rather thin. Rather than have politicians clothe themselves as technical experts, as they at times seem tempted to do,[26] would it not be preferable to limit their role to a number of basic policy choices and to grant them the right to intervene when issues they deem fundamental arise in the implementation phase? Indeed, this seems to be the solution contemplated in the recent comitology decision as regards regulatory decisions.

---

[23] Council Decision of 28 June 1999 laying down the procedures for the exercise of implementing powers conferred on the Commission, OJ L 184/23 of 17 July 1999.

[24] Bradley, 'European Parliament', 234.

[25] See the analysis of V. Eichener, 'Social Dumping or Innovative Regulation? Process and Outcomes of European Decision-Making in the Sector of Health and Safety at Work Harmonization', European University Institute Working Paper SPS 92/28.

[26] C. Landfried, 'Beyond Technocratic Governance: The Case of Biotechnology', 3 *European Law Journal* (1997), 255.

Rather than systematically participating in the adoption of implementing legislation, the European Parliament has been given the right to step in whenever it feels a political input is needed, and to ask that a proper legislative procedure be followed.[27] Although such an opinion would not be binding, it would be likely to enjoy considerable weight, but only because the Parliament has given ample evidence of its willingness to go to court whenever it feels its prerogatives are being ignored.

Admittedly, such a division of labour would better correspond to the respective functions of legislator and executive in modern societies. Of particular importance, given the technical character of many issues tackled within European committees, is the Parliament's power to hold hearings. This technique could be used more systematically, as a means of obtaining independent expertise and facilitating a dialogue with interested parties. It would also enable the Parliament to exert greater control over the Commission, as the latter would be called upon to react to the views expressed by witnesses. Furthermore, hearings would very likely attract media attention to particular issues, thereby contributing to improved public awareness of the decisions taken at the European level. Such an approach, which emphasizes accountability and the European Parliament's function as a forum where the important political issues of the day can be debated, would be better suited both to the structure of comitology as a system of regulatory networks, and to the technical character of the issues tackled through comitology, than parliamentary involvement in the day-to-day work of committees.

But would enhanced monitoring by a supranational legislature suffice as a ground for legitimacy? There are reasons to be sceptical. Representative democracy has become the focus of widespread criticism in Western Europe, where it is often perceived as a system that enables a cartel of elites to exert tight control over the policy agenda.[28] Arguably, the gap between the rulers and the ruled may be even wider at the Community level. To many European citizens, the Parliament still appears a remote assembly, whose work remains largely unknown and whose members do not always represent the mood of the populace. More importantly, in a system where primary allegiances remain firmly rooted at the national level, national ties may prove to be more important than the supranational logic of parliamentary democracy. To put the matter bluntly, German or Danish

---

[27] Article 5(5) of Council Decision of 28 June 1999.
[28] Y. Mény, 'The People, the Elites and the Populist Challenge', European University Institute, Jean Monnet Chair Paper RSC 98/47.

consumers might feel more effectively represented by, say, a delegate from a national consumer organization than by Greek or Portuguese MEPs.

Reflections on the legitimacy of the European policy process must also come to terms with the polycentric character of the European populace. Not only is there no European 'demos',[29] but 'we the people' cannot simply be read in the plural as a reflection of the coexistence of different states within the European Union. The truth is that the peoples of the Member States, too, come from a kaleidoscope of regions, cultures and interests not always identified with the state apparatus, and can all legitimately claim to voice their views and be heard at the European level. After all, even at national level, the reductive nature of representative democracy, distorted even further by the structure of many electoral systems, makes it impossible for parliaments to mirror perfectly the broad range of interests and feelings that coexist within a single polity. Hence the attractiveness of alternative forms of legitimation, which provide for some form of direct participation of affected parties in the decision-making process.

The procedural avenue: transparency, openness and participation

So far, I have argued that several of the approaches traditionally used in order to legitimate delegated legislation are ill-adapted to the specific needs of comitology. Reliance on the expertise model is no longer sufficient in a world where technocracy has become the focus of much mistrust. Legislative mandates cannot always be sufficiently clear, as it is impossible to set down precise standards and objectives consistently. Although more promising, an approach based on parliamentary control over expert decisions is still far from sufficient, as the European Parliament cannot claim to represent *all* the interests, be they national, local or sectorial, that coexist within the European Union. Additional techniques ought therefore to be considered if the legitimacy of European governance is to be put on firmer ground.

Bearing in mind what has just been said about the growing gap between citizens and government in Europe, one such technique might be to empower all the parties affected by comitology decisions to express their concerns before the relevant committees. The main advantages of such an approach would be twofold. An extensive dialogue with the various segments of civil society would obviate some of the shortcomings of

---

[29] J. H. H. Weiler, 'Does Europe need a Constitution? Reflections on Demos, Telos and the German Maastricht Decision', 1 *European Law Journal* (1995), 219.

representative democracy at the European level, by enabling those who so wish to have a say in the decision-making process.[30] In so doing, one might enhance the legitimacy of decisions taken by European bodies, for there is empirical evidence to suggest that decisions taken by public bodies (even non-representative ones, such as courts) are more readily accepted when they appear to be taken according to fair procedures.[31] A greater openness of the decision-making process also improves public awareness of the issues discussed at the European level, thereby contributing to the emergence of a truly pan-European public sphere.

From the standpoint of openness to the populace at large, the present situation is defective in several respects. As any scholar who has done research on comitology knows, information on the actual operation of committees is difficult to find. The total number of committees remains a mystery.[32] In 1994, the Parliament had to freeze a share of the appropriations for committees in order to obtain more information from the Commission on the number of meetings and their work output.[33] Committees' rules of procedure are difficult to get hold of. When formal rules do exist, they appear to focus on the internal operation of committees: regulating deliberation among experts, i.e. relationships between the Commission and national representatives, is their main target.[34] In contrast, little or no attention is paid to the relationship between the comitology web and the outside world. True, in some areas, committees have been created specifically for the purpose of allowing organized interests to give their input. In the food sector, for instance, an ad hoc committee has been set up to represent the views of various socio-economic interests. Yet the Advisory Committee on Foodstuffs offers a good illustration of the limits of what has been achieved so far.[35] As its members are appointed by

---

[30] See D. Curtin, 'Civil Society and the European Union: Opening Spaces for Deliberative Democracy', in *Collected Courses of the Academy of European Law* (The Hague: Kluwer Law International, 1999), 185.

[31] T. Tyler, *Why People Obey the Law* (New Haven, CT: Yale University Press, 1990).

[32] See e.g. E. Vos, 'The Rise of Committees', 3 *European Law Journal* (1997), 210 at 213; J. Falke, 'Comitology and Other Committees: A Preliminary Empirical Assessment', in R. H. Pendler and G. F. Schaefer (eds.), *Shaping European Law and Policy: The Role of Committees and Comitology in the Political Process* (Maastricht: EIPA, 1996), 117 at 136–7.

[33] Bradley, 'European Parliament', 242.

[34] See e.g. the rules procedure of the standing committee for foodstuffs, a consolidated version of which has been prepared by the Commission (doc. III/3939/93 83/260/90-EN of 11 May 1993).

[35] Commission Decision 75/420/EEC of 26 June 1975, OJ L 182/35 of 17 July 1975; amended by Commission Decision 78/758/EEC, OJ L 251/18 of 14 September 1978. See the analysis of E. Vos, 'Institutional Frameworks of Community Health and Safety Regulation: Committees, Agencies and Private Bodies', PhD thesis (Florence, 1997), 152–4.

the Commission, the latter may privilege certain interests; for instance, representatives of environmental interests have been excluded. Moreover, the committee can only act at the Commission's request, which explains why it has remained inactive for long periods.

Rather than ad hoc representative fora, greater openness in the work of *all* committees is needed. This could be achieved with a standard set of procedural rules regulating the interface between comitology committees and civil society at large. What kind of principles should these rules contain? Without entering into a detailed examination of the question, it may be useful to point out some basic elements. Thus, for instance, the agenda of committee meetings, the draft proposals to be discussed and the minutes should be made public.[36] Interested persons should be given the opportunity to express their views on any item on the agenda; public hearings could even be envisaged for matters of particular importance. Committees should also be required to explain the considerations that underlie their eventual choices.

How could such a proceduralization be brought about? A number of scholars have warned against the danger of 'ossification' of administrative procedures through codification in a legislative act.[37] It is fair to say that both the European Court of Justice and the Court of First Instance have displayed a growing awareness of the necessity to protect 'process' rights, such as the right to be heard and the duty to state reasons, when individual rights are directly affected by Community decisions.[38] However, judicial decisions are necessarily ad hoc, rendered in concrete cases; they are therefore not the best avenue for injecting new principles into decision-making processes. Moreover, the overall object of the exercise should not be forgotten. What matters for legitimacy purposes is not only that justice be done, but also that it be *seen* to be done. Put together, these considerations point in the same direction: the best way to introduce the principles discussed here would be through a basic decision, adopted in the most solemn of manners, which would apply to all kinds of bureaucratic decisions.

---

[36] This could be achieved by exploiting the potential of the Internet. See in this respect the proposals put forward by Joseph Weiler, 'The European Union Belongs to its Citizens: Three Immodest Proposals', 22 *European Law Review* (1997), 150 at 153.

[37] J. Schwarze, *European Administrative Law* (London: Sweet & Maxwell, 1992); C. Harlow, 'Codification of EC Administrative Procedures? Fitting the Foot to the Shoe or the Shoe to the Foot', 2 *European Law Journal* (1996), 3.

[38] See e.g. Cases C-269/90 *Hauptzollamt München* v. *Technische Universität München* [1991] ECR I-5469; T-364/94 *France Aviation* v. *Commission* [1995] ECR II-2845; and the comments by H. P. Nehl, 'Principles of Administrative Procedures in Community Law', LL M thesis (Florence: European University Institute, 1997).

The framework comitology decision of 17 July 1999[39] took a significant number of steps in the right direction. It provides for the adoption
of standard rules of procedure, which will be used by committees to draft
their own rules of procedure, although they retain the right to make
the adjustments they deem necessary.[40] It also renders applicable to the
committees the principle and conditions governing public access to Commission documents[41] – a decision of considerable importance as both the
Amsterdam Treaty and recent rulings of the European Court of First Instance appear to have reversed the hierarchy of values that prevailed in the
past: public access to documents has become the rule, and confidentiality
an exception to be interpreted narrowly.[42] In a ruling rendered only two
days after the adoption of the framework decision, the European Court
of First Instance indicated that, as most committees do not have a staff of
their own, for the purpose of access to documents they are deemed to be
under the Commission, which is in charge of their secretariat.[43]

All these developments should ease access to committee documents,
thereby enabling those who so wish to keep track of their work. In terms
of public awareness of policies conducted at the European level, this is certainly more important than the annual report on the working of committees which the Commission is now required to produce.[44] However, does
it suffice? In my opinion, the answer can only be negative. Transparency
is of course important, but only as a means to ensure a greater openness
of decision-making procedures. For the latter objective to be attained,
some provision must be made for participation of individuals in such
procedures,[45] and on this the framework decision is remarkably silent.
Moreover, if the idea is really to enhance the legitimacy of EU decision-
making by granting individuals a say in decisions affecting their fate, then
this right should be granted adequate recognition. From that standpoint
too, the solution that has prevailed falls short of the objective. True, the
standard rules of procedures to be adopted could formally sanction some
participatory rights, but it would remain legitimate for each committee to

---

[39] Council Decision of 28 June 1999 laying down the procedures for the exercise of implementing powers conferred on the Commission, OJ L 184/23 of 17 July 1999.
[40] Article 7(1).   [41] Article 7(2).
[42] See e.g. Cases T-105/95 *WWF* v. *Commission* [1997] ECR II-313; *Svenska Jornan-
listförbundet* v. *Council* [1998] ECR II-2289; T-188/97 *Rothmans International BV* v. *Commission*, ECR [1999] II–2463; T-14/98 *Hautala* v. *Council*, ECR [1999] II–2489.
[43] Case T-188/97 *Rothmans International BV* v. *Commission*, at para. 62.
[44] Article 7(4) of the framework decision.
[45] A similar plea can be found in P. Craig, 'Democracy and Rule-making within the EC: An
Empirical and Normative Assessment', 3 *European Law Journal* (1997), 105.

adopt more restrictive procedures if it so wished. For the process-oriented approach to legitimacy outlined here to be taken seriously, the rights in question should be given a legal status that would protect them against arbitrary decisions of the rulers. In other words, what appears to be required is a decision of a constitutional nature, namely a formal recognition of participatory rights to be enshrined in the Treaty itself.

A procedural approach of this nature, with its participatory ethos, would bolster the legitimacy of comitology. It should not however be seen as an alternative to parliamentary control. On the contrary, proceduralization, because it would foster public debate, might significantly reinforce the accountability of committees. One can imagine, for instance, that if a committee were to overlook the concerns of, say, consumer groups, the European Parliament might be interested in knowing why. In this case, procedural and accountability concerns, far from being at odds with one another, would actually be mutually reinforcing.

Conclusion: the need for a process-based approach

It is often said that the functionalist approach followed by the Founding Fathers is no longer able to ensure the legitimacy of the integration process. True, integration can be credited with a number of benefits – peace and prosperity being the most important – but now that it has become clear that decisions taken at European level influence people's lives in so many ways, *legitimation by outputs* is not sufficient. People no longer accept that the quality of decisions is all that matters: they want a say in policy choices which affect their destiny. As a result, calls for an *input-based* approach have gradually intensified. However, such calls are often inspired by an idealized, Rousseauian vision of parliamentary democracy, in which representatives of the people serve the collective interest of a polity and translate it into legislative decisions. This understanding of democracy is so deeply rooted in Western European political culture that it is espoused by two camps that are at odds with each other: the self-professed European Federalists, advocating the upgrading of the powers of the European Parliament, and the *souverainistes* and Eurosceptics of all kinds, for whom there can be no real democracy outside national parliaments.

This approach is fraught with difficulties. It rests on a mechanical, transmission-belt vision of public policy, in which voters control the Parliament, the Parliament controls the executive, and the latter is supposed to keep the bureaucracy under control. However, real-life situations tend to be much more complex. Each link of the chain develops interests of its own and may be captured by specific interests of some kind. Moreover, the sovereign which is to be represented, the people, is far from being a homogeneous creature: behind this convenient abstraction, one finds a complex constellation of conflicting interests and preferences, which cannot easily be reconciled. These structural problems, which undermine the functioning of representative democracy at national level, are magnified at European level. The sheer size of the polity affects the representativeness of governing bodies: an assembly of some 600 members cannot claim to mirror all the interests that coexist within a polity of over 400 million people. The longer the command chain gets, the looser the ties between rulers and ruled. Consider, for instance, the position of citizens vis-à-vis the two dominant institutions of the European Union. The European Council is composed of sixteen members, out of whom fourteen escape their control: they are without any influence on their appointment or their dismissal. As to the European Commission, even though the European Parliament now exerts an incommensurately higher control over its destiny than used to be the case, it embodies a complex compromise between the partisan backgrounds and the national origins of the commissioners, which makes it difficult for citizens to identify with the institution. Finally, the existence of multiple vetoes at various levels makes it nearly impossible to assign the responsibility for most decisions to a single body, thereby weakening democratic accountability.[46] All these elements are undoubtedly necessary to preserve the consensus-based character of the decision-making process, which is as crucial a constitutional feature in the EU as in any polycentric community. However, they make it illusory to hope that representative democracy will suffice to endow European institutions with all the legitimacy they need. As Robert Dahl has shown, changes in the scale of the polity unavoidably affect the way in which a democratic political system must respond to the preferences of its citizens: new paradigms are needed.[47]

This contribution has pleaded for a radically different approach. Adopting a resolutely inductive approach, it has taken as a starting point the growing importance of the post-legislative phase in public policies, and the difficulties faced by parliaments in keeping abreast of complex decision-making processes, which often invoke delicate technical issues.

---

[46] This latter point is developed in Scharpf, 'Legitimacy', 270–5.

[47] 'A Democratic Dilemma: System Effectiveness versus Citizen Participation', 109 *Political Sciences Quarterly* (1994), 23.

Some may of course deplore this evolution, but one should take notice of structural developments of this magnitude, rather than insisting on a romantic vision of the past. Thus, it is argued, the input-oriented approach which has so far dominated discussions on the legitimacy of European institutions needs to be supplemented by a *process-oriented* one, in which interested citizens would be given a say in the post-legislative, bureaucratic phase. Unlike other approaches, this one attaches less importance to the quality of the inputs received by decision-makers (citizens' votes, legislative mandates) than to the fairness of decision-making procedures: what matters is not that the eventual decision can be formally reduced to the will of the citizenry, but rather that those who so wish be given a chance to express their views. Not only would such an approach, with its emphasis on transparency, openness and participation, appear to be more finely tuned to the evolution of European governance, but it could also contribute to informing the citizenry of the problems that are addressed at the European level, thereby facilitating the development of public deliberation, which is as essential an element of democracy in a transnational system as it is in a national one.

Admittedly, such an approach departs from classical understandings of European constitutionalism, which focus on the demarcation of the respective powers of the Union and of the Member States and on the balance of power between European institutions. At the same time, however, its ambition is identical to that of liberal constitutions: to keep power, wherever it lies and whatever its form, under control, and to ensure the fairness of decision-making processes. Moreover, the procedural avenue outlined here should not be seen as a substitute for the control exercised by political institutions. On the contrary, the emergence of a public debate on 'implementing' decisions might reinforce the accountability of otherwise obscure bodies, ultimately contributing to the emergence of a transnational public sphere. Governance, particularly in present-day complex societies, is a multifaceted phenomenon, which cannot be encapsulated in one single model.

7

Finality vs. enlargement: constitutive practices and opposing rationales in the reconstruction of Europe

ANTJE WIENER

Introduction

[I]n the coming decade we will have to enlarge the EU to the east and south-east, and this will in the end mean a *doubling in the number of members*. And at the same time, if we are to be able to meet this historic challenge and integrate the new member states without substantially denting the EU's capacity for action, we must put into place the last brick in the building of European integration, namely *political integration*. The need to organize these two processes *in parallel* is undoubtedly the biggest challenge the Union has faced since its creation...

Crucial as the [2000] intergovernmental conference is as the next step for the future of the EU, we must, given Europe's situation, already begin to think beyond the enlargement process and consider how a future 'large' EU can function as it ought to function and what shape it must therefore take... Permit me therefore to remove my Foreign Minister's hat altogether in order to suggest a few ideas both on the nature of this so-called *finality* of Europe and on how we can approach and eventually achieve this goal.

(German Foreign Minister Joschka Fischer, Humboldt University, Berlin, 2000)[1]

For comments on earlier versions of this chapter I would like to thank the participants of the Research Seminar Series in the Department of Politics at the University of Edinburgh in January 2002, the participants of the European Integration/International Relations Colloquium at the Institute of European Studies, Queen's University, Belfast, and the participants of the annual ARENA conference, in March 2002. Particular thanks go to Elizabeth Bomberg, Lynn Dobson, Richard Bellamy, Uwe Puetter, Guido Schwellnus and Ben Muller. For extensive and thorough comments on the most recent version I am very grateful to Karin Fierke and Jo Shaw. The responsibility for this version is the author's. The British Academy's support through two small research grants as well as a Social and Legal Studies Association small research grant are gratefully acknowledged.
[1] Fischer 2000, http://www.auswaertiges-amt.de/www/de/eu_politik/aktuelles/zukunft/ausgabe_archiv?bereich_id = 0&type_id = 3&archiv_id = 97 (emphases added).

The issue of compliance in the international system of states, on the one hand, and why citizens obey the law, on the other, follow different trails of philosophical reasoning. Yet, as Thomas Franck points out, while 'there are differences between law's place in national society and the place of rules in the society of nations . . . those differences do not justify the closing of the international rule system to philosophical inquiry aided by the insights developed by the study of national and sub-national communities. On the contrary, the differences create a tantalizing intellectual symbiosis' (Franck 1990, 5). This observation raises the question of why legal philosophy has been mostly applied to national as opposed to international systems. In turn, this chapter's interest is in the dimension of international law – and international relations theory – that is brought into the European constitutional debate with the current enlargement proceedings. In other words, if the European legal order does not fall under international law, can enlargement be reasonably judged and its impact on the constitutional process be understood by applying the theoretical assumptions about compliance set out by international law/international relations theory? In the event of a negative response, what theoretical approach would be more helpful instead?

To elaborate on these questions, the chapter highlights the policy of conditionality, i.e. compliance with the accession *acquis*, as harbouring the rationale of rule-following that involves obeying rules without the possibility of reasoned change. It is pointed out that, while according to compliance procedures under international law rule-following behaviour is not considered as puzzling, as long as it is identified as legitimate based on transnational legal practices of internalization (Koh 1997, Chayes and Chayes 1995) or successful political processes of persuasion, shaming, learning and so forth,[2] with a view to the pending membership of the designated rule-followers in the enlargement process, the rule-following rationale is potentially anachronistic and therefore puzzling. It is even more puzzling given that the Europolity is neither an international organization nor a state but a new type of transnational politico-legal order with an evolving proto-constitutional framework. In this framework a key problem with compliance is that norms are often not properly specified. While the participants in the constitutional debate find it hard to agree on a compromise towards thinning out a thicket of institutionalized rules

---

[2] See Finnemore and Sikkink 1998; Risse, Ropp and Sikkink 1999; and Checkel 2001 among others.

and norms, the candidate countries are often forced to comply with norms which remain dubious and under-specified in the EU's very own context.[3] While the constitutional debate attaches an 'in progress' label to the EU institutional order,[4] the accession process requires clear reference to the status quo set by the 1993 Copenhagen criteria[5] and the related accession procedures, chapter developments and proposals. In other words, the EU's nature as a community, not a club, does not run well with the compliance rationale and its focus on the past.[6] Assessing the finality debate based on the logic of national constitutional law, i.e. based on a hierarchy of norms towards 'enhancing stability and predictability',[7] would imply squaring the circle. After all, and unlike most polities, the EU's commitment to accept democratic and European states as new members means that its external borders are, in principle, not fixed but in flux in a long-term perspective.[8]

While the EU's constitutional saga has long moved beyond the dichotomy of national and international law,[9] with many students of European integration treating the EU as a *sui generis* case with its own logic of European constitutional law,[10] or transnational law, the current situation of massive enlargement brings back elements derived from the logic of

---

[3] See, for example: De Witte 1998; Dimitrova 2001; Schwellnus 2001; Phinnemore and Papadimitriou 2002; and Amato and Batt 1998.

[4] As Wolfgang Wagner notes, for example, 'the dynamic character of the EU leads to the particularity that her institutional order is subjected to an almost permanent bargaining process' (Wagner 1999, 415) (translation from original German text by AW).

[5] For the criteria, see the Commission website at http://europa.eu.int/scadplus/leg/en/lvb/e40001.htm.

[6] For a critical perspective towards the 'club' approach, see Wallace 2002.

[7] On the hierarchy of norms in European law, see Bieber and Salome 1996.

[8] According to Article 49 TEU: '[A]ny European state which respects the principles set out in Article 6(1) may apply to become a member of the Union.'

[9] For a debate over the role of international and European constitutional law, see the 'Schilling–Weiler/Haltern Debate' (Schilling, Weiler and Haltern 1996) in which Schilling insists on distinguishing between the two approaches (Schilling 1996) while Weiler and Haltern argue that '*the blurring of this dichotomy* [international and constitutional] *is precisely one of the special features of the Community legal order and other transnational regimes*'. See Weiler and Haltern 1996, 1 (emphasis added). According to the latter authors, the key features that distinguish the European legal order from public international law involve 'the different hermeneutics of the European order, its system of compliance which renders European law in effect a transnational form of "higher law" supported by judicial review, as well as the removal of traditional forms of State Responsibility from the system'. See, Weiler and Haltern 1996, 2 at www.jeanmonnetprogram.org/papers/96/9610.htm.

[10] The existence of European constitutional law is usually derived from the constitutionalization of the Treaties.

international law[11] which deserve attention. The case is interesting since it has aroused little attention from either lawyers or political scientists despite raising analytical questions with relevance to a more interdisciplinary approach in both academic fields.

The case at hand can briefly be summarized as follows. The candidate countries are involved in complying with the internationally agreed conditions for membership according to the Copenhagen accession criteria up until the point of accession. At this point their status changes from candidate to law-abiding member bound by the EU's constitutional texts. Meanwhile, the Member States take part in a constructive approach towards finalizing the constitutionalization of the Treaties according to the provisions agreed in the Amsterdam Treaty of 1997[12] and the subsequent declarations at the 2000 Nice intergovernmental conference (IGC) and at the 2001 Laeken Summit[13] to the point of constitutional change at the forthcoming IGC in 2004. This change will put them into the position of having to obey the rules they created.

This chapter's focus on what are termed the opposing rationales of enlargement and finality re-invokes the question about separate or blurred disciplinary boundaries from a political scientist's point of view. The intention is to raise the critical question about the actual absence of blurring disciplinary boundaries and the impact of that absence on studying seemingly separated but, as it is argued, ultimately related action rationales that guide policy and politics in the EU, and which are constitutive towards a new transnational politico-legal order.

As part of the constitutional process leading up to the 2004 IGC, the two rationales – compliance with the accession criteria, on the one hand, and the debate over political finality, on the other – embody traits of the intellectual symbiosis highlighted above. They are interrelated and

---

[11] That is, 'international laws are thought *not* to be obeyed and the governance of international institutions and their norms *not* to be accepted' (Franck 1990, 6; emphases in text) unless discursive practices 'internalize' the interpretation of a new norm into the other partner's 'normative system' thus creating an interest in compliance with international conventions or treaties through 'transnational interactions' (Koh 1997, 2646; see also Chayes and Chayes 1995).

[12] On the necessary reforms for enlargement, see Protocol No. 7 to the Amsterdam Treaty; for a detailed timetable on institutional reform between the Amsterdam IGC and the Nice IGC, see the Commission's website at http://europa.eu.int/comm/archives/igc2000/geninfo/index_en.htm.

[13] For the Laeken Declaration, see http://belgium.fgov.be/europ/en_decla_laken.htm; for the Presidency Conclusions of the Nice Council Meeting (7–9 Dec. 2000), see http://ue.eu.int/Newsroom/LoadDoc.asp?BID = 76&DID = 64245&LANG = 1.

constitutive towards the evolving institutions of a new transnational order. Yet, while both enlargement and finality involve interactive practices, interaction in the enlargement process excludes the possibility of changing the rules that guide the practice of compliance. In turn, interaction in the finality debate is precisely geared towards innovation and change. This chapter highlights the apparent anachronism of the two action rationales by situating both within a 'larger process of transformation' (Tilly 1984). As part of this process, the practices of both enlargement and the finality debate are constitutive towards transnational institution building.[14] Considered from this analytical angle, the hermeneutic limits of a 'behaviourist approach to compliance', that values structure over agency and hence reduces the possibility of changing the rules, can be circumvented. It therefore allows a fresh view of the very practices that are part of the enlargement process, i.e. the interactions between the involved actors such as the candidate countries, Member States and EU representatives which are constitutive for institution building in the transnational realm, forging socio-cultural trajectories and social institutions in the process. Both are central to norm resonance and the implementation of legal rules, as will be discussed further below. Viewed within this larger context then, this chapter seeks to demonstrate that both the compliance and the finality rationale do have an impact on the substance of the evolving proto-constitutional setting in Europe.

Case: logics and action rationales

Both the enlargement process and the constitutional bargaining process are expressions of the same structural pressure, namely the logic of integration which states that all European and democratic states which have achieved particular economic, administrative and political standards defined in the accession *acquis* may join the EU. Yet, both processes differ considerably according to their respective action rationales. The difference between the processes lies in the possibility of institutional change (i.e. of norms and rules) entailed in each, and which may or may not result from social interaction in each process.[15] For example, the rule-following

---

[14] On the relational approach to state building, see Tilly 1975; on the discussion of constitutive practices and institutional change towards a new political order in world politics, see March and Olsen 1998.

[15] For a conceptual discussion of the possibility of change as a result of political process according to realist and constructivist approaches in international relations theory, see in particular Fierke 2002.

rationale that guides the enlargement process excludes contestation and change of norms and rules. Its only potential opening towards negotiation is the bargaining situation in which compliance rules are agreed.[16] This situation, in which rule-following action is structured with legal or normative pressure, is therefore the key arena in which understanding and a potential for norm resonance is developed through interaction.[17] In turn, the constructive rationale in the process of constitutional bargaining is geared precisely towards institutional change as the outcome of contentious deliberation. It is argued that the logic of integration (i.e. all European and democratic states will eventually come together to collaborate within one polity) which has replaced the logic of anarchy in the international realm (i.e. in the absence of government, states will not cooperate) as the context of political (inter)action in Europe exerts structural pressure for institutional adaptation on all actors – Member States, candidate countries and EU political organs.

Yet the two processes of enlarging the EU and debating its finality unfold according to two types of action rationales which differ crucially in their respective impact on change as a consequence of social interaction. Thus, the finality debate in preparation for the constitutional bargain at the 2004 IGC not only allows but also explicitly asks for the contestation and change of substantive and formal rules of the Europolity. After all, the goal of the constitutional debate is to change the current constitutional framework based on a negotiated compromise which refers to shared frameworks of reference. This constructive rationale thus entails social interaction such as deliberation and argument with a view to identifying and changing the formal institutional framework, i.e. the Treaties. Even though the interaction will largely remain limited to the exchange between elites, in this process social interaction is not a mere rule-following

---

[16] Key debates on why actors comply have been generated within international relations theories that relate political decisions and behaviour to the concept of law. Friedrich Kratochwil pinpointed the key question of this debate as 'why actors follow rules, especially in a situation of alleged anarchy' (Kratochwil 1984, 685). The elaborations on this question involve discussion of, for example, Zürn's point on the significance of the 'manner in which norms are generated' in a supranational context: for example, whether or not they are 'produced in the context of legitimate norm-forming processes' (Zürn 2000, 2). On the development of informal bargaining contexts that create frames of reference, see Risse 2000 and Puetter 2001.

[17] On the contested role of the 'legalness' of such norms, see in particular Finnemore and Toope who raise the question 'if policy makers do not know and do not care about the legal status of . . . rules, what reason do we have to think that "legalness" matters at all in compliance with norms?' (Finnemore and Toope 2001, 701).

activity but a constructive activity as well. In turn, compliance with the accession *acquis* excludes the possibility of contestation and change of substantive and formal issues. The compliance rationale states that, in order to acquire membership in a club, newcomers need to accept, adopt and follow the rules of that club. The rules are clearly stated and are not up for debate. For the candidate countries this implies a straightforward carrot–stick or means–end oriented behaviour. They are expected to initiate the adaptation of their respective administrative, judicial, political and regulative institutions according to European standards and conditionality so as to ensure compatibility with the Europolity. The logic of the compliance rationale is then set by this behaviour. It is neither expected nor supposed to change as a result of social interaction in the duration of the compliance process.[18]

Timing

The logic of collaboration towards integration and enlargement has created a situation of time pressure towards constitutional change in the EU. In light of this pressure, not only the substance of the forthcoming constitutional bargain but also the resonance with it in the 'fifteen-plus' domestic constitutional settings raise questions. While it has been observed that 'the timing is simply wrong' (Schmitter 2000, 1), the countdown of the constitutional process with a view to producing a constitutional agreement in 2004 has nonetheless begun. Notwithstanding the long, ongoing constitutionalization that has inspired countless more or less specific, if repeatedly stated, definitions among lawyers and political scientists which largely focus on 'the formation of a fairly structured polity' in the EU,[19] the prospect of moving towards a particular point at which massive widening and decisive deepening are scheduled has raised expectations and concerns about substantive and specific formal changes of the EU's constitutional framework. The relatively quick move has two major implications which this chapter will address in turn. The first implication is the much discussed issue among political scientists of institutional adaptation in the candidate countries, the Member States and the Europolity. That is: first,

[18] The constructive impact of social practices both on the evolving norms of constitutionalism within the Europolity over time and on the rule-following practice in the process of compliance with European (double) standards in the enlargement process is dealt with in more detail later in this chapter.

[19] See Castiglione 2002, 1; for discussion of the term see an overview in Schepel 2001, and extensive discussion in Craig 2001.

the candidate countries are under pressure to produce institutional change according to the conditions for accession; second, the Member States are expected to adapt to changes in a number of core policy areas including budget policy, agricultural policy, and justice and home affairs; and third, the Europolity's formal institutional framework will have to change as well. The second implication is the debated issue – particularly in legal and public and/or party-political circles – of political finality and substantive constitutional change. It involves philosophical issues of constitutional principles, the practices that forge and identify these principles, and the procedures to establish and safeguard these principles in the long run.

Institutional mis/fit

Analyses of institutional adaptation raise the question of 'fit/misfit' that has been studied extensively within the framework of Europeanization and the compliance literature.[20] By contrast, studying the implementation of, and/or resonance with, constitutional principles is less straightforward because it leads the researcher beyond the boundaries of 'material resources' towards exploring the terrain of 'associative resources'[21] and, depending on research perspective and interest, into the intellectual territories of law and sociology. In other words, in addition to the familiar material resources that define formal institutional fit or misfit, studying constitutional principles requires an analytical focus on informal and less tangible phenomena such as meanings and interpretations. In the social sciences, both types of resources are defined as institutions, albeit on a range from formal to informal (or 'soft' institutions).[22] They guide action and result from interactive social practices. The difference in studying each type of resources, material and associative, lies in understanding the way in which their respective impacts on politics unfold. Thus, formal institutions, such as administrative rules and procedures, are tangible and can be changed or adapted relatively quickly, to the extent that, in cases of misfit with the European model, change and adaptation are required.[23] In

[20] See, for example, Börzel and Risse 2000; Joerges and Zürn 2003.
[21] On the former, see Pierson 1996; on the latter, Wiener 2001.
[22] On the definition of soft institutions such as norms and rules, see in particular: March and Olsen 1989; Finnemore and Sikkink 1998; March and Olsen 1998; Jepperson, Wendt and Katzenstein 1996; Ruggie 1998; Kratochwil 1989; and Wendt 1999.
[23] Here, the Europeanization literature would add that misfit, and hence friction, increases the chance of Europeanization: see in particular the contributions in Cowles, Caporaso and Risse 2001.

the case of informal institutions, e.g. constitutional principles of equality or norms such as minority rights or gender rights, the question of fit or misfit is not as easy to establish (since the boundaries of associative resources are fuzzy), nor are constitutional principles as quick to adapt to predefined rules (since their meaning is embedded in particular contexts in which socio-cultural trajectories facilitate interpretation and understanding). While the degree of fit with European constitutional principles can hence be qualitatively assessed according to variation in associative connotation, adaptation to the respective European standards is less easily achieved, for constitutional principles are fuzzy in all contexts, European and domestic alike. It is this fuzziness which makes the associative resources that are central to the current constitutional process analytically so hard to handle.[24]

Theoretical framework and argument

The argument draws on two theoretical perspectives which are inter-disciplinary in so far as they straddle the boundaries of law and the social sciences. The first perspective is a societal approach to compliance that builds on Habermas's facticity–validity tension (Habermas 1992) in order to elaborate on the societal impact on norm resonance across different contexts in world politics.[25] The second perspective draws on critical approaches to law in society, stressing the interrelation between social practices, the constitution of social institutions, and the impact of the law.[26] Since they do not begin with the assumption that successful implementation and institutional design are directly related, both offer helpful insights into addressing the mismatch between nominally agreed constitutional rules and norms (facticity), on the one hand, and their interpretation within their respective contexts of implementation, i.e. the EU Member States and candidate countries (validity), on the other. Underlying the following elaborations is an understanding of the term 'institution' as 'a group of laws, usages and operations standing in close relation to one another, and forming an independent whole with a united

---

[24] At the same time, however, fuzziness can be an asset, as this chapter seeks to reveal.

[25] For an elaboration of the 'societal approach' as opposed to the 'compliance approach' and the 'arguing approach' to norms in world politics, see Wiener 2002.

[26] For several contributions to this perspective which do not necessarily share a theoretical approach yet which all stress the interrelation between societal institutions, social practices and the impact of legal rules, see in particular: Shaw 1996; Curtin and Dekker 1999; and Finnemore and Toope 2001.

and distinguishing character of its own'.[27] The advantage of this rather
flexible definition of an institution as including norms, rules and procedures over narrower definitions that understand institutions as social
facts which entail behavioural rules either as collections of practices and
rules or as standardized norms,[28] is the respective impact on, and relation
with, actors' behaviour.

Law and society: social institutions

According to an Aristotelian perspective: '[C]onstitutions institutionalize
the whole even as they themselves consist of an aggregate of institutions.'[29]
The particular role of a constitution, from this perspective, lies in the fact
that 'institutions also protect rules from changes in society *and* make it
possible for rules to change with such changes'.[30] A constitution is then
understood as a set of rules, norms and procedures which are rooted in a
particular system of core constitutional values. These values include, most
importantly, understandings about the legitimate organization of internal
and external sovereignty, i.e. citizenship and borders, within this constitutional system. A constitution thus entails the legally confirmed rules that
ought to be respected and followed within a particular polity. Whether
or not the thus established substance of a constitution is, however, socially accepted, i.e. whether or not it resonates within a particular societal
context, depends on the matching network of social institutions, or more
generally on socio-cultural trajectories.[31] 'In other words, there is a direct relation between legal norms and rules – as objective thoughts – and

[27] See Onuf 2002, 218; cf. Lieber 1859, 305. As Onuf adds, '[E]ven today, it would be difficult
to improve on this definition, which makes rules working together "through human
agents" the central feature of any institution.'

[28] For a political science perspective to norms/institutions, see Finnemore and Sikkink 1998,
891; for an organizational approach see March and Olsen 1998, 948.

[29] See Onuf 2002; 218; cf. Lieber 1859, 343–6.

[30] See Onuf 2002, 222 (emphasis added); cf. Bull 1977, 56.

[31] As Deirdre Curtin and Ige Dekker write, '[T]he definition of legal institutions as a presentation of a state of affairs that ought to be made true in practice brings with it two conceptual
realities. In addition to legal institutions, which are valid by virtue of a comprehensive legal
system, so-called "social" institutions exist, in other words societal practices corresponding
to the system of norms and rules of the legal institutions' (Curtin and Dekker 1999, 90).
For a similar perspective, see Max Weber's observation that '[T]he legal rule perceived as
an "idea" is not an empirical pattern or "organized rule", but a norm which is thought of
as "ought to apply", that is surely not a form of being, but a value standard according to
which the factual being can be evaluated, if we want juridical truth' (translated from the
original German citation by the author) (Weber 1988, 349).

social reality' (Curtin and Dekker 1999, 91). Or, more broadly speaking, '[t]o be effective, obligation needs to be felt, and not simply imposed through a hierarchy of sources of law' (Finnemore and Toope 2001, 754). While it remains to be established how to measure this 'feeling' according to academic perspective and approach (e.g. behavioural or relational), for the time being it is important to note that, in order to be effective, the norms, principles and procedures of the constitutional text need to be matched by a set of social institutions in order to facilitate resonance with the constitution's substance.

In contrast to the constitutional text, social institutions are generated through social practices. They provide a contextualized filter, so to speak, through which the constitutional text gains meaning and political power. Depending on context, then, interpretations of constitutional substance differ. This variation in interpretation increases in situations where the constitutional substance is constituted outside the boundaries of a domestically established state of law, such as in the Europolity. That is, in situations where the socio-cultural trajectories and social institutions provide little overlap, divergence in associative connotation of constitutional substance prevails. This divergence is further increased by a number of contextual variables that enhance difference in associative connotations with 'Western' constitutional substance. As will be demonstrated, the emerging transnational order of the Europolity does indeed include social institutions that enhance the interpretation of, and resonance with, European transnational law. It also reveals, however, that, given this order's status of becoming, the enlargement rationale seems increasingly to lack legitimation. As the case studies below will show, the candidate countries are obliged to follow (double) standards, an interactive process which by itself creates standards that are not conducive to resonance with European constitutional norms.

The link between the 'oughtness' of legal texts and societal conditions that facilitate understanding and realization of constitutional rules and norms can be summarized in two propositions. First, the more inter-related constitutional rules and norms are with socio-cultural trajectories, the better the match between constitutional substance and societal acceptance. Second, the likelihood of resonance with constitutional norms increases with the degree of organic interaction that precedes the constitutional agreement. It follows that, in order to assess the degree of domestic resonance with European constitutional substance, it is necessary to identify the respective societal institutions such as rules, norms and procedures, in addition to the constitutional substance, in the three types of contexts involved.[32] Both are difficult to assess since the oft-mentioned, albeit still analytically challenging, perspective on the EU as an ongoing stage of 'becoming' puts on academics and politicians alike a constant pressure of acting or arguing 'as if' the EU were an international organization or a state, despite being perfectly clear about the constraint entailed in the EU's status as both 'anti-state' and 'near-state' (Shaw and Wiener 1999). The enormous constructive potential of this analytical fuzziness has proved particularly difficult to exploit for the dogmatic legal tradition that prevails on the European continent and for political scientists, most notably those lawyers and political scientists who follow the conceptual trails laid down by the discipline of 'state sciences' (*Staatswissenschaften*) or, indeed, rational choice approaches to politics. In turn, theorists who are primarily interested in analysing process and change find the EU a less challenging object of study. Indeed, it is probably fair to say that to this group of academics (which includes lawyers and political scientists with a focus on meta-theoretical, socio-historical, cultural and constructivist theorizing) the EU represents a case that demonstrates most clearly processes that are less obvious or visible in other circumstances, namely the crucial role of process, practices and becoming in world politics. It is this focus on process, practices and becoming which suggests that the two apparently opposing rationales of rule-following and constructive debate are actually constitutive towards the transnational European order. Absent supranational statehood,[33] it is precisely the perspective of impossibility attached to constitution building beyond the state that enhances the dynamic of the constitutional debate.[34]

Facticity and validity: social practices

The societal approach to compliance centres on the observation that norms entail a 'dual quality' of both structuring and construction. It states that norms acquire social properties through their relation with social practices in particular contexts. Their meaning thus reflects, and is

---

[32] This chapter's limits do not allow for such an extensive empirical study. Instead it explores the link between social practices and institution-building, on the one hand, and societal institutions and law, on the other, as two conditions for resonance with the constitutional substance that stands to be negotiated at the forthcoming IGC in 2004.

[33] See the *Maastricht* ruling of the Second Chamber of the German Constitutional Court, 1993, BVerfGE 89, 155 – Maastricht.

[34] See also Bruno de Witte's cautionary use of the term 'European constitution' which he finds to 'presuppose a broad understanding of the term "constitution", cutting the umbilical cord connecting the constitution and the nation-state' (De Witte 2002, 39).

reconstructed by, social interaction (Wiener 2002). Absent social interaction, the meaning of norms is neither produced nor recognized (Kratochwil 1989, Onuf 1989). It follows that, to understand the role and function of norms, it is necessary to recall the practices that contributed to their origin. According to this approach, it is not only norms that are contested (which norm is valid?) but also their meanings (which meaning of a norm is valid?). Furthermore, norm validation does not exclusively take place in supra- or transnational contexts, but in domestic contexts as well. The transfer of norm validation between political arenas therefore must be considered as posing an additional challenge to norm resonance. Finally, norms entail varying degrees of prescriptive force. While 'thick' norms entail clearly defined, albeit contestable, prescriptive normative force, 'thin' norms usually lack clear prescriptions that would work like standardized rules. They are therefore open to various projected meanings.[35] Thin supranational norms raise the stakes for norm resonance in domestic contexts. They cause political reaction and make norm resonance unlikely. The type of political reaction depends on the socio-cultural trajectories that inform the interpretation of norms, as, for example, the nationally informed expectations about Union citizenship demonstrated.[36] It can be expected that, in the absence of a constitutional compromise on the supranational level, i.e. an agreement on 'thick' constitutional norms including shared norm validation and meanings, the potential for projected meanings of norms will undermine norm resonance and hence the political success of the constitutional process in the EU. That is, the absence of knowledge about what constitutional substance means in the current and future Member States opens the field for normative projection, which in turn is prone to generating political unrest, objection and backlash.

The type of constitutional change resulting from the supranational constitutional bargain is likely to entail 'thin' as well as 'thick' institutions. In contrast to substantiated and clearly defined thick institutions that entail standardized rules for behaviour, such as the EU legislation on the environment or on equal pay,[37] thin institutions carry few or no prescriptions for behaviour. They are therefore likely to bring conflicting expectations and public contestation to the fore. In other words, resonance with the institution's substance cannot be taken for granted. While compliance with

---

[35] I thank Theresa Wobbe for this specification (conversation in Berlin on 31 August 2002).

[36] These expectations were not informed by the 'thin' supranational institution of Union citizenship, but were rooted in national practices of citizenship, thus expecting Union citizenship to mean something akin to national citizenship (Wiener 2001).

[37] See Articles 175 and 141 EC Treaty, respectively.

either type of institution depends on whether or not the institution as a fact (facticity) resonates with the expectations raised in their respective contexts of implementation (validity), thin institutions are more likely to cause contention, as the reactions to Union citizenship[38] demonstrate. Politically, thin institutions pose a potentially greater hazard, precisely because clear rules of prescription undermine the certainty of behavioural predictions. The detached existence of Union citizens from 'their' polity, or, for that matter, the lack of social glue between the citizens and the European institutions, enhance the possibility of unintended consequences triggered by institution-building in the European non-state as the lack of prescriptive rules is enhanced by the perception of the Treaties as distant and empty.

In order to bridge this gap, a dialogic approach to politics builds on the two basic principles of constitutionalism and democracy; it is expressed by a third principle of constitutional recognition. The principle of constitutionalism implies that the discussion of successful norm-implementation needs to consider the (conceptually ingrained) power of norms. In other words, the fact that '[r]easonable disagreement and thus dissent are inevitable and go all the way down in theory and practice' must be appreciated, since there 'will be democratic agreement and disagreement not only *within* the rules of law but also *over* the rules of law' (Tully 2002, 207). It implies that deliberation over norms in bargaining situations is unlikely to cover the whole story if it is dealt with exclusively as a 'snapshot' situation. Instead, deliberation – as communicative action – is not reduced to a mere performance within a system of rules, but bears the potential for changing that system at the same time. In turn, the principle of democracy

> requires that, although the people or peoples who comprise a political association are subject to the constitutional system, they, or their entrusted representatives, must also impose the general system on themselves in order to be sovereign and free, and thus for the association to be democratically legitimate ... These democratic practices of deliberation are themselves rule governed (to be constitutionally legitimate), but *the rules must also be open to democratic amendment* (to be democratically legitimate).[39]

It follows that, in principle, democratic procedures are a precondition for establishing the validity of norms. '[I]nstitutionalized deliberation and public debate, must, indeed, interact' (Joerges 2002, 146). According to

---

[38] See Articles 17–22 EC Treaty.   [39] See Tully 2002, 205 (emphasis added).

the principle of constitutional recognition (Tully 1995), it is not the act of staking out more or less overlapping individual claims but the process of discussing the validity of such claims which will eventually produce shared constitutional norms. The challenge for the constitutional bargain thus, according to this principle, lies in establishing some sort of constitutional mechanism that warrants ongoing dialogue about cultural diversity. As Tully writes:

> [P]erhaps the great constitutional struggles and failures around the world today are groping towards a third way of constitutional change, symbolized in the ability of the members of the canoe to discuss and reform their constitutional arrangements in response to the demands for recognition *as they paddle* . . . [A] constitution can be both the foundation of democracy and, at the same time, subject to democratic discussion and change in practice.[40]

The ongoing debate over constitutional claims sets a framework in which agreement on shared values can be forged – and contested. This type of dialogical interaction between differing claims offers an alternative to competing over often mutually exclusive constitutional standpoints. Indeed, '[r]ealising this dialogical approach involves rethinking the role of both constitutions and democracy within the EU' (Bellamy and Castiglione 2001, 13). Establishing fair and equal conditions for the participation in dialogical interaction on constitutional substance thus has implications beyond the participatory dimension. It is constitutive for the evolving constitutional meaning itself. Yet, it has been observed that, as it stands, the EU does less to encourage and safeguard such dialogues than it does to 'circumnavigate' them.[41]

Argument

In the context of the wider Europe the compliance rationale leads to a focus on institutional adaptation within the national polities of the candidate countries. The most remarkable aspects of the compliance process are twofold. On the one hand, the norm-following candidate countries are not supposed to 'bargain' over the accession criteria once these have been set. Their performance is judged on strictly formal changes in the respective national institutional arrangements. On the other hand, and

---

[40] See Tully 1995, 29 (emphasis added).
[41] This is precisely where Bellamy and Castiglione (2001, 14) locate 'tensions within the EU'.

following the static and past-focused compliance rationale, the candidate countries are required to comply with norms that are *per se* defined in the past, and which, in addition, have been found to lack precision themselves. Compliance in the current enlargement process means institutional adaptation so that full membership in a community becomes possible. Yet, in the light of the ongoing constitutional debate and the focus on political finality, it is not even obvious what this membership will eventually mean: for example, 'Membership in *what*?'[42] Club or community? And, if the latter, what type? Here, recent efforts to theorize enlargement suggest membership in a club[43] while, by and large, the constitutionalism literature stresses membership in a community, if reluctantly and for want of a better term. According to the argument presented in this chapter, both assumptions need to be discarded as they provide insufficient information in the light of the social practices involved in the compliance process, on the one hand, and the evolving and contested norms that emerge in relation to these practices, on the other. After all, the boundaries of the EU are in flux, its political and legal rules are under ongoing construction, its constitutional status is one of becoming. In this context, the role of shared informal rules and practices, or the emerging soft institutions of postnational governance, provides an increasingly stabilizing function for politics.[44] This potentially important role notwithstanding, norms are subject to contention and reconstruction in relation to social practices. Their origins, roles and functions are therefore central to understanding governance in postnational times.[45]

When considered as a social practice as opposed to a mere act of rule following, compliance processes offer an additional angle that exceeds the behavioural dimension and brings the constructive dimension to the fore. This dimension matters in the European context in particular, since the EU is neither a club with clear boundaries or rules of entry, nor is it a constitutionally entrenched community with shared values and a common identity. From this background I seek to demonstrate how and

---

[42] See James Caporaso who wrote, with reference to citizenship in the Europolity, '[I]f citizenship is still thought of as membership, this approach raises the question "membership in *what*?"' (Caporaso 2001, 4).

[43] See Schimmelfennig and Sedelmeier 2002; for criticism see Wallace 2002.

[44] They may be likely to turn into something akin to a *Grundnorm* which provides guidance on the nature of legitimate governance beyond state boundaries.

[45] On the observation that studying the role of norms does not only involve their impact, but also their origin, see Ruggie 1998, 13.

why the opposing rationales of enlargement and constitutional process in the EU are interrelated, and how their interrelationship has an impact on emerging transnational institutions and hence the resonance of European constitutional substance.

The argument develops as follows. The behavioural approach identifies the reasons for actors' *interest* in compliance with norms, including, for example, acceptance, pressure, shaming or membership in either informally or formally constituted international communities, such as the global security community, the global society of civilized states or the OECD community, on the one hand, or the EU, on the other. Here, the research focus is on strategic choice at one point in time. In turn, the societal approach raises questions about the *impact* of compliance, e.g. how does compliance with norms resonate within particular contexts? The research focus is on the social practices in context. Put this way, the rules and norms defined by the different types of international documents can be studied within one single research framework as the research interest is no longer defined according to the central question of why comply?, but instead elaborates the constitutive dimension about the impact of compliance (Wendt 1998).

The distinctive action rationales, it is held, have political impact in the long term. According to a behavioural approach to compliance, the firm conditions for accession that structure the enlargement process are expected to lose political impact once enlargement is completed. The societal approach to compliance contradicts that claim. Building on the assumption that norms entail dual qualities, it is suggested that, as a practice, rule-following during the enlargement process is constitutive and therefore has an impact on the meaning of, say, minority rights. The general rule here is that the less clearly defined a norm, the more prone to projection and change through social practices it becomes. This is the case with a number of accession standards, a prime example being minority rights, which are not defined under the Treaty yet have been added to the accession *acquis*.[46] The meaning of minority rights is therefore likely to be coined by the enlargement process. It is expected that this meaning will loop back into the EU context. To elaborate on these observations, this chapter thus goes beyond the obvious question for political scientists about the likely outcome of a constitutional bargain and the likelihood

---

[46] For this observation and analyses see De Witte 1998; Amato and Batt 1998; Schwellnus 2001; and Wiener and Wobbe 2002.

of a constitutional compromise vs. a highest common denominator outcome at the 2004 IGC. Instead, it is argued that even if a constitutional
bargain is struck, the question of domestic resonance with the rules and
norms agreed among elites during the IGC remains. The bottom line of
the argument is thus not to make normative claims about the necessity
of a European constitution, nor is it to provide a political outlook on the
future of the Europolity. Instead, I am interested in the long-term impact of compliance as a social practice and its constructive impact on the
evolving norms of constitutionalism in the transnational European order.
To suggest but a few possibilities as to how this constructive impact might
evolve, given that the routinization of practices in particular policy areas
establishes procedural rules that guide subsequent policy making (Tilly
1975, Koslowski and Kratochwil 1994), possible outcomes of the current
enlargement process may be, for example, the institutionalization of the
policy of conditionality as a resource with a view to slowing down future
enlargement processes; and the redefinition of the interpretation of minority rights which may turn out to be relevant beyond the enlargement
process, for example by having an impact on the definition and application of minority rights policy in the 'old' Member States as well as raising
critical questions about the EU's equality norm.

Evolving constitutional norms: a societal perspective

The structural pressure exerted on enlargement and constitutional change
by the logic of collaboration towards further integration leaves little room
for choice about the large issues, i.e. whether or not to enlarge and whether
or not to change the EU's constitutional framework. The smaller issues,
i.e. the policies which address the how and when of institutional adaptation and constitutional change, leave more room for strategic choices. In
this situation of major change and normative entrapment,[47] the spotlight
is on the practices and policy choices that are part of the processes of enlargement (e.g. conditionality) and constitution-building (e.g. the constitutional convention). While enlargement and constitutional change are by
and large considered to be unchangeable and beyond critical discussion,[48]

---

[47] See Sedelmeier 1998; Schimmelfennig 2001; and Schimmelfennig and Sedelmeier 2002.

[48] Thus, Joschka Fischer, then President of the Council of Ministers, stressed: '[A]fter the
Cold War the EU must not be limited to Western Europe, instead at its core the idea of
European integration is an all-European project. Geopolitical *realities do not allow for a serious alternative anyhow. If this is true, then history has already decided about the "if" of eastern
enlargement, even though the "how" and "when" remains* to be designed and decided.' See

the way both processes are orchestrated does create space for debate. Indeed, the practices underlying both processes do leave room for manoeuvre, adaptation and critical assessment. The intention of this and the following sections is therefore to explore this window of opportunity by relating the 'how', i.e. the impact of constitutive practices first on evolving European constitutional norms, second in the process of compliance, and finally in the current constitutional debate, with a view to offering an empirical basis from which to assess the 'what', i.e. the outcome that results from routinized practices, norms and shared understandings in the evolving transnational order.

European constitutional norms

In the following sections, I first identify a selection of evolving constitutional norms in the long-term process of European integration, and then turn to the compliance process.

Cooperation towards integration

It is by now commonly accepted that the EU, although once 'merely' a regime, has developed institutional features that reach beyond its original institutional and political design, and certainly beyond the purpose of managing economic interdependence.[49] While it was originally 'conceived as a legal order founded by international treaties negotiated by the government[s] of states, the high contracting parties, under international law and giving birth to an international organization' (Weiler 1997, 97), its current political quality is significantly different. As it now stands, it is not exclusively based on the original set of political and legal institutions, but has come to include shared norms, commonly accepted rules and decision-making procedures. Indeed, the 'constitutionalism thesis' would argue that 'in critical aspects the Community has evolved and behaves as if its founding instrument were not a treaty governed by international law but, to use the language of the European Court of Justice, a constitutional charter governed by a form of constitutional law' (*ibid.*). Decision-making in the 'European' polity is not only guided

---

Die Zeit, 21 January 1999, 3 (emphases added). See also the Nice Summit Presidency Conclusions which state that: '[T]he European Council reaffirms the historic significance of the European Union enlargement process and the political priority which it attaches to the success of that process.' See http://ue.eu.int/Newsroom/LoadDoc.asp?BID = 76&DID = 64245&LANG = 1, at III.

[49] See Bogdandy 1999 and Pernice 1999.

by the shared legal and institutional property, the *acquis communautaire*, it is also both the result and part of an ongoing process of construction. For example, overriding national interest in particular issue areas has become a shared principle that is legally grounded in the practice of qualified majority voting in the Council of Ministers. In accepting this rule, *cooperation between states* has acquired the meaning of *cooperation towards European integration*. In the Europolity cooperation, therefore, entails more than the sum of the cooperating actors and the rules that guide them. It represents a belief – however contested and diffuse – in the project of integration.[50]

Shared democratic norms

General principles underpinning shared democratic norms in the EU include, for example, 'the right to equality' or the 'principle of legal certainty'. More generally, the Treaty involves four main groups of general principles, including rules and standards, economic freedoms, an emerging group of political rights, as well as a yet to be properly defined body of fundamental rights (Shaw 2000, section 9.2). From a legal perspective, the validity of these four groups of rights has been demonstrated by frequent and key references in court rulings.[51] From a political science perspective, democratic norms mainly include election procedures which allow citizens to vote and be elected in their community of residence.[52] This right has been brought to the fore in frequent contributions to the process of 'European' citizenship practice. Specifically, the European Commission has referred to the norm of equal access to political participation in the community where an individual is a resident with a view to establishing voting rights for EU foreigners (Wiener 1998, ch. 8). It has hence been taken on and referred to by advocacy groups that seek to establish voting rights not only for all EU nationals, but also for third-country nationals.[53] The important contribution of practices in the process of establishing shared norms has been specifically demonstrated by citizenship studies, reflecting the observation that a constitution is as legitimate as the procedure that has

---

[50] Helen Wallace makes a similar point in relation to the little-developed discussion about alternatives to European integration or, for that matter, European enlargement: see Wallace 2002.

[51] See, for excellent overviews of the courts' rulings and their impact on integration, among many others: Craig and De Burca 1998; De Burca and Weiler 2002; and Shaw 2000.

[52] See Article 19 EC Treaty.

[53] On the legal conditions for third-country nationals, see an overview by Hedemann-Robinson 2001. See also Shaw 2002; Day and Shaw 2002, 2003. On the normative reasoning for third-country nationals 'as Euro Citizens', see Follesdal 1998.

led to its implementation.[54] This dictum is as valid for citizens as for states as the constituent units of a polity.[55] Based on the discussion of different types of norms (social and legal), the distinction between the dual quality of norms (constructed and constitutive) and the impact of different types of norms in relation to their respective institutional and constitutional contexts, the following sections focus on the analysis of compliance and finality in the European constitutional debate.

Compliance with European (double) standards

As this section demonstrates, emerging 'double standards' in various policy areas such as human rights, minority rights, budget policy and freedom of movement for workers fly in the face of equality as a shared European constitutional norm and a key value in the finality debate.[56] Indeed, the lack of shared reference frames provided by the norm-setting EU for the norm-following candidate countries even with regard to accession criteria such as respect for minority rights or rules for national administration has been noted (Dimitrova 2001, 27). If the project of building, designing, revising or otherwise working on a European constitution is pursued, this context makes a successful development of the basic functions of a constitution, i.e. the foundation of legitimate authority and the task of social integration, problematic.[57] The following paragraphs briefly summarize the emerging two-class approach to EU membership by pointing to emerging deviations from the principle of equality in various policy areas.[58]

---

[54] See Wiener and Della Sala 1997; Lord 1998; and Hansen and Williams 1999.

[55] For example, studies on the concept of 'good international citizenship' which promotes an ethical foreign policy stressing the impact of moral principles such as the respect for human rights norms, over material gains in international politics (Wheeler and Dunne 1998).

[56] Note that equality is understood here as a norm that evolves through social practices and which therefore does not necessarily offer a sound basis for a legal case. Thus, the nature of that equality norm has always been a problem, in that it has always at least partially distinguished between insiders and outsiders (Article 12 EC), and also, so far as it is a general norm (e.g. equality in treatment of traders under the CAP or the customs union), it has always had to cede ground, as appropriate, to countervailing policy reasons, i.e. a lack of equal treatment can be justified. (I thank Jo Shaw for this observation.)

[57] On the basic functions of a modern constitution, see Frankenberg 2000, 258.

[58] See, for example, the observation by Danner and Tuschhoff, who find that candidate countries are about to turn into 'second-class members' (Danner and Tuschhoff 2002) at 2, www.aicgs.org/at-issue/ai-konzept.shtml.

Agricultural policy

Reactions to the Commission's proposals for enlargement negotiations,[59] in particular on the extended transition procedures in the area of free movement and agricultural policy, suggest that some Member States and candidate countries feel that they do not get what they have bargained for.[60] The lack of enthusiasm demonstrated by the Polish reaction to transition arrangements in the current eastern enlargement process of the European Union has not been received well in the EU. Jaroslaw Kalinowski, the Polish farm minister, 'attacked the European Commission's proposals [for incorporating new Member States into the EU's farm subsidy regime] as discriminatory, saying they were likely to leave the most efficient Polish farmers worse off after EU membership than they were before' and 'accused the EU of *double standards* for wanting to set in stone what new members would receive for the next 10 years, when the budget for the current EU was only set until 2006'.[61] This intervention was not well received in Brussels. Indeed, Poland was seen as causing 'irritation by demonstrating *an attitude of bargaining* that is often irreconcilable as well as by its *difficulties in understanding*'.[62]

Commission officials, like German Foreign Minister Fischer, tend to perceive enlargement and the political debate in the EU as two parallel events. Indeed, they insist on the separation of bargaining for membership from deliberation over substantive issues when stating that, for example, 'they [the candidate countries] *have to accept the rules of the game of the club* (of the 15 old member states), they have to implement our rules'.[63] When asked whether the participatory conditions for candidate countries in the accession process should be enhanced, another commission official replied: 'No, I don't think so...these are rules...and when you want to

---

[59] Note that the Commission proposes the draft negotiating positions. The Commission is in close contact with the applicant countries in order to seek solutions to problems arising during the negotiations. See: http://europa.eu.int/comm/enlargement/negotiations/index.htm.

[60] As the *Financial Times* reported, for example: 'Arguments over financing farm and regional aid in an enlarged EU represent the biggest potential obstacle to the successful conclusion of accession negotiations by the end of this year. Under the Commission's proposals, unveiled last month, enlargement would cost £40.2bn between 2004 and 2006. Poland, the biggest of the 10 states hoping to join the EU in 2004, rejects the Commission's proposals to phase in direct aid to farmers in new member states over 10 years. Meanwhile, existing EU states, such as Germany, the biggest contributor, are already manoeuvring to keep a lid on spending after enlargement.' *Financial Times*, 12 February 2002, 8.

[61] *Ibid.* (emphasis added).

[62] See *Frankfurter Allgemeine Zeitung*, 8 February 2002, 5. Translated from the original German text by the author (emphases added).

[63] *Ibid.* Translated from the original German text by the author.

become a member of the club, then these rules must be complied with...
the rest can be negotiated once they are members of the club... I think
that *for accession, one should set up a hurdle which they will have to deal
with, see and accept.*'[64]

Instead of exploring the reasons for misunderstandings, the diplomatic
discourse reveals the view of the candidate countries' duty to comply and
the expectation that club membership comes at the cost of compliance.
In a long-term perspective, however, such rigid expectations of compliance with EU rules may cause backlashes. A situation of lacking norm-
resonance, such as the contested chapters on budget policy, might not even
be in the EU's very interest once electoral politics come into play.[65] For example, Polish voters may feel compelled to vote against accession in order
to maintain economic survival. As Mr Kalinowski pointed out, 'I need to
convince our farmers to vote for accession... But how am I supposed to
convince them if they will expect lower incomes after accession?'[66] Later
that year Wladyslaw Serafin, president of the largest Polish farmers' union,
'Kolka Rolnicza', said that his organization would urge a 'no' vote on EU
membership, adding that '[i]f EU proposals concerning the direct pay-
ments – I do not say 100 per cent – will not guarantee competitiveness to
a Polish farmer, we will vote "no" in a referendum'.[67]

Minority rights

Observations on the request to comply with respect for minority rights as
a condition of enlargement raise similar questions about double standards
and a lack of resonance with accession norms in the candidate countries.
Notwithstanding the Treaties, the European Commission added respect
for minorities as a new condition for accession.[68] Thus the Copenhagen
criteria stipulate:

> The Copenhagen European Council not only approved the principle of
> the EU's enlargement to embrace the associated countries of Central and
> Eastern Europe, it also defined the criteria which applicants would have to
> meet before they could join the Community.

---

[64] Interview with Commission official, EU Commission, Brussels, 28 August 2001 (emphasis
added; this and all other interviews have been conducted by the author and are on file
with the author).

[65] See, for example, Danner and Tuschhoff 2002; Merlingen, Mudde and Sedelmeier 2000.

[66] *Financial Times*, 12 February 2002, 8.

[67] See http://www.euobserver.com/index.phtml?aid = 7488 (9 September 2002).

[68] De Witte 1998; Fierke and Wiener 1999; Williamson 2000; Pentassuglia 2001; and
Schwellnus 2001.

These criteria concern:

- the stability of institutions guaranteeing democracy, the rule of law, human rights *and respect for and protection of minorities* (political criterion);
- the existence of a functioning market economy as well as the capacity to cope with competitive pressure and market forces within the European Union (economic criterion);
- the ability to take on the obligations of membership including adherence to the aims of political, economic and monetary union (criterion concerning adoption of the Community *acquis*).[69]

While in the Amsterdam Treaty conditions for enlargement are defined according to Articles 7 and 6(1) TEU, these conditions have been creepingly extended by informal EU policies. As Bruno de Witte noted less than a month after Amsterdam, 'the European Commission, in its opinion on the request for accession to the EU of a number of Central and Eastern European countries, insisted on the importance of what it called "respect for minorities" as one of the political criteria for membership in the European Union'.[70] Respect for minorities has hence been included in the EU's package of conditions for accession. Crucially, the acceptance of this condition is not expected as a result of formal procedures, since there are no legal instruments to put it into practice. Indeed, as de Witte observes,

> among the famous 'political criteria' set out by the European Union as conditions for the accession of, or – more generally – closer cooperation with, the CEECs [Central and Eastern European Countries], *the insistence on genuine minority protection is clearly the odd one out*. Respect for democracy, the rule of law and human rights have been recognized as fundamental values in the European Union's internal development and for the purpose of its enlargement, whereas *minority protection is only mentioned in the latter context*.[71]

Free movement

In the Chapter on Free Movement, the Commission also proposes limitations for the candidate countries. As the Commission explains:

> Research suggests that the impact on the EU labour market of *the freedom of movement of workers after accession should be limited*. However, it is expected that the predicted labour migration would be concentrated in

---

[69] See the Commission website at http://europa.eu.int/scadplus/leg/en/lvb/e40001.htm (emphasis added).
[70] See Agenda 2000 – Volume I: 'For a stronger and wider Union', 15 July 1997, 52, cited in De Witte 1998, 3.
[71] De Witte 1998, 5 (emphases added).

certain member states, resulting in disturbances of the labour markets there. Concerns about the impact of the free movement of workers are based on considerations such as geographical proximity, income differentials, unemployment and propensity to migrate. The EU was also worried that this issue threatened to alienate public opinion and to affect overall public support for enlargement.

The EU has not requested a transition period in relation to *Malta* and *Cyprus*. However for all other countries where negotiations are under way, a common approach has been put forward. Negotiations with the candidate countries are ongoing. The essential components of the transition arrangement are as follows:

- A two year period during which national measures will be applied by current Member States to new Member States. Depending on how liberal these national measures are, they may result in full labour market access.
- Following this period, reviews will be held, one automatic review before the end of the second year and a further review at the request of the new Member State. The procedure includes a report by the Commission, but essentially leaves the decision on whether to apply the acquis up to the Member States.
- The transition period should come to an end after five years, but it may be prolonged for a further two years in those Member States where there are serious disturbances of the labour market or a threat of such disruption.
- Safeguards may be applied by Member States up to the end of the seventh year.[72]

According to the transition rules agreed to among the negotiating partners of the current association procedures, the freedom of movement for citizens of the candidate countries will remain restricted, if for a limited period. Here, citizens may experience a growing feeling of unequal treatment under the EC Treaty that has all the potential to spark conflict in the Union.

Conclusion

The constitutional debate and the enlargement process follow internationally acknowledged, albeit informally constituted, rules of legitimacy. Thus, the constitutional process allows all EU Member States to participate in the bargaining process. Following the logic of consequentialism, argument and/or appropriateness, they are entitled and enabled to make their

---

[72] See the Commission website at http://europa.eu.int/comm/enlargement/negotiations/chapters/chap2/index.htm (emphasis added).

point within, first, the framework of the constitutional convention and, second, during the IGC itself. In the compliance process of EU enlargement, the rule-following candidate countries follow the internationally established procedural norms of good compliance, i.e. as applicants for membership in a club, they know that their interest in membership comes at the cost of rule-following. If both processes are perfectly in agreement with the shared rules of social legitimacy, why does this chapter challenge the fact that they are addressed as parallel rather than interrelated processes? Two reasons appear justified. First, the particular situation of a constitutional debate in relation to the forthcoming enlargement in the EU entails an important shift of actor identity from candidate to Member State role which is not without influence on behaviour. Indeed, as the enlargement case shows, with progress in compliance and reasonable expectations of the candidates to achieve membership relatively soon, the compliance rationale is taken less seriously by the candidate countries. As a consequence, notions of contention are gradually beginning to be mixed with rule-following behaviour on the part of the candidates. This deviation from the compliance rationale, while causing irritation on the part of the norm setters who expect the norm followers to comply, is not as problematic once placed within a long-term perspective. On the contrary, according to the societal approach to compliance, contestation is a crucial and necessary factor in the process of establishing the validity of a norm's meaning. Indeed, in the absence of contestation, norm validity is expected to be less stable, as the meaning of the norm remains thin and therefore prone to projections – a classic situation of unintended consequences of institution-building.[73] Secondly, the rules which the newcomers are expected to follow are not always clearly defined.

The constitutional debate: finality and compliance with evolving norms

The massive enlargement process currently under way has created pressure for institutional change in the EU. Member States and candidate countries, as well as the Europolity itself, are affected by the impending changes and pushed to (re)act in preparation for constitutional change and the enlargement which stands to be settled by a constitutional

---

[73] As Nicholas Onuf notes: '[T]he alternative to institutions by design are those that arise as the unintended consequences of self-interested human action' (Onuf 2002, 212). See also North 1990 and Pierson 1996.

bargain at the 2004 IGC. In contrast to previous enlargement rounds, at this point not only institutional adaptation but also constitutional reform have become a major political issue. It is reflected in a constitutional turn in European integration studies stretching beyond the boundaries of the legal discipline.[74] Indeed, constitutional issues appear in the jargon of European public and analytical discourse to the extent that it seems 'astonishing that so many scholars and politicians speak about the future constitution of Europe' (Zuleeg 2001, 1). As the Fischer speech emphasized, the major changes ahead reinforce the necessity to define the oft-mentioned 'finality' of European integration. Finality, as it was cast into the European constitutional debate, was intended to mean finishing the project of European integration, by adding the building block of political integration. As Joschka Fischer put it,

> what I want to talk to you about today is not the operative challenges facing European policy over the next few months, not the current [2000] intergovernmental conference, the EU's enlargement to the east or all those other important issues we have to resolve today and tomorrow, but rather the possible strategic prospects for European integration far beyond the coming decade and the intergovernmental conference. So let's be clear: this is . . . a contribution to a discussion long begun in the public arena about the 'finality' of European integration. (Fischer 2000)

Fischer thus clearly distinguished between the organizational or governance business that had been part of European integration for a long time, and the future project of constructing a common political community.

Finality

While the issue of finality has often caused little reaction apart from stifled yawns, at the current stage of massive enlargement discussions of finality are no longer as leisurely and idealistic as those of the European enthusiasts in the early decades of integration which resulted in papers on European identity, federal constitutions and political union which rarely passed the declaratory stage. Instead, the current pressure for institutional change requires a more hands-on approach to finality, i.e. identifying the

---

[74] However, the European constitutional debate is characterized by the absence of a shared constitutionalist approach. As Armin von Bogdandy notes: '[T]he divergence in approach and even the lack in systematic approaches to European Union law render an assessment of key approaches, main directions, and plausible decisions in the constitutional debate, an enormously complex exercise' (Bogdandy 2000, 209).

goal, purpose and limits of integration and specifying the measures for
institutional reform for the more mundane reasons of political survival and perspective. If anything, Fischer's much-commented-on speech
brought that message home. It was an invitation to think constructively,
and the responses came from across Europe in debates over constitutional
reform in politics, the media and academia. During the two years that
followed the speech there were in fact few politicians or academics who
denied an interest in the constitutional debate in Europe and a plethora of
proposals were produced and discussed in public or semi-public settings.
As a result, Ingolf Pernice observes that the 'constitution is no longer a
taboo' in integration discourse (Pernice 2001, 3–4) and the 'constitutionalisation of the Treaties' has turned into an accepted policy objective.[75]
Yet, this quantitative shift towards constitutional issues by no means indicates that a similar qualitative shift towards shared views on constitutional
issues, let alone the emergence of shared European constitutional norms,
is discernible as well. In fact, it is pretty obvious that the facticity of things
constitutional and their validity do not go hand in hand. In other words,
the constitutional debate brought a plethora of considerably diverging
constitutional models to the fore, with little agreement on type, shape,
legal status or substance of a constitutional text.[76]

The constitutional process seeks to revise the EU's Treaties with a view to
enabling the EU to cope with the pending round of massive enlargement,[77]
possibly adding to, but in any case changing, the constitutional quality of the Treaty. The enlargement process, in turn, follows primarily
the logic of rule-following with a view to club membership.[78] While the
constitutional process is relatively open regarding the substantive changes

---

[75] See, for example, European Parliament, Committee of Institutional Affairs, 2000, Report
on the Constitutionalisation of the Treaties, Final A5-0289/2000, PE 286.949. Brussels:
European Parliament. In this document the term 'constitutionalization' is applied to mean
the drafting of a constitutional document, as opposed to the academic definition of the
term as a process including sets of social practices that contribute to constituting and
constructing the meaning of constitutional norms.

[76] The 2001 special issue of the *German Law Journal* expresses it thus in its editorial comments:
'[T]he discussion about a European constitution, newly reignited by German Foreign
Minister Joschka Fischer's speech last May, has been – so far – as thrilling as it has been
disconcerting.' *Special Issue: Ever Closer, Ever Larger: European Constitutionalism – Quo
Vadis?*, www.germanlawjournal.com, 1.

[77] Thirteen states currently have accession partnerships that entitle them to make membership applications to the EU. They are Bulgaria, Cyprus, the Czech Republic, Estonia,
Hungary, Latvia, Lithuania, Malta, Poland, Romania, the Slovak Republic, Slovenia and
Turkey. See the Commission website on enlargement at http://europa.eu.int/comm/
enlargement/intro/index_en.htm.

[78] Schimmelfennig and Sedelmeier 2002; but see Fierke and Wiener 1999.

(yet not flexible regarding the time-frame), the enlargement process is not flexible at all in terms of its substantive compliance rules (yet not clearly limited regarding the time-frame). The bottom line regarding the role of norms is thus the following: first, in the constitutional process, rules and norms as well as their respective meanings leave room for constructive impact; secondly, in the enlargement process, rules and norms have a structuring role. Yet, it is the constitutional process which will identify rules and norms with a clear structuring role in the future. After all, the constitutional bargain that is expected to be struck at the forthcoming intergovernmental conference in 2004 will have legal implications for all Member States. Furthermore, depending upon the type of constitutional choice eventually made, the constitutional bargain is expected to develop not only structuring qualities, i.e. a power-limiting function that judicializes existing power such as in the English and German constitutions, but also constructive qualities based on the constitutional document that initiates a power-founding function of the constitution, such as in the US and French traditions.[79]

The lack of convergence in constitutional politics among EU Member States is to be expected within the fragmented multi-levelled Europolity.[80] It is an expression of multiple socio-cultural trajectories which have shaped the institutional and ideational framework that sets the conditions for institutional fit, informs Member State preferences and defines the need for adaptation. It is, however, interesting to observe that nationally distinguishable positions have become even more pronounced in the process, i.e. the French prefer to know what a constitution is for, the British prefer to experience constitutionalization as they go along and the Germans know what they want to control and how to do it.[81]

---

[79] For an overview of the respective traditions, see Möllers 2003.

[80] See Olsen 2002 for a critical assessment of the lack of institutional convergence in the European polity despite European integration.

[81] The differing positions on constitutional change include rifts even among political allies. For example, a project for a constitution drafted by Elmar Brok, the chairman of conservatives from the European Parliament, in cooperation with a German professor of constitutional law, was criticized by leading EU conservatives as being 'too academic' and 'too German'. Subsequently, seven conservative prime ministers meeting in Sardinia on 9 September 2002 would have to 'struggle to patch significant rifts over crucial points concerning in particular the election of the Commission's president and the rotating EU presidency ... Their task will be difficult as several competing projects for a European constitution have so far been drafted by conservative politicians, and they all fail to gather support amongst right forces across Europe. Moreover, a persistent rift between a more federalist view, put forward by German Christian democrats, and a vision favoring keeping more powers for the EU governments will have to be healed.' See http://www.euobserver.com/index.phtml?aid = 7463 (6 September 2002).

Indeed, the constitutional proposals and/or blueprints demonstrate a radical shift from 'state-neutral wording' in constitutional language towards a remarkable lack of 'semantic precaution' (Haltern 2002, 8). This observation indicates a hardening of national bargaining positions in the constitutional debates that are expected at the end of the post-Nice process in 2004.[82]

The constitutional convention

Despite a lack of agreement about the how, why and what among promoters of a European constitution, let alone the critical voices of its opponents and, at best, cautious public enthusiasm for the project, since March 2002 a Convention on the Future of Europe[83] has been institutionalized. As a prelude with no precise formal link to the forthcoming IGC it offers, in principle, a new space for transnational deliberation. It may therefore have an important impact on preparing a European constitutional compromise. The convention entails three key issues. First, do Europeans want a constitution? Second, do Europeans have a constitution already? And third, do Europeans want the constitution they have?[84] It provides a space in which representatives of governments (member and candidate states), parliaments (member and candidate states, and the European Parliament), the Commission and the Council deliberate in preparation for the constitutional bargain that is to be struck at the 2004 IGC.[85] That bargain will entail the revision of the current Treaties in both formal and substantial ways. According to Declaration 23 on the future of the Union,[86] the following key issues need revision: the delimitation of powers between the European Union and the Member States (the principle of subsidiarity); the status of the Charter of Fundamental Rights proclaimed in Nice; the simplification of the Treaties 'with a view to making them clearer and better understood without changing their meaning'; and the role of

---

[82] This shift of perspective towards identifying national interest positions has been supported by Beate Kohler-Koch's work: see, for example, Kohler-Koch 2000.

[83] For the 2001 Laeken Council Declaration which set the rules and procedures for the Convention, see http://europa.eu.int/futurum/documents/offtext/doc151201_en.htm.

[84] As one MEP states: 'To me, the question is not whether Europe has a constitution, instead the question is, whether Europe has the constitution it needs. And the answer is clear; the European Union does not have the constitution it needs.' Interview with MEP official, Brussels, 29 August 2001 (on file with the author).

[85] The convention provides strictly limited space for civil society organizations. For details, see Shaw 2003.

[86] As appended to the Nice Treaty signed on 26 February 2001.

national parliaments.[87] As the outcome of the expected bargain, a revised
constitutional framework will set the standards for compliance in the fifteen Member States as well as the candidate countries who are soon to
join. It will contain changes regarding institutional and substantive issues.
More specifically, it will involve agreement among the participating heads
of state and/or government about the formal institutional changes and
procedures, such as the number of commissioners, the role and composition of the Council of Ministers, the establishment of new committees[88]
and so forth. It will also involve agreement about substantive change, such
as the type of constitutional document, and accordingly the role the TEU
texts are to play in the future of the EU. For example, are they meant to
limit political power based on a constitutional contract as some would
wish,[89] or are they expected to create unity based on the constitutional
moment?

While offering a new space for deliberation, the preparatory Convention will have little influence on remedying the expected gap in resonance
with the new supranational constitutional norms, on the one hand, and
the associative connotations they evoke in the respective domestic contexts of the fifteen-plus Member States in which they stand to be implemented, on the other. The gap, I would argue, is due to the detached
and speedy way in which the constitutional process takes place, without leaving space for interaction or contestation over the meaning of
the norms that are at stake. As a result, the revised institutions will be
kept at that proverbial distance from the citizens who simply will not
recognize them as 'theirs' and will keep seeing them as 'empty shells'
(Haltern 2001, 5). Expressed in the language of political science, such
empty texts mean 'thin' institutions that entail few prescriptions for behaviour; according to the societal approach, they offer little match with

---

[87] See 'Editorial Comments', 38 *Common Market Law Review* (2001), 493–7 at 494.
[88] See, for example, Pernice's proposal to establish a parliamentary subsidiarity committee:
Pernice 2001, 8.
[89] As the British Foreign Secretary Jack Straw told the Edinburgh Chamber of Commerce:
'The convention's main aim must be to design a written constitution for the people and
communities of Europe, not the political elites. This need not mean a long list of each
and every activity of government, setting out in detail who should do what and at which
level. But *there is a case for a constitution which enshrines a simple set of principles, sets
out in plain language what the EU is for and how it can add value, and reassures the public
that national governments will remain the primary source of political legitimacy.* This would
not only improve the EU's capacity to act, it would help to reconnect European voters
with the institutions which act in their name.' See the *Guardian*, 27 August 2002, at
http://politics.guardian.co.uk/eu/story/0,9061,781293,00.html (emphasis added).

social institutions. Instead of providing clear rules for compliance, they are therefore likely to provoke unintended consequences. That is, they are likely to raise expectations based on associative connotations that have been developed within the respective contexts in which the norms stand to resonate.

The lack of closeness or mutual understanding between the EU's institutions and the citizens is nothing new in the history of European integration, and, one could add, why should it matter at all, if the Euro-polity is not expected to turn into anything akin to a nation state? I would argue that it does matter in the light of the fast unfolding constitutional discourse that could run the risk of creating a situation of what might be called 'constitutional entrapment'.[90] That is, a constitutional revision of the Treaties is expected at the 2004 IGC in any case, despite the lack of closeness (i.e. European identity, belonging), despite the absence of an interest in establishing a supranational community and despite the uncertainty about the outcome of the forthcoming IGC. Its substance is largely validated through deliberations among western European elites notwithstanding the (if now increasingly invited) contributions of central and eastern European participants at the convention and in day-to-day political deliberations in Brussels and Strasbourg.[91] Its final shape stands to be negotiated at the 2004 IGC. While the thus increased access to participation will prove important in the long run, it is unlikely to create the shared validity of European constitutional norms, given the short time-span and the divergence in socio-cultural trajectories involved. In the

---

[90] On the situation of 'entrapment' in the enlargement process, see the argument offered by Frank Schimmelfennig (Schimmelfennig 2001).

[91] See, for example, the 'repossess enlargement' initiative of the European Parliament. As the President of the European Parliament Pat Cox said in a parliamentary speech in Strasbourg on 15 January 2002: 'The greatest transformation in hand of course is enlargement. The time has come for us, the political class, to repossess enlargement. It is inevitably the case that the *acquis communautaire* requires an enormous amount of work on the part of the European Commission and on the part of the public service in the candidate states to deal with all of the detail. But surrounding that detail is the wider political challenge – and that is our challenge. This House is uniquely well-placed to lead the politics of the transformation towards an enlarged Europe... *I would like to ask you, especially in the political groups, to consider a formula where we can invite MPs from our political families from the candidate states to participate in our enlargement debates with us this year*, to create a sense of vitality, to create a moment which is a very European moment, and to do it in terms which allow us to hear the different voices. They may be voices of accord or discord on some of the issues, but it is a really vital time and I hope the House will find within its mechanisms, and through the groups, a willingness to explore and create this platform, to express in a parliamentary sense this new Europe' (emphasis added). See http://www.europarl.eu.int/president/speeches/en/sp0002.htm.

absence of time and space for contestation a constitutional compromise will therefore prove difficult to achieve.[92]

Learning from experience?

The cases of enlargement and finality demonstrate an interesting paradox. While the compliance conditions have been fixed, the candidate countries are judged not only by their performance as good norm-followers, i.e. their ability to implement the accession *acquis* and initiate institutional adaptation accordingly, but also by their *capacity to understand*.[93] Furthermore, while the accession criteria are not up for debate at this point in the accession procedure, the candidate countries are invited to participate in the finality debate, nonetheless. This invitation is double-edged though. Thus, on 25 January 2002 German Foreign Minister Joschka Fischer 'encouraged Poland and the other east and central European countries which apply for membership in the European Union, to *participate in the debate over EU finality*'.[94] As Fischer explained, the EU was to take on board more 'responsibility in the transatlantic realm'; hence 'closer European integration' was necessary. Debate over these issues, Fischer emphasized, would contribute to '*increase understanding for one another*'. Soon afterwards, the Laeken Declaration agreed on the procedural rules for the Constitutional Convention which sustains this invitation to participate in the European dialogue. Yet, at the same time, voice is not paralleled by vote. In other words,

> [T]he accession candidate countries will be fully involved in the Convention's proceedings. They will be represented in the same way as the current Member States (one government representative and two national parliament members) and will be able to take part in the proceedings *without, however, being able to prevent any consensus which may emerge among the Member States*.[95]

---

[92] Absent a constitutional compromise, the IGC is likely to fall back on constitutional bargaining in which national preference formation (Moravcsik 1991, 1998) and experience with national constitutional norms will provide the core guidance for actors' decision-making. Elsewhere I take this assumption further, based on a model that discusses four positions in the constitutional debate that negotiators are likely to draw on in the case of constitutional bargaining under time pressure (Wiener 2003, 3–5). For reasons of space, this line of argument will not be further elaborated here.

[93] See citation in n. 62 above in *Frankfurter Allgemeine Zeitung*, 8 February 2002, 5.

[94] *Frankfurter Allgemeine Zeitung*, 26 January 2002, 4 (emphasis added).

[95] Laeken Declaration, http://europa.eu.int/futurum/documents/offtext/doc151201_en.htm (my emphasis); for the participating government and parliamentary representatives of the accession countries, see http://european-convention.eu.int/Static.asp?lang = EN&

The invitation to participate in order to overcome a lack of under-standing, on the one hand, and the rigorous application of the policy of conditionality, on the other, bring rationales to the fore which are not only distinct and potentially counterproductive, but which at the same time may turn into an important asset in the constitutional debate. They are counterproductive for the project of establishing shared reference frames in the constitutional debate. After all, if the candidate countries remain excluded from processes of norm-validation, the likelihood of norm-resonance in the domestic contexts of the candidate countries will decline. In turn, they might become an asset, if the conflict over enlarge-ment procedures and substance gains ground in the political debate. As Danner and Tuschhoff note, for example, the 'leaders took off their gloves and switched off the autopilot of enlargement negotiations. They *politi-cized the previously automatic process and charged the issues with conflicts.'*[96] While these authors predict a negative outcome of such politicization for the enlargement process, stating that 'that will be very difficult to settle. It is highly unlikely that the enlargement negotiations will be finalized according to the timeline established at Gothenburg. In fact, the added conflicts have the potential to prevent enlargement altogether',[97] a societal approach to compliance would not exclude a constructive outcome with a view to finality and the resonance of European constitutional substance. Thus, as the dialogic approach to politics suggests, access to participating in a potentially conflictive debate over accession criteria could contribute to enhancing the debate over constitutionalism which has long been con-sidered as 'axiomatic, beyond discussion, above the debate' and as some-thing which 'seemed to condition debate but not be part of it' (Weiler 1997, 98).

Compliance with evolving norms

While making actors comply depends on the interaction between norm-setters and norm-followers, compliance still remains an action which is structured by a bargaining outcome in the past. During that debate, norm followers' capacities for adaptation to the norm-setting identities are as-sessed, and rules and procedures to guide future behaviour are settled. The finality debate, in turn, entails constructive possibilities. While the

Content = Candidats_Gouv and http://european-convention.eu.int/ Static.asp?lang = EN&Content = Candidats_Parl, respectively.
[96] See Danner and Tuschhoff 2002, 1 (emphasis added).   [97] *Ibid.*

outcome of this debate does not necessarily mean producing a genuinely new structure, participants will inevitably bring their respective experience and beliefs to bear (Weber 1988, 153). In the absence of signposts in that debate, they are likely to draw on familiar constitutional concepts. However, given that a debate under conditions of truth-seeking does take place, the finality debate is *potentially open towards change*. In principle then, there is room for a constructive dimension in which deliberation can play an important part. The focus on 'fit' implied by the static character of the compliance rationale conflicts with the finality rationale then. If compliance thrives on establishing the 'goodness of fit' or rule-following for whatever reasons, then change is not the intended outcome and deliberation serves the single purpose of ensuring compliance. Subsequently, good norm-followers will rather abide by the rules than bend and contest them, and it has been noted that the candidate countries were good norm-followers – until early 2002. The compliance rationale suggests a successful outcome if and when actors can be successfully socialized into accepting the rules in a given context. In the absence of equal access to norm-construction under truth-seeking conditions, this socialization includes the pressure and even coercion – albeit, not overtly applied[98] – to fit in. Compliance is hence imposed rather than established interactively. Subsequently, the absence of shared validity of norm interpretation and meaning is likely to undermine resonance – as, for example, documented by the Polish case discussed above.

In sum, to comply with firm rules within the context of continuous change and adaptation to widening and deepening implies a counter-movement; to comply with these rules with a view to achieving the right to participation in the finality debate – after the constitutional bargain – raises normative questions about the EU's democratic equality norm on the one hand, and political questions about the gap between validation and resonance of constitutional norms on the other. In other words, according to the societal approach to compliance, the candidate countries' exclusion from norm-validation in the compliance process, in addition to the lack of a clear identification of compliance standards (norms) – in the Copenhagen accession criteria – by the norm-setters in the enlargement process, enhances the resonance gap with supranational norms. An unintended outcome of the parallel procedures of finality and compliance

---

[98] As Checkel puts it, 'I define persuasion as a social process of interaction that involves changing attitudes about cause and effect in the absence of *overt* coercion' (Checkel 2002, 2) (emphasis added).

is a double pattern of identity formation. Like all interactive processes, both contribute to particular identity constructions. They result however in different identities, potentially in favour of European integration for those who participate in the finality debate and share the norm of collaboration towards integration (see above); while creating Europe as the 'other' for the designated norm-followers in the compliance process who have to deal with the double standards of minority rights, and the transition rules of delayed freedom of movement for workers, for example. While, in principle, the discourse which sets the 'border of order' (Kratochwil 1994) is open and contested in the finality debate, it is uncontestable and fixed in the compliance process. The compliance process therefore has the potential to create new borders of inclusion/exclusion within the wider Europe. The borders are set by belonging to a wider Europe in the finality debate, and by being assigned the position as norm-follower in the compliance situation.

Conclusion

In this chapter, I have argued that, according to the societal approach to compliance, interactive processes that establish and/or reproduce norms as well as the interrelation between context and socio-cultural trajectory of norms are key conditions of norm resonance. Guidelines for norm resonance include the following. Norm resonance is achieved with acceptance and shared interpretation of a norm's meaning by different actors, in different contexts, and over time. Three factors are central to analysing the potential for norm resonance across contexts: first, the plausible *validity* of a norm to both norm-setters and norm-followers established through interactive processes between both types of actors; second, the *transferability* of this validity between different contexts, e.g. supranational, transnational, domestic or other political arenas; and third, the *durability* of norm validity over time. It follows that contestation in the process of norm construction sustains the validity of a norm and hence lowers the stakes for norm resonance. In turn, despite clearly defined prescriptive standards of norms and strong behavioural indicators of rule-following, including institutional adaptation, the absence of possibilities for norm contestation raises the stakes for norm resonance. *In sum, the success of compliance with supranational norms increases with the degree to which norm contestation is possible in each context and stage of the compliance process.*

Accordingly, a policy of conditionality, in other words the 'take-it-or-leave-it approach' of the EU's accession policy, prevents norm-followers' access to norm validation. As a consequence, compliance is often simply performed in order to gain access to the club, and once that goal is achieved, interest in the supranational norms wanes. While it could be argued that this approach to accession is by now established enlargement practice in the EU, and hence raises no major political issue, it is contended that the massive enlargement round ahead differs in significant ways from previous rounds. For example, first of all, the current widespread and actively conducted finality debate defines a constitutional dimension that has been absent in previous enlargement situations. Thus, a number of concrete measures, e.g. the establishment of the Convention, have been taken since the Amsterdam IGC set the institutional conditions for adaptation in view of the forthcoming massive enlargement round. Secondly, the constitutional substance in most candidate states has been influenced by the context of command economies for a number of decades. Thirdly, and following up on the difference in political context conditions set by the cold war, the candidate countries' expectations towards EU membership are shaped by the previous East–West gap between freedom and democracy (Fierke and Wiener 1999). Finally, the candidate countries have established firm links and an emerging group identity amongst themselves: for example, the *Visegrad* group (V4) includes Hungary, Poland, Slovakia and the Czech Republic who have announced that they will continue to work together – similarly to the Benelux countries – after joining the EU.[99]

Instead of claiming that compliance with the accession conditions undermines successful resonance with a constitutional bargain, I have argued in this chapter that the more the conditions for access to participation in the process of validating constitutional norms are enhanced, the more likely it is that the constitutional bargain resonates well within the fifteen-plus domestic contexts. In turn, the more exclusive are the deliberations over constitutional change, the more likely is the growing resonance gap with the constitutional bargain. Following the dual quality of norms assumption of the societal approach, it was argued that, despite norm validation in the supranational Brussels arena, i.e. agreement on a type, style

---

[99] According to the Polish Prime Minister Leszek Miller, they 'are determined to speak with one voice as then it is stronger and will be respected at the end of accession talks with the EU'. See http://www.euobserver.com/index.phtml?aid = 7467 (6 September 2002).

and contents of a document of constitutional quality, the validity of that document's contents – such as the expected constitutional text(s) at the forthcoming 2004 IGC – remains likely to be contested in the domestic arenas of the EU Member States and candidate countries. The impact of the context-specific constitutional baggage brought to the negotiating table by the Member State representatives is expected to increase in relation to the absence of shared European constitutional norms. While these might be more pronounced in some policy areas than in others, the fact that the current constitutional process focuses on broad constitutional changes leaves sectoral constitutional revisions that stand to be more successful regarding the establishment of shared constitutional values unexplored. While the bargain in 2004 matters, it is not the end of the story but a mere stage in the process of constitutional change in the EU. *The litmus test of the bargain's success lies in the degree to which the agreed constitutional norms on the supranational level resonate within the domestic contexts.* Empirical studies will have to establish the degree of resonance, i.e. the fit between the supranationally established European bargain and the respective domestic constitutional norms; the main intention here is to flesh out the opposing action rationales and social practices towards the construction of constitutional norms with a view to the long-term success of the envisaged constitutional bargain.

I argued that, in order to establish constitutional norms that not only reflect the validation attached to them by norm-setters but also potentially resonate with the designated norm-followers, it is necessary to take a long-term perspective, instead of a snap-shot approach to constitutional bargaining. Only thus can crucial information about the socio-cultural trajectories of norms be gathered. For work on the EU's constitutional debate this implies a need to back away from staking out constitutional positions according to national interests, and to reconstruct the emergence of constitutional norms according to different, if at times overlapping, socio-cultural trajectories instead. Indeed, interests in and by themselves do not offer much information as to whether or not norms stand a chance of resonating. In other words, not only the fixed interests at the point of constitutional negotiation but also the constructed values and norms must be brought to interact in order to identify the emergence of European constitutional norms. Empirically, such a perspective needs to bring dialogues within different constitutive policy areas to bear. The key is to identify and allocate such processes in the Europolity, and to establish an institutional or constitutional mechanism which safeguards it over time. According to the principled perspective on dialogical politics, a main challenge to be addressed by the current constitutional debate lies in establishing a space for deliberation and in making sure that the access conditions are fair and equal. The societal approach to compliance advanced in this chapter cast the view on the conceptual issue of how to institutionalize procedures according to a dialogic conception of politics which defines 'politics as contestation over questions of value and not simply questions of preference' (Habermas 1994, 3). Along this line, much recent work in European integration studies has pursued the question of how to establish institutionally procedures of deliberation that would accommodate the pluralist and multi-level character of political and legal procedures in the EU's fragmented polity. These studies all discuss how to maintain the principle of contestedness as a normative basis for democratic politics in the Habermasian sense that 'allows for the institutionalization of a public use of reason jointly exercised by autonomous citizens [and thus] accounts for those communicative conditions that confer legitimating force on political opinion and will formation' (Habermas 1994, 3). Work that tackles citizens' choices in a pluralist postnational polity (Maduro 2002), or that seeks to identify spaces for deliberation in processes of governance that are neither guided by a shared community nor organized according to liberal politics (Joerges and Neyer 1997), addresses 'precisely the conditions under which the political process can be presumed to generate reasonable results' (Habermas 1994, 3).

References

Amato, G. and J. Batt (1998), 'Minority Rights and EU Enlargement to the East. Report of the First Meeting of the Reflection Group on the Long-Term Implications of EU Enlargement: The Nature of the New Border', European University Institute, RSC Policy Paper No. 98/5

Bellamy, R. and D. Castiglione (2001), 'Normative Theory and the European Union: Legitimising the Euro-polity and its Regime', Queen's Papers on Europeanization, No. 13/2001

Bieber, R. and I. Salome (1996), 'Hierarchy of Norms in European Law', 33 *Common Market Law Review* 907

Bogdandy, A. von (1999), 'The Legal Case for Unity: The European Union as a Single Organization with a Single Legal System', 36 *Common Market Law Review* 887

(2000), 'A Bird's Eye View on the Science of European Law: Structures, Debates and Development Prospects of Basic Research on the Law of the European Union in a German Perspective', 6(3) *European Law Journal* 208

Börzel, T. A. and T. Risse (2000), 'When Europe Hits Home: Europeaniza-
    tion and Domestic Change', European Integration online Papers (EIoP)
    http://eiop.or.at/eiop/texte/2000-015a.htm 4(15)
Bull, H. (1977), *The Anarchical Society: A Study of Order in World Politics*
    (Basingstoke: Macmillan)
Caporaso, J. (2001), 'Citizenship and Equality: A Long and Winding Road', paper
    prepared for presentation at the International Association Annual Meeting,
    22–25 February 2001, Chicago
Castiglione, D. (2002), 'Comments on Carlos Closa: "The Implicit Model of
    Constitution in the EU Constitutional Project"', ARENA Conference 3–4
    March 2002, http://www.arena.uio.no/events/Conference2002/documents/
    Castiglione.doc
Chayes, A. and A. H. Chayes (1995), *The New Sovereignty. Compliance with Interna-
    tional Regulatory Regimes* (Cambridge, MA and London: Harvard University
    Press)
Checkel, J. (2001), 'Why Comply? Social Norms Learning and European Identity
    Change', 55(3) *International Organization* 553
    (2002), 'Persuasion in International Institutions', ARENA Working Paper 02/14,
    http://www.arena.uio.no/publications/wp02˙14.htm
Cowles, M. G., J. A. Caporaso and T. Risse (2001), *Transforming Europe: Euro-
    peanization and Domestic Change* (Ithaca, NY: Cornell University Press)
Craig, P. (2001), 'Constitutions, Constitutionalism, and the European Union',
    7(2) *European Law Journal* 125
Craig, P. and G. de Burca (1998), *EU Law – Text, Cases, and Materials*, 2nd edn
    (Oxford: Oxford University Press)
Curtin, D. and I. Dekker (1999), 'The EU as a "Layered" International Organiza-
    tion: Institutional Unity in Disguise', in P. Craig and G. de Burca (eds.), *The
    Evolution of EU Law* (Oxford: Oxford University Press)
Danner, F. and C. Tuschhoff (2002), 'Derailing EU Enlargement: Why Negotiations
    Stutter and How to Get Back on Track', American Institute for Contemporary
    German Studies (comment)
Day, S. and J. Shaw (2002), 'EU Electoral Rights and the Political Participation of
    Migrants in Host Polities', 8 *International Journal of Population Geography* 183
    (2003), 'The Boundaries of Suffrage and External Conditionality: Estonia as an
    Applicant Member of the EU', 9(2) *European Public Law* (forthcoming)
de Burca, G. and J. H. H. Weiler (eds.) (2002), *The European Court of Justice* (Oxford:
    Oxford University Press)
de Witte, B. (1998), 'Ethnic Minorities, the European Union and its Enlarge-
    ment', Reflection Group on 'Long-Term Implications of EU Enlargement: The
    Nature of the New Border', European University Institute, Florence
    (2002), 'The Closest Thing to a Constitutional Conversation in Europe: The
    Semi-Permanent Treaty Revision Process', in P. Beaumont, C. Lyons and

N. Walker (eds.), *Convergence and Divergence in European Public Law* (Oxford: Hart Publishing)

Dimitrova, A. L. (2001), 'Governance by Enlargement? The Case of the Administrative Capacity Requirement in the EU's Eastern Enlargement', paper prepared for presentation at the ECPR General Conference, 6–8 September 2001, University of Kent at Canterbury

Fierke, K. M. (2002), 'Beyond Agents and Structures: Logics, Rationality and the End of the Cold War', Queen's University, Belfast, unpublished paper

Fierke, K. M. and A. Wiener (1999), 'Constructing Institutional Interests: EU and NATO Enlargement', 6(5) *Journal of European Public Policy* 721

Finnemore, M., and K. Sikkink (1998), 'International Norm Dynamics and Political Change', 52(4) *International Organization* 887

Finnemore, M. and S. J. Toope (2001), 'Alternatives to "Legalization": Richer Views of Law and Politics', 55(3) *International Organization* 743

Fischer, J. (2000), 'Vom Staatenverbund zur Föderation – Gedanken über die Finalität der europäischen Integration' (Berlin Humboldt University)

Follesdal, A. (1998), 'Third Country Nationals as Euro Citizens: The Case Defended', ARENA Working Papers WP 98/9

Franck, T. (1990), *The Power of Legitimacy* (Oxford: Oxford University Press)

Frankenberg, G. (2000), 'The Return of the Contract: Problems and Pitfalls of European Constitutionalism', 6(3) *European Law Journal* 257

Habermas, J. (1992), *Faktizität und Geltung* (Frankfurt am Main: Suhrkamp)
(1994), 'Three Normative Models of Democracy', 1(1) *Constellations* 1

Haltern, U. (2001), 'Europe Goes Camper: The EU Charter of Fundamental Rights from a Consumerist Perspective', Constitutionalism Web-Papers (ConWEB) 3, http://www.les1.man.ac.uk/conweb/papers/conweb3-2001.pdf
(2003), 'Gestalt und Finalität Europas', in A. von Bogdandy (ed.), *Europäisches Verfassungsrecht. Theoretische und dogmatische Grundzüge* (Heidelberg: Springer)

Hansen, L. and M. C. Williams (1999), 'The Myths of Europe: Legitimacy, Community and the "Crisis" of the EU', 37(2) *Journal of Common Market Studies* 233

Hedemann-Robinson, M. (2001), 'An Overview of Recent Legal Developments at Community Level in Relation to Third Country Nationals Resident within the European Union...' 38 *Common Market Law Review* 525

Jepperson, R. L., A. Wendt and P. J. Katzenstein (1996), 'Norms, Identity, and Culture in National Security', in P. J. Katzenstein (ed.), *The Culture of National Security. Norms and Identity in World Politics* (New York: Columbia University Press)

Joerges, C. (2002), 'The Law in the Process of Constitutionalizing Europe', Arena Annual Conference (2002), Oslo, http://www.arena.uio.no/events/Conference2002/Papers.html

Joerges, C. and J. Neyer (1997), 'From Intergovernmental Bargaining to Deliberative Political Processes: The Constitutionalisation of Comitology', 3 *European Law Journal* 273

Joerges, C. and and M. Zürn (eds.) (2003), *Compliance in Modern Political Systems* (forthcoming)

Koh, H. H. (1997), 'Why Do Nations Obey International Law? Review Essay', 106 *Yale Law Journal* 2599

Kohler-Koch, B. (2000), 'Ziele und Zukunft der Europäischen Union: Eine Frage der Perspektive', 23(3) *Integration* 185

Koslowski, R. and F. Kratochwil (1994), 'Understanding Change in International Politics: The Soviet Empire's Demise and the International System', 48(2) *International Organization* 215

Kratochwil, F. (1984), 'The Force of Prescriptions', 38(4) *International Organization* 685

  (1989), *Rules, Norms, and Decisions. On the Conditions of Practical and Legal Reasoning in International Relations and Domestic Affairs* (Cambridge: Cambridge University Press)

  (1994), 'Citizenship: The Border of Order', 19 *Alternatives* 485

Lieber, F. (1859), *On Civil Liberty and Self-government* (Philadelphia: J. B. Lippincott)

Lord, C. (1998), *Democracy in the European Union* (Sheffield: Sheffield Academic Press)

Maduro, M. P. (2002), 'Where to Look for Legitimacy?' Arena Annual Conference, Oslo, http://www.arena.uio.no/events/Conference2002/Papers.html

March, J. G. and J. P. Olsen (1989), *Rediscovering Institutions. The Organizational Basis of Politics* (New York: Free Press)

  (1998), 'The Institutional Dynamics of International Political Orders', 52(4) *International Organization* 943

Merlingen, M., C. Mudde and U. Sedelmeier (2000), 'Constitutional Politics and the "Embedded Acquis Communautaire": The Case of the EU Fourteen against the Austrian Government', Constitutionalism Web-Papers (Con-WEB), http://www.qub.ac.uk/ies/onlinepapers/const.html(4/2000)

Möllers, C. (2003), 'Begriffe der Verfassung in Europa', in A. von Bogdandy (ed.), *Europäisches Verfassungsrecht. Theoretische und dogmatische Grundzüge* (Heidelberg: Springer)

Moravcsik, A. (1991), 'Negotiating the Single European Act: National Interests and Conventional Statecraft in the European Community', 45(1) *International Organization* 19

  (1998), *The Choice for Europe* (Ithaca, NY: Cornell University Press)

North, D. C. (1990), 'The Path of Institutional Change', in D. C. North (ed.), *Institutions, Institutional Change and Economic Performance* (Cambridge: Cambridge University Press)

Olsen, J. P. (2002), 'The Many Faces of Europeanization', ARENA Working Paper WP 01/2

Onuf, N. (1989), *World of Our Making: Rules and Rule in Social Theory and International Relations* (Columbia: University of South Carolina Press)

(2002), 'Institutions, Intentions and International Relations', 28 *Review of International Studies* 211

Pentassuglia, G. (2001), 'The EU and the Protection of Minorities: The Case of Eastern Europe', 12(1) *European Journal of International Law* 3

Pernice, I. (1999), 'Multilevel Constitutionalism and the Treaty of Amsterdam: European Constitution-Making Revisited?' 36 *Common Market Law Review* 703

(2001), 'The European Constitution', 16th Sinclair-House Talks in Bad Homburg, May 2001

Phinnemore, D. and D. Papadimitriou (2002), 'The Europeanisation of Romania: The Contribution of Twinning', 1st Pan-European Conference on European Union Politics, Bordeaux, 26–28 September 2002

Pierson, P. (1996), 'The Path to European Integration: A Historical Institutionalist Analysis', 29(2) *Comparative Political Studies* 123

Puetter, U. (2001), 'The Informal Eurogroup: A New Working Method and an Institutional Compromise', Constitutionalism Web-Papers (ConWEB), No. 2/2001, http://www.les1.man.ac.uk/conweb/papers/conweb2-2001. pdf

Risse, T. (2000), "Let's Argue!: Communicative Action in World Politics', 54(1) *International Organization* 1

Risse, T., S. C. Ropp and K. Sikkink (eds.) (1999), *The Power of Human Rights. International Norms and Domestic Change* (Cambridge: Cambridge University Press)

Ruggie, J. G. (1998), *Constructing the World Polity* (London: Routledge)

Schepel, H. (2000), 'Reconstructing Constitutionalization: Law and Politics in the European Court of Justice', 20(3) *Oxford Journal of Legal Studies* 457

Schilling, T. (1996), 'The Autonomy of the Community Legal Order: An Analysis of Possible Foundations', Harvard Jean Monnet Working Paper 96/10

Schilling, T., J. H. H. Weiler and U. R. Haltern (1996), 'Who in the Law is the Ultimate Judicial Umpire of European Community Competences? The Schilling–Weiler/Haltern Debate', Harvard Jean Monnet Working Paper 96/10

Schimmelfennig, F. (2001), 'The Community Trap: Liberal Norms, Rhetorical Action, and the Eastern Enlargement of the European Union', 55(1) *International Organization* 47

Schimmelfennig, F. and U. Sedelmeier (2002), 'European Union Enlargement – Theoretical and Comparative Approaches', 9(4) *Journal of European Public Policy* (special issue)

Schmitter, P. C. (2000), 'An Excursus on Constitutionalization', Constitutionalism Web-Papers (ConWEB), No. 3/2000, http://www.les1.man.ac.uk/conweb/papers/conweb3-2000.pdf

Schwellnus, G. (2001), 'Much Ado About Nothing? Minority Protection and the EU Charter of Fundamental Rights', Constitutionalism Web-Papers (ConWEB), No. 5/2001, http://www.les1.man.ac.uk/conweb/papers/conweb5-2001.pdf

Sedelmeier, U. (1998), 'The European Union's Association Policy Towards the Countries of Central and Eastern Europe: Collective EU Identity and Policy Paradigms in a Composite Policy', PhD thesis, University of Sussex

Shaw, J. (1996), 'European Union Legal Studies in Crisis? Towards a New Dynamic', 16(2) *Oxford Journal of Legal Studies* 231

(2000), *Law of the European Union*, 3rd edn (Houndmills, Basingstoke and New York: Palgrave Law Masters)

(2002), 'Sovereignty at the Boundaries of the Polity', in N. Walker (ed.), *Sovereignty in Transformation* (Oxford: Hart Publishing)

(2003), 'Process Responsibility and Inclusion in EU Constitutionalism', 9(1) *European Law Journal* 45

Shaw, J. and A. Wiener (1999), 'The Paradox of the "European" Polity', Harvard Jean Monnet Working Paper 10/99

Tilly, C. (1984), *Big Structures, Large Processes, Huge Comparisons* (New York: Russell Sage)

Tilly, C. (ed.) (1975), *The Formation of National States in Western Europe* (Princeton: Princeton University Press)

Tully, J. (1995), *Strange Multiplicity: Constitutionalism in an Age of Diversity* (Cambridge and New York: Cambridge University Press)

(2002), 'The Unfreedom of the Moderns in Comparison to Their Ideals of Constitutional Democracy', 65 *Modern Law Review* 204

Wagner, W. (1999), 'Interessen und Ideen in der europäischen Verfassungspolitik. Rationalistische und konstruktivistische Erklärungen mitgliedstaatlicher Präferenzen', 40(3) *Politische Vierteljahresschrift* 415

Wallace, H. (2002), 'Enlarging the European Union: Reflections on the Challenge of Analysis', 9(4) *Journal of European Public Policy* 658

Weber, M. (1988), 'Die "Objektivität" sozialwissenschaftlicher und sozialpolitischer Erkenntnis. 1904', in M. Weber (ed.), *Gesammelte Aufsätze zur Wissenschaftslehre* (Tübingen: J. C. B. Mohr (Paul Siebeck))

Weiler, J. H. H. (1997), 'The Reformation of European Constitutionalism', 35(1) *Journal of Common Market Studies* 97

Weiler, J. H. H. and U. R. Haltern (1996), 'The Autonomy of the Community Legal Order – Through the Looking Glass', Harvard Jean Monnet Working Paper 96/10

Wendt, A. (1998), 'On Constitution and Causation in International Relations', in T. Dunne, M. Cox and K. Booth (eds.), *The Eighty Years' Crisis: International Relations 1919–1999* (Cambridge: Cambridge University Press)

(1999), *Social Theory of International Politics* (Cambridge: Cambridge University Press)

Wheeler, N. J. and T. Dunne (1998), 'Good International Citizenship: A Third Way for British Foreign Policy', 74(4) *International Affairs* 847

Wiener, A. (1998), *'European' Citizenship Practice – Building Institutions of a Non-State* (Boulder, CO: Westview Press)

(2001), 'Zur Verfassungspolitik jenseits des Staates: Die Vermittlung von Bedeutung am Beispiel der Unionsbürgerschaft', 8(1) *Zeitschrift für Internationale Beziehungen* 73

(2002), 'The Dual Quality of Norms: Stability and Flexibility', Queen's University, Belfast, unpublished paper

(2003), 'Editorial: Evolving Norms of Constitutionalism', 9(1) *European Law Journal* 1

Wiener, A. and V. Della Sala (1997), 'Constitution-Making and Citizenship Practice – Bridging the Democracy Gap in the EU?', 35(4) *Journal of Common Market Studies* 595

Wiener, A. and T. Wobbe (2002), 'Norm Resonance in Global Governance – Contested Norms in the Process of EU Enlargement', paper prepared for presentation at the Annual Meeting of the International Studies Association, New Orleans, 24–27 March, New Orleans Archive, http://www.isanet.org/noarchive/wiener_wobbe.html

Williamson, A. (2000), 'Enlargement of the Union and Human Rights Conditionality: A Policy of Distinction?' 25 *European Law Review* 601

Zuleeg, M. (2001), 'Comment', 2(14) *German Law Journal* http://www.germanlawjournal.com/

Zürn, M. (2000), 'Introduction – Law and Compliance at Different Levels', paper presented at the 41st Annual ISA Convention, Los Angeles

Epilogue
Europe and the dream of reason

PHILIP ALLOTT

The sleep of reason produces monsters.

F. Goya, *Los Caprichos* (1799)[1]

Ideal self-constituting

What we need is a *metaphysics of Europe's self-constituting*. What we do not need is a rationalization of 'European integration'. Still less should we act as apologists of the current incoherent state of the public realms of Europe, a state of affairs which is an unwilled and irrational outcome of countless coordinated and uncoordinated acts and events – a leviathan of shreds and patches. 'European Union' is an *Ungeheuer* which is an *Unganze*.

There was Europe – as place, as subjectivity, as potentiality – before there were the social systems ('states') which the usual conception of 'European integration' presupposes. The true *self-constituting* of the people and the peoples of Europe requires a new concept (*Begriff*) of their perennial unity, not merely an explanation of a particular negating of their recent disunity.

---

[1] *El sueño de la razon* [sic] *produce monstruos.* The full explanatory text accompanying the engraving is: 'La fantasia abandonada de la razon, produce monstruos imposibles: unida con ella, es madre de las artes y origen de sus marabillas.' 'Imagination abandoned by reason produces impossible monsters: united with her, she is the mother of the arts and the source of their wonders.' F. Goya y Lucientes, *Los Caprichos* (tr. H. Harris; New York: Dover Publications, 1969), plate 43 (pre-modern spelling and accenting retained).

The Spanish word *sueño* means 'dream' as well as 'sleep', giving Goya's text a more complex resonance. Also, and of particular interest in the present context, it has been suggested that Goya based the iconography of this engraving on the frontispiece to a work, published in Paris in 1793, on the philosophy of J.-J. Rousseau. (*Ibid.*, introduction by P. Hofer, p. 2.)

Europe – as place, as subjectivity, as potentiality – is not the natural product of organic processes. It is a product of, and in, consciousness. Societies constitute themselves ideally by imagining collectively their identity, their unity and their purpose. The ideal self-constituting of a society is a process of collective thinking, embracing every kind of thinking, theoretical and practical, disinterested and subjective, rational and irrational.

If we choose to call such a phenomenon the *ideal self-constituting* of a society within the *public mind* of a society,[2] then we are conscious of adding one more thread to a substantial tradition within the self-contemplating of the European public mind: Montesquieu's *spirit or mind (esprit)* of the constitution; Vico's *social poetics*; Herder's *Volksgeist* (spirit or mind of a people); Goethe's *felt world (gefühlte Welt)*; Destutt de Tracy's *ideology*; Hegel's *Geist* (particularized in the consciousness of society and state); Dilthey's *life expressions (Lebensäusserungen)*; Marx's *consciousness*; Sorel's *social poetry*; Freud's *collective mind*; Durkheim's *psychic life* of society and *collective representations*; Mannheim's *collective spirit* and *collective conscious*.

All such ideas themselves participate in the phenomena which they organize. Europe's self-constituting self-consciousness is an unbroken 3,000-year continuum, perpetually making itself, and reflecting on its making of itself. The public mind of Europe contains a history of itself, and a history of its history, perpetually re-imagining what it has meant to itself. A constant feature of that history has been the occurrence of phase-shifts of consciousness, discontinuities within the continuum. From time to time, the people and the peoples of Europe re-imagine themselves at the level of the ideal, specifically and purposively, and not merely routinely and accretively. We may call such events *ecthetic moments*.

Ecthesis is the step in a Euclidean proof which says: *let ABC be a triangle.* The mathematical proof links the ideal and the actual by way of the mathematically necessary. In the ecthetic moment the proof particularizes the universal (the ideal triangle) and universalizes the particular (any actual triangle). At the beginning of the twenty-first century, Europe is living such a moment. *Let Europe be a unity!*

---

[2] For the concept of the *ideal constitution* (as well as the *real* and *legal* constitutions), see P. Allott, *Eunomia – New Order for a New World* (Oxford: Oxford University Press, 2001), ch. 9. For the concept of the *mind politic* of the nation, see P. Allott, 'The Nation as Mind Politic', 24 *Journal of International Law and Politics* (1992), 1361. For the concept of the *public mind*, see P. Allott, *The Health of Nations, Society and Law beyond the State* (forthcoming), §1.15.

Two primordial ecthetic moments[3] in Europe's ideal self-constituting have together been the first source of Europe's unique ideal identity, making Europe's self-constituting ('European civilization') a particular in the universal social self-constituting of all humanity.

The first ecthetic moment is Europe's appropriation of the book of Genesis, an *Urtext* of European self-consciousness. The account of the creation of the universe contains the reiterated ecthetic formula: *let there be...*; in Latin, *fiat!* It is a subjunctive which is hypothetical, optative and dispositive (idea, wish and command). The divine *fiat* expresses the ideal, real and legal constituting of the universe, the image and model of the self-constituting of every human society and of every human personality. It is an archetype of humanity's self-creating, of the *progressive dynamic* at the heart of European civilization.

On this view, the Fall of Man in the Garden of Eden is the archetype of humanity's power of self-destroying, the necessary corollary of the power of self-creating, the negation which reveals itself in all the grandeurs and miseries of European civilization, not least in the twentieth century. Human self-evolving is not necessarily human self-perfecting. We have the unique species-characteristic that we can adapt our habitat to fit our imperfection. We can make human beings in test tubes and destroy human beings in gas chambers.

The other primordial ecthetic moment is the making, and the repeated rediscovery, of another *Urtext* of European self-consciousness: Plato's *Republic*, book VII.[4] In the parable of the cave, Plato placed the self-enlightening work of the mind at the centre of the activity of being human, but placed the activity of being human within the activity of the whole universe – idea, wish and command reconceived as knowledge, liberty

---

[3] 'Moment' is here used in approximately the Hegelian sense (*das Moment* – as opposed to *der Moment*, a moment in time), which has a deep-structural semiotic relationship with the use of the word in mechanics (the tendency of a force to rotate a body). In this sense, a moment is a determinative element in a social structure (static) or a determinative development in a social system (dynamic).

[4] Each rediscovery of Plato has been a re-creation of Plato and also an ecthetic moment in the development of social consciousness: Aristotle, the Stoics, the neoplatonists (of the third century and after), the ninth-century renaissance (centred on the court of Charlemagne), the twelfth-century renaissance (centred on the University of Paris), the Italian humanists of the fifteenth century, the Cambridge Platonists of the seventeenth century, Hegel. Even Francis Bacon acknowledged the achievement of Plato, provided that his 'metaphysique' is put on a different basis (proceeding from the particular to the universal, rather than by prior postulation of the universal). Bacon also noted that, in the Genesis account, the first created thing is Light. F. Bacon, *The Advancement of Learning* (1605) (ed. G. W. Kitchin; London: J. M. Dent (Everyman), 1915), 91ff.

and necessity. Through the power of mind we can freely create a *human reality*, but it is a reality which cannot escape the reality of all that which transcends human reality, including the necessity of the natural world and the unknowable reality of the universe of all-that-is.

And, as in the moment of self-creating, so in the moment of self-knowing, humanity found itself in possession of the knowledge not only of good but also of evil, the necessary corollary of the power to imagine our own reality, a power of human self-denying. Shackled prisoners remain, unenlightened, in the cave of unknowing. Human self-knowing is not necessarily human self-surpassing. Our reason produces quantum mechanics. Our reason produces slavery.

Social metaphysics

To revise and reverse the empiricist slogan: there is nothing in society which was not first in the mind. Social consciousness is the product of the interacting of individual consciousnesses, but it produces a reality-for-consciousness which is not merely the consciousness of individual human beings, and which lives longer than the lives of individual human beings.

The making of human reality is made possible by a capacity of the human mind to create what we may call *paratheses*. A parathesis (*a triangle ABC*) is the product of an ecthesis (*let ABC be a triangle*).[5] God, immortality, the soul, the universe, nature, species, humanity; society, law, freedom, right, obligation; tribe, king, *polis*, nation, empire, republic, state, community, union; property, wealth, money, the market, capital, labour, equilibrium: there are countless metaphysical paratheses of human social self-consciousness. They are more than words, and less than things. They flow, in an endless reciprocating dialectic, from society's *ideal* self-constituting (in the form of ideas) to its *real* self-constituting (as the form and content of social struggle) and so to its *legal* self-constituting (as the form and content of legal relations), and back again from the legal to the real to the ideal. They are the product of a society's social process, and yet they determine the forms and formulas of that process.

---

[5] This use of the word *parathesis* is proposed as an innovation. In ancient Greek it meant 'a putting beside, juxtaposition, comparison', and also 'suggestion, advice' (Liddell and Scott). The Greek preposition and root *para* conveys the idea of 'alongside'. The general sense of *ekthesis* in ancient Greek was 'putting out, exposing'.

Like *the triangle ABC*, a parathesis can give form and substance to any appropriate content. It is the universalization of countless possible particulars, each of which is the particularization of the same universal. Among *poleis* there can be Athens and Sparta. Among empires there can be the Church of Rome, the Holy Roman Empire and the European Union. Human beings use such products of social struggle to recognize themselves and to recognize each other in a universalized parathetic form. They recognize each other by what they share (their universality) and by what they do not share (their particularity), their *quidditas* and their *haecceitas*.[6]

In Europe at the beginning of the twenty-first century, we are living through a profound crisis of *recognition*.[7] It is a metaphysical crisis, of our mutual self-knowing, of our consciousness, of our universality and of our particularities, of what we share and what we do not share. We are struggling socially to produce the parathesis *Europe*.

And twentieth-century European social struggle has taught us a lesson which humanity will surely never forget: that a metaphysical parathesis (nation, state, race, class) may become a *phenomenon*, that is to say, it may become the object of human perception as if it were not a product of human thought. A product of the world of mind is able to act as a phenomenon, as a cause of unlimited effects, like the phenomena of the physical world, that is, of mind's idea of a world of non-mind.

The social phenomenalizing of a metaphysical category is a matter of life and death. We can love metaphysical social phenomena, live for them, and we can hate them, die for them, kill for them. In twentieth-century Europe, more than 100 million people were killed by social violence in the name of metaphysical products of the human mind, and countless others were maimed in body and mind and in the actualizing of their personal potentiality.

---

[6] In medieval philosophy, *quidditas* was an answer to the question: what kind of a thing is this? *Haecceitas* was an answer to the question: what is the particularity of this thing? A given thing is thus seen as the universalization of a particular and the particularizaton of a universal. Metaphysics, it may be said, is the study which takes its origin in this distinction. One cannot know anything without knowing that which it is not but without which it cannot be known.

[7] The word 'recognition' (*Anerkennung*) cannot escape its Hegelian associations. For Hegel, the constituting of the self involves an interiorization of 'the other'. In a memorable formulation, he says (speaking of more than one consciousness): 'They *recognize* themselves as *mutually recognizing* one another.' G. W. F. Hegel, *Phenomenology of Spirit* (1807), §184 (tr. A. V. Miller; Oxford: Oxford University Press, 1977), 112. *The self and the other* is presented as one of the dialectically constitutive 'perennial dilemmas' of society in Allott, *Eunomia*, ch. 4 (and see below).

The dream of reason

It is possible to lay at the door of *philosophers* an important part of social responsibility for the way in which the European mind in the twentieth century disempowered itself in relation to its own metaphysical products, increasing its powerlessness in the face of its increasing powerfulness.[8]

Inspired by the anti-metaphysicalism of Hobbes and Locke and Hume and Rousseau, and provoked by the majestic metaphysical systems of Spinoza and Berkeley and Leibniz and Wolff, Immanuel Kant gradually discovered the purpose of his life-work, the ultimate challenge of philosophy. The great unsolved problem was the problem of metaphysics. How can the mind make sense of this very peculiar activity of the mind? In his *Dreams of a Spirit-Seer Elucidated by Dreams of Metaphysics* (1766),[9] Kant thought aloud about the problem, adopting a peculiar sardonic tone of voice (perhaps in imitation of Hume), a tone of voice which he would abandon in his great critical works twenty years later.

He called metaphysical philosophers 'builders of castles in the sky in their various private worlds' (*Luftbaumeister der mancherlei Gedanken-welten*). He said that there is a certain affinity between the *dreamers of reason* and the *dreamers of sense*. They both see apparitions. 'Both types of image are, in spite of the fact that they delude the senses by presenting themselves as genuine objects, hatched out by the dreamer himself.'[10] In words prophetic of his own later achievement, he said that metaphysics as a science might best be regarded as a science of the *limits of human reason.*[11]

In the first *Critique*, Kant explained what he meant by 'critique': 'It will...decide as to the possibility or impossibility of metaphysics in general, and determine its sources, its extent, and its limits...'[12] He will

---

[8] This argument is presented more fully in Allott, *Health of Nations*, ch. 1.

[9] Tr. and ed. D. Halford, *Immanuel Kant: Theoretical Philosophy 1735–1770* (Cambridge: Cambridge University Press, 1992), 301–55. The *Spirit-Seer* (*Geisterseher*) was explicitly directed against the Swedish philosopher-mystic Emanuel Swedenborg (1688–1772), whose version of 'theosophy' (co-ordinating the divine, the natural, the rational and the human) continues to have adherents.

[10] Halford, *Kant*, 329–30.

[11] *Ibid.*, 354. A century earlier, Thomas Hobbes had said, in his blunt mode, that, unlike animals, human beings have the power of reasoning which allows us to acquire knowledge, but also allows us 'to multiply one untruth by another' and 'to confuse *ratio* (reason) with *oratio* (speech), supposing that a thing must be true if we can say it'. T. Hobbes, *Human Nature: Or, The Fundamental Elements of Policy* (1640/50) (ed. J. C. A. Gaskin; Oxford: Oxford University Press, 1994), p. 38.

[12] I. Kant, *Critique of Pure Reason* (1781), preface to 1st edn (tr. N. Kemp Smith; London: Macmillan, 1929), 9. 'What we here require is a criterion by which to distinguish with certainty pure and empirical knowledge' (43).

demonstrate the possibility and the necessity of one privileged form of *a priori* thought (*a priori*, in the sense that it is 'knowledge absolutely independent of all experience'), namely, that which provides the 'universal modes of knowledge',[13] concepts which make possible our knowledge of the experiential world and without which we could not have such knowledge. Our understanding of such ideas is *metaphysical* in one sense of the word. It is, according to Kant, *transcendental* in the sense that they are ideas about the possibility of, and hence the proper limits of, ideas.[14]

There remained the other sort of non-experiential knowledge, namely, metaphysics in the widest sense of the word.

> But what is still more extraordinary than all the preceding is this, that certain modes of knowledge leave the field of all possible experiences and have the appearance of extending the scope of our judgments beyond all limits of experience, and this by means of concepts to which no corresponding object can ever be given in experience . . . Besides, once we are outside the circle of experience, we can be sure of not being *contradicted* by experience. The charm of extending our knowledge is so great that nothing short of encountering a direct contradiction can suffice to arrest us in our course; and this can be avoided if we are careful in our fabrications – which none the less still remain fabrications.[15]

As a direct result of Kant's treatment of these matters, three dramatic and fateful things happened in the subsequent development of European social consciousness.

The announcement of the death of metaphysics was premature. On the contrary, there has been a mass-production of social metaphysics, on a scale unprecedented in recorded human history. And feverish social energy has been applied to particular metaphysical paratheses, especially those of social totality, such as *nation, state*, and *economy*.

The development of the 'human sciences' has led to a massive naturalising of all human phenomena, including the products of social-metaphysical thinking, and this has had the effect of greatly increasing

---

[13] *Ibid.*, 43, 42.

[14] Kant claimed his new way as a Copernican revolution, in the sense that the human mind was no longer to be merely a passive recipient of perceptions but an active maker of reality. 'We must therefore make trial whether we may not have more success in the tasks of metaphysics, if we suppose that objects must conform to our knowledge.' (Preface to 2nd edn; *ibid.*, 22.)

[15] *Ibid.*, 45, 46. In the last pages of the first *Critique* (659ff.), Kant discussed the various senses of the word 'metaphysics', in order to isolate his own conception of the idea.

the power of those members of society who manipulate such things in the public interest, especially politicians and technocrats.

The renewed attack, in the twentieth century, on the possibility of metaphysics, and 'transcendental' philosophy in general, has left the institutional pragmatism of democracy-capitalism as the sole intellectual determinant of social identity, unity, and purpose. The products of social metaphysics are judged by the social systems that they make possible.

The unhappy state of consciousness known as 'European integration' is a direct, even necessary, product of these three closely related developments. The philosophical challenge at the beginning of the twenty-first century is to try, once again, to make sense of the social phenomenon of metaphysics, which flourishes as never before. The reconstituting of the self-consciousness of 'Europe' is an integral part of that challenge.

The metaphysics of totality

Even as Kant was defining the nature and prescribing the limits of the three forms of rationality (epistemic, moral and aesthetic), social practice was repudiating him. Emotional subjectivity began to take over the European public mind, combining rationalism and irrationalism, not only in the fine arts and literature (romanticism) but also in the conceiving of social totality (*the nation*). From 1789, the idea of the nation became a powerful metaphysical focus of social identity, social unity and social purpose, something to live for and to die for collectively.[16]

In philosophy itself, ultimate metaphysics, especially in Hegelian idealism (later in Schopenhauer and Marx), negated the Kantian separation of the real (unknowable) and the ideal (the product of the mind). And the surpassing of that separation could, among many other things, lead (as it did in Hegel) to the totalizing idea of *the state*, a metaphysical projection at the collective level of the self-knowing and self-governing of individual human consciousness. Human beings might recognize themselves individually as they recognized each other collectively in their common nationality, but they must also recognize themselves as subjects of that alienated externalization and systematization of the human mind and the human will which is the state.[17]

---

[16] For the significance of the idea in revolutionary France, see P. Allott, 'The Crisis of European Constitutionalism: Reflections on the Revolution in Europe', 34 *Common Market Law Review* (1997), 439 at 452ff.

[17] 'It has recently become very fashionable to regard the state as a contract of all with all ... This point of view arises from thinking superficially of a mere unity of different

From 1776 (publication of *The Wealth of Nations*), the European public mind found within itself the capacity to collectivize not merely subjectivity but also creative activity in the dual parathesis of the *economy* of a *nation*. The idea of the nation could set the framework of identity, unity and purpose for all of human effort, not merely the practical framework but also the ideal (aspirational) framework. The economy of the nation could harness the overwhelming power of collectivized energy in the self-developing of a society internally, and externally in competition and conflict with other societies which had undergone the same kind of development.[18]

These metaphysical totalities have been sustained by higher-level myth-theories of 'revolution', 'modernity', even 'Enlightenment', suggesting that they were something other than a new life for old metaphysics, very old wine in second-hand bottles. The tribalism of national subjectivity is as old as the tribe. The alienated state is as old as monarchy. The collectivist economy is as old as slavery. In their new manifestations they are sustained by complex hypothetical models of their functioning – history (in the case of nationalism), democracy (in the case of the state) and capitalism (in the case of the economy). These hypothetical models have proved to be most efficient means of 'legitimizing' the totalities, that is to say, of explaining and justifying their practice, and hence of arousing appropriate responses in the public mind of society and in the private minds of society-members.

The triune metaphysic of *nation–state–economy* actualizes its unity in the parathesis known as *law*, a society's legal self-constituting. Efficient law-making and law-executing are the efficient means of harnessing the troika of nation, state and economy. Law constructs and manages the economy. Law expresses and conditions the will of the nation. Law empowers and controls the state.

Nation–state–economy under the rule of law has proved to be of immense creative power, leading to a transformation of the conditions of human existence and, not least, to a new metaphysics of human self-knowing and self-judging. Europe's self-reconstituting at the beginning

---

wills ... But the case is quite different with the state; it does not lie within an individual's arbitrary will to separate himself from the state, because we are already citizens of the state by birth. The rational end of man is life in the state ...' G. W. F. Hegel, *The Philosophy of Right*, addition (*Zusatz*) to §75 (tr. T. M. Knox; London: Oxford University Press, 1952), 242.

[18] Adam Smith noted the fact that the 'very different theories of political oeconomy ... have had a considerable influence, not only upon the opinions of men of learning, but upon the public conduct of princes and sovereign states'. A. Smith, *An Inquiry into the Nature and Causes of the Wealth of Nations* (1776) (Oxford: Oxford University Press, 1993), 10.

of the twenty-first century is condemned either to be a surpassing of nation–state–economy in a new metaphysic of totality or, if not, to be a slow poisoning of that rich source of Europe's self-constituting and self-perfecting.

The naturalizing of the human

The failed nineteenth-century project of the 'human sciences' – German 'mind sciences' (*Geisteswissenschaften*), French 'social sciences', British 'moral sciences' – was a late flowering of an old idea, that the products of human consciousness could usefully be treated as if they were phenomena of the natural world, thereby increasing humanity's authority over human reality, its own creation.

Baconian scientism, the cultural relativism of Montesquieu, Humean scepticism (including the idea of moral sciences sharing the probabilistic character of the natural sciences), Voltairean demystificatory realism, the historicism of Condorcet, Kantian rationalism – all these had prepared the ground for the obsessive human naturalism which accompanied the remarkable development of the natural sciences in the nineteenth century.

We may now see that the whole idea rested on a *naturalistic fallacy* and has been productive of dire consequences. (a) Human naturalism (methodological prescription: 'treat social facts as things';[19] epistemological deconstruction: 'the superstition of the fact'[20]) empties human phenomena of their essential subjectivity, that is to say, of their essential humanness. (b) It treats systems in consciousness as if they were organic systems, with their own iron logic of self-development. (c) It condemns social phenomena to be what they are, rather than helping them to become what they might be. (d) It evades moral responsibility for one part of the work of the mind, implying that the activity of theory is independent of practice. (e) It legitimizes the actual by cloaking it with a spurious charisma of rationality. (f) It is a co-conspirator with the masters of the actual, who have their own processes of self-constituting, including their own self-ideals and self-interests. (g) It deprives social progress of its affective content, the passionate desire of self-preserving through

---

[19] E. Durkheim, *Les Règles de la Méthode Sociologique* (1895), preface to 2nd edn (Paris: F. Alcan, 1901), p. x.

[20] E. Husserl, *Phenomenology and the Crisis of Philosophy* (tr. Q. Lauer; New York: Harper & Row, 1965), 142.

self-surpassing through self-perfecting, which has been the motive-force of European civilization.

But it is two more practical consequences of human naturalism which are most relevant to the present state of 'European integration'.

In the first place, a naturalist intellectual ethos encourages the arrogance of the bureaucracy. It encourages the idea that social change, even profound constitutional change, can be imposed in rationalistic forms and on rationalistic grounds. It suggests that *politics* – social struggle about values, priorities, ends and means – is an add-on system for the mobilizing of acquiescence – ante hoc or post hoc – in the fiats of rationalistic governance. Fashionable talk in the twentieth century about the end of ideology, the end of politics, the end of history is music to the ears of those who know better than the people what the people want.

Secondly, human naturalism has enabled the life of the pre-1789 international social system to be prolonged for two more centuries. The metaphysical paratheses of nation, state and economy had made the pre-1789 international system. The artificially constructed nations of Europe were embodied externally in their sovereign, one of whose concerns was the mercantilist maximizing of national wealth in competition with the economies of other nations. *War* and *diplomacy* were the only organized means of inter-national interaction, marginally conditioned by a minimal 'law of nations'. With Vattel, the law of nations itself came to be the primary naturalizing force behind the relics of the old-regime metaphysics (sovereignty, sovereign equality, non-intervention, domestic jurisdiction, consent-based law, etc.).

> Nations or States are political bodies, societies of men who have united together and combined their forces, in order to procure their mutual welfare and security. Such a society has its own affairs and interests; it deliberates and takes resolutions in common, and it thus becomes a moral person having an understanding and a will peculiar to itself, and susceptible at once of obligations and of rights... The Law of Nations is the science of the rights which exist between Nations or States, and of the obligations corresponding to these rights.[21]

> I recognise no other natural society among Nations than that which nature has set up among men in general. It is essential to every civil society

---

[21] E. de Vattel, *The Law of Nations or the Principles of Natural Law applied to the Conduct and to the Affairs of Nations and Sovereigns* (1758), introduction (tr. C. G. Fenwick; Washington: Carnegie Foundation, 1916), 3.

that each member should yield certain of his rights to the general body, and that there should be some authority capable of giving commands prescribing laws, and compelling those who refuse to obey. Such an idea is not to be thought of between Nations [*On ne peut rien concevoir, ni rien supposer de semblable entre les Nations*].[22]

In the nineteenth century, even as the internal face of the state was re-imagined through the theories of democracy and capitalism, the external face continued to be that of the world according to Vattel, the world of war and diplomacy. 'European integration' in its present form is a technocratic attempt to surpass the European inter-state old regime without abandoning its metaphysical premises. It is the continuation of war and diplomacy by other means.

Democracy-capitalism

Democracy and capitalism are not inseparable. It is possible, as shown by pre-1945 Germany and Japan (and, perhaps, now in other countries), to operate what may be called statist capitalism. The requirement of capitalism for exceptionally efficient law-making and law-applying can be met by an energetic bureaucracy and/or by collusion between the bureaucracy and the most powerful economic operators. But, where democracy and capitalism are combined, democracy is the servant of capitalism. The function of democracy is then to provide the law and administration required by the current state of the economy. Democracy is efficient in so far as it performs that task in a way which the people in general, and leading economic operators in particular, can regard as appropriate and acceptable.

Democracy-capitalism is not merely a theory of a particular social system. It is a worldview. It combines all three levels of social theory.[23] It offers a *practical* theory to order the consciousness of those who participate in it as a social system, with ideas about the rights and responsibilities and legitimate expectations attaching to participation. It offers a *pure* theory to explain and justify that participation, with ideas about the nature of society, value and social responsibility. But it also implies a *transcendental* theory, in the Kantian tradition, about the bases of knowledge, obligation

---

[22] *Ibid.*, preface, 9a. For further discussion of the significance of Vattel's ideas, see P. Allott, *International Law and International Revolution: Reconceiving the World* (Hull: Hull University Press, 1989).

[23] For this threefold analysis of social theory, see Allott, *Eunomia*, §§ 2.45ff.

and judgement. And its transcendental theory is inherently pragmatist, suggesting that all such things are themselves to be determined within the social process.

Democracy and capitalism share the characteristic that they produce a product (respectively, law and wealth) which is more than the sum of its inputs. The totalized product is enhanced systematically through the peculiar aggregative principles which their theory presents as metaphysical paratheses – respectively, the *general will* and the *invisible hand*. The metaphysical character of these central features has had a profound effect on democratic-capitalist society. They hover at the frontier between the metaphysical and the magical. Over the forum of democracy and the market of capitalism there hover mysterious unseen powers, benign demi-gods.

The consequence of these characteristics of democracy-capitalism is that it is intrinsically a totalitarian system. It is complete in itself. Nothing human lies beyond its systematic grasp. Its value-system may contain non-pragmatic values (freedom, equality, justice even) but, to ground such values, it need not pay tribute to any system of ideas (religious, philosophical) beyond itself. Democracy-capitalism thus takes on the aspect of practical historicism. It seems to contain the logic of its own becoming, its own unfolding programme which becomes the programme of a democratic-capitalist society as a whole.

When democracy-capitalism was adopted as the basis of 'European integration', it was obvious that the process would take on an inexorable life of its own, a self-determining becoming. Opposition to any particular development in that process could be characterized as illogical and incoherent, a denial of the true nature of the whole enterprise. It was (and is) difficult to judge the development of the system other than in terms of the inherent logic of the system. It seemed as if Europe had discovered a way of self-reconstituting which is organic and naturalistic, naturally self-ordering and self-perfecting. It seemed that, through the intelligent application of well-established forms of social metaphysics, Europe's past could be surpassed, once and for all. But this dream of reason has proved to be a nightmare.

The metaphysics of contradiction

There is a difference between *dialectic* and *contradiction*. Dialectic is creative opposition. Contradiction is destructive opposition. The perilous state of 'European integration' is a reflection of the social metaphysics of contradiction which characterizes it. The task of rescuing the self-reconstituting of Europe from that perilous state is the formidable task of transforming a metaphysics of contradiction into a metaphysics of dialectical unity.

If Europe is to constitute itself as a dynamic society of the people and peoples of Europe, containing and surpassing its participating societies, then it must begin to be judged by the inherent logic of social self-constituting rather than by the inherent anomie of 'European integration'.

Judged by that logic, 'European integration' in its present condition is a mass of contradictions. They are not the creative dialectical oppositions of social self-constituting, but a self-constituting through deconstituting, a progressive, if haphazard, deconstituting not only of itself as a social system but also of the national constitutional orders which are caught up in the hazardous enterprise. The contradictions of 'European integration' are too numerous to list exhaustively. They include the following.

A treaty is not a constitution.   A treaty is an affirmation of multiplicity ('the contracting parties'). A written constitution is an affirmation of unity. Despite some half-hearted references by the European Court of Justice to the EC Treaty as a 'constitutional charter',[24] the morass of treaty texts has none of the dynamic society-making power of a true constitutional contract, the symbolic and psychic embodiment of the One from the Many, the physical form of the metaphysics of a society. The Community Treaties are unknown and unknowable not only for the mass of the people but also for the masters of the national public minds and of the national public realms.[25]

---

[24] Opinion 1/92 on the European Economic Area Treaty: [1992] ECR I-2821; [1992] 2 CMLR 217.

[25] The remarkable clear-mindedness of American constitution-making is an instructive precedent. George Washington's Letter of Transmittal to Congress of the 1787 Constitution said: 'It is obviously impracticable in the foederal government of the States, to secure all rights of independent sovereignty to each, and yet provide for the interest and safety of all – Individuals entering into a society, must give up a share of liberty to preserve the rest. The magnitude of the sacrifice must depend as well on situation and circumstances, as on the object to be obtained. It is at all times difficult to draw the line with precision between those rights which must be surrendered, and those which may be reserved; and on the present occasion this difficulty was encreased by a difference among the several States as to their situation, extent, habits, and particular interests. In all our deliberations on this subject we kept steadily in view, that which appears to us the greatest interest of every true American, the consolidation of our Union, in which is involved our prosperity, felicity, safety, perhaps our national existence.' In L. Wolf-Phillips (ed.), *Constitutions of Modern States: Selected Texts* (London: Pall Mall Press, 1968), 204–5.

The 'masters of the Treaty' heresy.   The idea that, after fifty years of 'European integration', the essential status and capacities of the 'Member States' are unchanged, internally and in relation to each other, was given undeserved respectability by the decision of 12 October 1993 of the German Federal Constitutional Court.[26] Such an idea is a perverse denial of the transformatory effect of the Community system, a social system which has clearly already transformed the internal orders of the 'Member States', their international status in relation to each other and to third parties, the distribution of ultimate legislative, executive and judicial powers, their authority over their own economies, the status of their citizens. To propagate such an idea not only spreads a sense of ultimate incoherence and confusion in relation to the whole enterprise. It is also a fraud on the people to suggest that nothing fundamental has changed.

The 'national constitutional order' heresy.   There are national superior courts which regard the Community system as deriving its validity from the national constitutional order, including the written constitution.[27] If and when EC law is applied, a mental reservation conceives of the event as being a continuing effect of the authority of the national constitution, rather than as the product of a new source of ultimate law-making authority. Such an idea is a lawyers' conceit and a deceit, because such a system as the Community system cannot possibly derive its everyday constitutional authority from the internal authority of fifteen separate national constitutional orders, none of which individually has authority over the total Community order.

A final court which does not have the last word.   The European Court of Justice has not established a psychic hegemony over the supreme national courts, notwithstanding the number of its decisions, the extent to which it has constructed a substantial common-law system out of the vagaries of litigation, and the constitutional imagination which it demonstrated

---

The splendid enacting words of the American Constitution are a supreme ecthetic moment of European social consciousness: 'We, the People of the United States, in order to form a more perfect Union, establish justice, ensure domestic tranquillity, provide for the common defense, promote the general welfare and secure the blessings of liberty to ourselves and our posterity, do ordain and establish this Constitution for the United States of America' (207).

[26] 89 BVerfGE 155; (1994) 33 ILM 393; [1994] 1 CMLR 57.

[27] This appears to be the view of the French superior courts. G. Teboul, 'Ordre Juridique International et Ordre Juridique Interne. Quelques Réflexions sur la Jurisprudence du Juge Administratif', *Revue du Droit Public* (1999), 697; J.-F. Flauss, *Note de Jurisprudence* (on the Conseil d'Etat's *Sarran* decision of 30 October 1998), *Revue du Droit Public* (1999), 919.

in a number of fundamental decisions. It has managed to alienate those who have seen it as overusing its jurisdictions, while, at the same time, seeming to live on sufferance in relation to superior national courts, who seem to behave as if they were making a graceful concession when they follow the line laid down by the Court in a particular matter, and some of which have indicated that, in the very last resort, they retain the very last word within their national systems.[28]

Fundamental rights which are not fundamental. The Court of Justice unfortunately misunderstands the nature of fundamental constitutional rights.[29] They are not 'general principles of law'. They are ultimate limits on the powers of all constitutional organs (legislative, executive and judicial). They are hierarchically separate from the rest of the law, since they are a condition of the validity of the rest of the law. The executive branches of the 'Member States', for obvious reasons of self-interest, support the European Court's misguided view which was reflected in the lamentable Articles F and L of the Maastricht Treaty.[30]

Disintegrated fundamental rights. Fundamental rights are the expression of a society's ultimate values of social organization, a unity of social nature which surpasses the plurality of the personal values of society-members. A society cannot organize itself in accordance with conflicting ultimate values of social organization. There are two and, in some 'Member States', three regimes of fundamental rights (national, EC, ECHR) which apply within the national constitutional orders. Apparently some of those orders even regard their regime as ultimately superior to the fundamental rights regime of the Community. There is no integrating concept at the Community level to resolve such multiplicities and divergences.

---

[28] The *Frontini* reservation of the Italian Constitutional Court ([1974] 2 CMLR 372) appears to be shared by the German Federal Constitutional Court (*Wünsche*: 73 BVerfGE 339; [1987] 3 CMLR 225; and *Brunner*: 89 BVerfGE 155; (1994) 33 ILM 393; [1994] 1 CMLR 57).

[29] The Court summarized its own jurisprudence in Opinion 2/94 on Community Accession to the European Human Rights Convention ([1996] ECR I-1759 at 1789; [1996] 2 CMLR 265 at 290): 'it is well settled that fundamental rights form an integral part of the general principles of law whose observance the Court ensures'.

[30] Article L of the Maastricht Treaty excluded the jurisdiction of the Court of Justice in respect of Article F(2) which provides that: 'The Union shall respect fundamental rights.' Since the Treaty leaves it entirely unclear what 'the Union' is, legally speaking, the precise effect of this exclusion was difficult to determine. The Treaty of Amsterdam conferred jurisdiction on the Court in respect of the provision (now Article 6(2)) 'with regard to action of the institutions, insofar as the Court has jurisdiction under the Treaties establishing the European Communites and under this Treaty', adding several further layers of obscurity.

A separation of powers which is a confusion of powers. The Community system involves a two-dimensional separation of powers: horizontal (Community national orders; national orders *inter se*) and vertical (Community national orders). The coexistence of 'regulations' and 'directives' has built into the system a fundamental confusion of the vertical separation, a confusion which has been seriously exacerbated by the concept of 'subsidiarity' which is either, on one view, a rule about the residual distribution of public powers in a federation or, on another view, a rule designed to entrench the primacy of the national order over the Community order. By its vacillations and incoherences, the Court of Justice has contributed much to the confusion. The idea of the 'direct effect' of Community law ensures that Community law is, on the contrary, not a true source of law in the national orders.[31] The Court's jurisprudence on Articles 30–6 EC has left the vertical and horizontal distribution of economic law-making powers in the most unsatisfactory state possible.[32]

A set of constitutional arrangements which is not a constitutional order. There is no concept (*Begriff*, parathesis) which could integrate the national constitutional orders with the Community constitutional order. Is the Community order an external order under international law which flows into the national orders, as if the Community were an advanced form of intergovernmental organization? Is the Community order an excescence from the national orders, an internal order with an external dimension, as it were, shared by the 'Member States'?[33] Or is the Community order a transcendent order which contains the national orders as a Many-in-One, a Self-from-Others, so that the national orders

---

[31] For an argument to similar effect, see P. Pescatore, 'The Doctrine of Direct Effect – An Infant Disease of Community Law', 8 *European Law Review* (1983), 155.

[32] The Court's line of retreat from any feasible conception of the common interest as the foundation of the common market (as opposed to the aggregation of national interests) may be plotted in *Dassonville* (Case 8/74 [1974] ECR 837); *Cassis* (Case 120/78 [1979] ECR 649); *Cinéthèque* (Case 60/84 [1985] ECR 2605); *Keck* (Case C-267-8/91 [1993] 1 ECR 6097); and, in relation to intellectual property, in a line from *Deutsche Grammophon* (Case 78/70 [1971] ECR 487) to *Hag II* (Case C-10/89 [1990] ECR I-3711) and *IHT Internazionale Heiztechnik* (Case 9/93 [1994] 4 ECR I-2789).

[33] The cynical wording of the Maastricht amendment (1992) to the French Constitution (Article 88) is a sad symbol of the poverty of the constitutional philosophy of 'European integration' after four decades. It speaks of the Member States 'having freely chosen to exercise certain of their powers in common', as if that were all the vast world-transforming enterprise amounted to. The *Brunner* decision of the German Federal Constitutional Court said that the Member States created the Union 'in order to perform some of their duties and to exercise some of their sovereignty jointly' (p. 423 of ILM text).

are both independent and dependent in relation to each other? No one knows, and many have an interest in seeing to it that no one shall know. 'European integration' is a normative order without a *Grundnorm*, and with no immediate prospect of getting one.

'Member States' as oxymoron. The expression 'Member States' is an oxymoron in a constitutional order such as the Community system. A 'state' cannot be a 'member' of such a thing. A state (in the *external* aspect of that parathesis) is imagined to be a unitary social system, with a single ultimate source of law and exclusive authority within its territory and over persons subject to its jurisdiction (the defining aspects of so-called 'sovereignty'). Participation in the Community system is a fundamental negation of these characteristics. The 'Member States' cannot be Member 'States'.

'Member States' as metonymy. The expression 'Member States' is a metonymy in the Community context. The members of the Community are not merely the states but the societies and their peoples, the people and the peoples of Europe. 'Member States' suggests that the Community is a community of public realms, one aspect only of the national societies. It legitimizes the representation of those societies by only one part of that totality, namely, 'the state' in the *internal* aspect of that parathesis, which is, in practice, a reference to the controllers of the public realm, that is to say, the government. And the phrase is used to support a fraudulent conception of 'representation', that central parathesis of liberal democracy, as if a government were able to 'represent' as a single policy or interest the inchoate mass of competing policies and interests which each national society contains in relation to all the matters which are dealt with in the Community system. Such a false notion of representativity is counter-revolutionary, in that it empowers the executive branch of government to behave in the Community system in a way in which it can no longer behave in the national constitutional orders. *Les états, c'est nous.*

Diplomacy-democracy. Oxymoron + metonymy = diplomacy-democracy. Such an unlikely formula expresses one aspect of the central contradiction of the Community system. The Community is Athens and Sparta in cloudy confusion. It is seeking to provide the operational basis (law-making and law-applying) of a capitalist economy by means of a system in which the internal state (public realm) of democracies is externalized, and then behaves as the external state behaved in relation to other 'states' in the past, that is, diplomatically, by negotiation among governments purporting to represent their peoples, and purporting to give effect to their respective national interests. Aspects of the national democratic apparatus are produced at the Community level as simulacra (parliament, courts, the Council as Cabinet, the Commission as executive branch, etc.), in order to disguise the monopolizing of the political process by the executive branch.

Statist-capitalism. Metonymy + oxymoron = statist-capitalism. Such an unlikely formula expresses the other aspect of the central contradiction of the Community system. The Community is a Second Reich Europe, a Meiji Europe. It is a partial integrating of democratic-capitalist national economies in the form of a multinational statist-capitalist system. The crudely aggregative Community economic system is different in conception and operation from the economic systems of the national societies. The economic self-constituting of the Community is statist in the sense that it is an artificial construction stage-managed by the managers of the public realms (the governments and the Community institutions), using the law-making and law-applying systems of the Community.

The heresy of national legitimation. In recent years the idea has gained ground, and has proved particularly popular with politicians, that the activities of the governments of the 'Member States' in the Council are legitimated by the legitimacy which they derive from their national constitutional orders, including especially the accountability of individual ministers to their national parliament. This heresy has gained added respectability, once again, from the decision of 12 October 1993 of the German Federal Constitutional Court, which even managed to suggest that the European Parliament has a secondary role in the legitimation of the activities of the Council.[34] More correctly seen, Ministers in the Council are two-persons-in-one: they are respresentatives, however improper and inadequate, of their national societies, but they are also servants and agents of the Community common interest. The decisions of the Council, in the form of Community law and policy, are actualizations of the general will of the Community as a whole. As J.-J. Rousseau saw with obscure clairvoyance, the general will is not the same thing as the will of all. The general will of the Community is not merely an aggregate of the national will-forming processes. It is the universalizing of the interests of all the people and peoples of Europe through law-making and law-applying in the Community common interest.

An economy which is not an economy. A capitalist economy is a mystical and magical integrating of three things – human psychology

---

[34] The Court calls the role of the European Parliament a 'supportive function' (p. 421 of the ILM text).

(self-consciousness, desire, preservation of self and family), the market (other-consciousness, the totalizing of human effort and human will) and the law (finding and disaggregating the common interest, including the distribution and control of governmental decision-making powers). The integrated and integrating systematic totality of the economy is the cause and the effect of the capitalist social system, including the democratic system. The Community economy has no such integrative totality. It is an artificial and piecemeal aggregation of parts of the national economies, an aggregation which undermines but does not supplement, let alone re-totalize, the totalities of the national economies. There are national markets and national market-behaviour and there is an incoherent and inefficient Community market demanding aberrant forms of market behaviour. This means that the EC is doomed not to achieve at the Community level the vast wealth-creating and self-surpassing effect of a true capitalist economy of 350 million people, and may, on the contrary, be undermining the capacities of the national economies to produce that effect and to succeed competitively against the other global super-economies.

A common interest which is not common.   Central to the success of democracy-capitalism is the immeasurably complex and subtle day-to-day finding of the common interest, through the processes of an open society and, above all, through politics in the widest sense, a common interest which is then actualized in law-making and law-applying. Older constitutional writers spoke of society as a *commonwealth*, something in which all society-members have a stake, so that, in working for themselves, they are working for the common good and vice versa. In modern mixed-economy capitalism, the citizens do this not only through their socially systematized work but also through contributing up to 40 per cent of their working time to serve the public good (counting direct and indirect taxation together for this purpose). The subjects of the Community system have no such sense of commonwealth. There is no real Community politics and nothing which is clearly Community taxation. We may reverse the grand ecthetic of Anglo-American constitutional history and say: *no representation without taxation!* Taxation is the best way of making the citizen into a very interested party in government. To carry out government using the taxpayers' money but without acknowledging its source (as if 'own resources' fell like manna from heaven) is an act of structural dishonesty, however convenient it may be for those who benefit from the largesse (including the technocrats themselves). The European Community is not a European Commonwealth but merely a European

Aggregation. It is a community without a sense of community, a *Gemein-schaft ohne Gemeinsamkeit*.[35]

Transparency not accountability. A democratic-capitalist society depends on accountability for the exercise of public powers, not merely in the courts under the rule of law, but day by day in the conversation of an open society. Accountability means the permanent threat of public anger at the abuse of power, incompetence and the waste of public money. Technocrats (rationalistic politicians, narrow-minded judges, and civil servants)[36] believe that the needs of accountability are met by the provision (*en clair*, the management) of public information. They suppose that a relatively high level of transparency guarantees a relatively high level of democracy. Because of the absence of a sense of common interest, the absence of Community taxation and the absence of a Community political system, those who manage the Community system are relatively immune from the awful reality of accountability. They are also past masters at the gracious gesture in the name of so-called transparency (as if government were a matter of accountancy rather than of accountability), including that *fine fleur* of technocratic cynicism, the establishing of a 'Court of Auditors' as an 'institution' alongside Parliament, Court, Council and Commission.

Forward to the past. The Austro-Hungarianization of the European Community has been a story of steady progress backwards. Each of the accessions, beginning with that of 1973, has been a decline in the coherence and efficacy of the system. The Maastricht Treaty was a great leap forward backwards, towards the inexorable goal of the Congress System of the 1820s. The splendid confusion of the structures of 'integration' – worthy of the *K und K, K–K, and K* of Austria-Hungary, and comprehensible, if at all, only to a chosen very few – looks set to be carried to new heights and lengths as the European Union Treaty allows for 'closer cooperation' (greater disintegration) and as the 'integration' of waves of new 'Member States' gradually recreates the sublime miscellany which, for a thousand years, was known as the Holy Roman Empire.[37] And, sublimest of all, there is an Economic and Monetary Union, the promised land of the

---

[35] It is 'civil society' in Hegel's social metaphysics which engages the subjectivity of the citizen, by contrast with the 'state', as a particular manifestation of social self-constituting, whose source is elsewhere (spirit actualizing itself as reason). Hegel, *Philosophy of Right*, §§182ff.

[36] The *Beamtementalität* is found also in commercial corporations and, not least, in universities.

[37] The metaphysics of totality of Austria-Hungary was never clearly established, but its parts were labelled Imperial and Royal (*K und K*), Imperial–Royal (*K–K*), and Royal (*K*). According to a famous old saying, of which Austria was not ashamed: *Alii bellum faciunt. Tu, felix Austria, nube.* 'Others make war. You, fortunate Austria, make marriages.' EU

Euro, protected by a trans-European economic *limes*, like a latter-day Roman Empire. In my beginning is my end.

The necessity and the irrelevance of political union. 'Economic and Monetary Union is impossible without a profound transformation of Community and national constitutional systems.' 'EMU is possible on the basis of existing constitutional systems.' Either proposition may be correct or, perhaps, both. What is clear is that the constitutional consequences of EMU, at the Community and national levels, will simply be faced pragmatically and *ambulando*, as and when necessary, if necessary. EMU is a leap into the constitutional dark, and into a profoundly new era in the history of the people and peoples of Europe, a paper revolution made by rationalistic collusion among politicians, central bankers and civil servants.

An international person without a personality. The EC has international legal personality. The EU may, now or in the future, have international legal personality. Neither has the personality of the people and peoples of Europe, the 3,000-year-old civilization to which so many of the grandeurs and miseries of the current condition of humanity are attributable. The so-called Common Foreign and Security Policy is a meaningless survival of nineteenth-century conceptions of diplomacy and of an obsolete international situation. It is a hopeless irrelevance in a world which is now governed by systems and forces which are far beyond the reach of traditional diplomacy, an emerging, if incoherent, global society and an emerging global economy.[38] Europe's failure, over a period of almost fifty years, to create a viable form of European society suggests that it will, at long last, be obliged to watch as others dominate the making of world history in the future.

Reason's dream of Europe's unity

These nineteen contradictions of 'European integration' (and no doubt more could be identified) are outward signs of a failure of social metaphysics. They are the consequences of a failure to conceive of the European enterprise as a process of European social self-constituting (ideal, real and legal). They are a consequence of the fact that the process has been almost

'enlargement' is a series of arranged marriages with more or less eager, more or less suitable, partners.

[38] See P. Allott, 'European Foreign Policy: After-Life of an Illusion', in M. Koskenniemi (ed.), *International Law Aspects of the European Union* (Amsterdam: Kluwer Law International, 1998), 215–29.

entirely in the hands of technocrats (rationalistic politicians, narrow-minded judges, and civil servants), for whom social metaphysics is a fact of life rather than a transformatory potentiality, and for whom the actual is presumed to be rational.

The present state of 'European integration' is a Ptolemaic system of social cosmology. In the Ptolemaic system of the universe ever greater complexity and ever greater unreality were required to 'save the appearances' (rationalize actual observational fact) in a system which was fundamentally flawed in its Aristotelian metaphysics (a geocentric system of bodies in perfectly circular motions). Epicycle after epicycle, and epicycles of epicycles, had to be added (Article 189b, *Cassis de Dijon*, variable beef premiums, *Francovich*, mixed agreements, convergence criteria, horizontal direct effect, representative rates, etc.). The Copernican revolution (Copernicus, Galileo, Kepler and Newton) had to establish a new cosmological metaphysics, making possible the triumphant new cosmological science.[39]

Europe is sleepwalking in a nightmare of reason towards a European super-state or towards terminal disintegration or, possibly, to both. It will require unprecedented efforts of reason and imagination to produce one more ecthesis in the long history of European constitutionalism, perhaps the most difficult that we have ever been required to attempt, a new European genesis and a new European enlightenment. It is a rescue operation which must consist of the constructing of a metaphysical superstructure around the actual, like scaffolding around a fragile building. We must construct an exogenous constitutional skeleton within which Europe's unity can flourish with new and healthy growth. We must engage the social consciousness of the people and peoples of Europe in an ultimate act of recognition, the recognition of their unity-in-diversity.

A first attempt at such a Copernican ecthetic, a metaphysics of Europe's totality, might contain the following four paratheses.

One constitutional order.   The European Union is a union of all the national constitutional orders and the Europe-wide constitutional order, in which the two kinds of constitutional order are not anomalous in

---

[39] It is interesting that Einstein specifically acknowledged his debt to Ernst Mach for uncovering the *metaphysics* of the Newtonian system, which enabled Einstein to imagine the metaphysics of his new view of the universe. See P. G. Frank, 'Einstein, Mach, and Logical Positivism', in P. A. Schilpp (ed.), *Albert Einstein: Philosopher-Scientist* (La Salle, IL: Open Court, 1949), 272. It seems that his obsessive interest in alchemy may have played a significant part in the making of Newton's physics. See M. White, *Isaac Newton. The Last Sorcerer* (London: Fourth Estate, 1998).

relation to each other or in competition with each other. Each is a necessary part of the other. The national constitutional orders, with their long and complex histories and their distinctive cultural foundations, must flourish within the flourishing of the European order, which also has a long history and a distinct cultural foundation.

One economy.   The economy of the European Union is a unitary economy in which the national economies participate, not as anomalies in relation to each other nor in competition with each other. Each is a necessary part of the other. The self-surpassing wealth-creating capacity of a capitalist economy at the level of all-Europe involves the capacities of the national economies in the form of the economic competition which is inherent in the capitalist system.

One common interest.   The interest of each member of the European Union is the interest of all, as in any liberal democratic society. The function of European Union politics and European Union law is to find the common interest of the Union from all the infinite variety of competing interests of all subordinate societies and of each individual citizen. The task of the managers of the public realm of the Union and the public realms of the national constitutional orders is to assist in the finding, the actualizing and the implementing of the common interest.

One person.   The members of the European Union are the people and the peoples of Europe, in all their infinite cultural and social diversity, and in all their profound unity – a unity of place, of subjectivity and of potentiality. Together they constitute one person, not least among the persons forming the international society of all-humanity.

INDEX

accession *see also* enlargement
  accession *acquis*, 160, 161, 163, 173,
    177
  candidates, 160, 163, 167, 171, 179,
    180, 182, 193
  constitutional bargaining, 161, 162,
    171
  Copenhagen criteria (1993), 159,
    160, 179, 191
  flexibility, 107, 111
  institutional adaptation, 163, 172,
    174
accountability
  comitology, 154
  democracy, 155
  legitimacy, 144, 145, 149
  representation, 136
  transparency, 222
acquis communautaire
  accession *acquis*, 160, 161, 163, 173,
    177
  derogations, 105
  disintegration, 120
  enhanced cooperation, 117
  European constitution, 7, 121
  Europolity, 175
  internal market, 112
  Kerneuropa, 109
  less developed states, 111
  preservation/extension, 120
  Reflection Group, 115
  rule-following, 146
  Treaty of Maastricht (1992), 114
action rationale
  finality, 162
  logics and action rationales, 161–5
  rule-following, 161

added value
  democracy, 75, 85
  experts, 148
  public goods, 49
administration *see also* public
  administration
  decentralized, 143
Advisory Committee on Foodstuffs,
  151
Africa, customary law, 64
agriculture
  BSE crisis, 139, 143, 147
  Common Agricultural Policy, 72
  enlargement, 178–9
  France, 139
aliens
  boundary removal, 19
  identity, 19
  other, 19
  relationships, 18
Allott, Philip, 4, 120, 202
Aristotle, 15, 166
Australia, 8
Austria, 18

Bacon, Francis, 211
Balladur, Eduard, 109, 110, 112
banana dispute, 17, 96
Belgium, 107
Benelux, 108, 110
Berkeley, George, 207
Berlin, Isaiah, 15
Bohannan, P., 64
boundaries
  aliens, 19
  constitutionalizing process, 66
  constitutions, 67, 104